PATTON'S GAP

PATTON'S GAP

An Account of the Battle of Normandy 1944

Major - General

RICHARD ROHMER

Arms and Armour Press

LONDON   MELBOURNE

Published in Great Britain by
Arms and Armour Press, Lionel Leventhal Limited,
2-6 Hampstead High Street, London NW3 1QQ
and at 4-12 Tattersalls Lane,
Melbourne, Victoria 3000

Published in Canada by
General Publishing Co. Limited, 30 Lesmill Road
Don Mills, Ontario M3B 2T6

Published in the United States by
Beaufort Books, Inc., 9 East 40th Street
New York, N.Y. 10016

© Richard Rohmer 1981

Designed by E.J. Carson

British Library Cataloguing in Publication Data:
Rohmer, Richard, 1924-
Patton's gap

1. Falaise Gap, Battle of, 1944- 2. World War,
1939-1945 - Campaigns - Normandy. I. Title.

940.54'21   D756.5.F34R63

ISBN 0 85368 118 X

Printed and Bound in Canada

*Thanks are due to the following for their kind permissions to include the many
quotes, maps, and photographs which appear throughout this book:*

Fred Cleverly of *The Winnipeg Free Press* for the excellent, autographed photo
of Field Marshall Montgomery.
The Comptroller of Her Majesty's Stationery Office (London), for use of the
maps (British Crown copyright).
The Estate of the late Field Marshal Montgomery of Alamein, for the maps and
numerous excerpts from *Montgomery of Alamein*, Volume II, Normandy to
the Baltic Invasion.
The Public Archives of Canada (Ottawa).
The Trustees of the Imperial War Museum (London). Photo of meeting of
General Patton, Lieutenant General Omar N. Bradley, and Field Marshal
Sir Bernard L. Montgomery at a field conference in France (photo reference:
NYF 48420). Photo of General Patton (photo reference: S & G 66084).

To all wartime
and peacetime members
of 430 Squadron

Acknowledgements

Beyond those people I mention in the prologue I wish to give recognition to others who have been of invaluable assistance in the preparation of this book.

Mrs. A. White of the Canadian Public Archives in London, England, who was most helpful in the search for documents and photographs; and for their editorial comments, Dr. Mervyn Franklin, the President of the University of Windsor, Major General Dan Loomis, MC, CD, of the Canadian Armed Forces, and Colonel C.P. Stacey, OC, OBE, CD, the renowned Canadian military historian; and for his research efforts, Professor Christopher Bart who has assisted me in digging out facts for many of my books, both fiction and non-fiction; and for her perceptive comments, advice and ever-supportive patience, my wife Mary-O.

Richard Rohmer

Prologue

There were four unusual research 'accidents' that allowed this book to be written.

The first of these was my finding of the wartime log book of 430 Squadron of the Royal Canadian Air Force. As a pilot, I was a member of that squadron from September 1943 to the end of November 1944. The log has a descriptive record of the daily activity of the unit and of every operational mission that was carried out during the period of its wartime existence. In fact, I was the author of a part of it.

Thirty-one years later, in my then capacity as the Commander of the Air Reserve Group of the Canadian Armed Forces, I was invited to a ceremony at Canadian Forces Base Valcartier, Quebec. 430 Squadron, equipped with helicopters, was to be presented with its Queen's Color, a symbolic flag bearing the unit's badge and the names of the places where the squadron had won its battle honors. To qualify for presentation of the Queen's Color, a unit must have been in existence for more than twenty-five years. I was the guest of honor and the only wartime 430 Squadron pilot to appear for the festivities. My wife and I were treated to much hospitality and courteous attention. We were taken on a tour of the squadron's facilities — the hangar, maintenance shops, administrative offices and the aircrew's 'waiting room' as we used to call it. That room I inspected with high interest, looking at all the pictures, paraphernalia and trophies hanging on the walls. Sitting on a table at the side of the room was an unusual looking book. It had a gray binding. It was large — about one and a half feet long, one foot wide and three inches thick. My memory told me that it had the look of an ancient Royal Air Force record book I had seen many times before. As I lifted the cover to look at the first page, I was astonished to find that this was 430 Squadron's original wartime log complete with signatures!

The discovery brought a moment of excitement as well as intense nostalgia. I leafed through the pages with their terse descriptions of our operational sorties, especially those of the D-Day period and the time of the closing of the Falaise Gap.

I had to have the original so I could photocopy it for my personal records. Would the commanding officer let me take it? Of course he would.

It was that discovery which made this book possible. My own personal log book covering the invasion period had been lost when a Dakota transport aircraft was shot down carrying our tents and personal gear from an airstrip near Evreux in France to another strip at Diest in Belgium. So I had no records of my own from those long gone days. Therefore, the find of the squadron log book was a surprising, unexpected bonanza. In 1975, putting together an account of the Battle of Normandy had not even crossed my mind.

The second research accident has to do with the finding of two aerial photographs I had taken during 1944. One is found at page 24 and the other at page 165. As with my log book, all the important reconnaissance photos I had taken during the invasion period were lost. There was one particular photograph I wanted to find in the photographic archives in the United Kingdom. It was a picture taken on 17 August 1944 in the Falaise Gap. It was of a two-abreast column of German tanks, trucks, horse-drawn artillery, ambulances and other vehicles moving in broad daylight without fear of any attack from the Allied air forces — this for reasons explained in the text. If I could have found that picture it would explain with dramatic impact the scope and scale of the massive day and night exodus by the enemy out of the pocket in which we had the German army trapped.

A search was conducted in the two institutions in the United Kingdom that might have had a negative of that photograph and all others taken by my squadron during World War II. The British are notorious hoarders. That picture could not be found. In the meantime I asked those of my wartime 430 Squadron colleagues I was able to track down, including army intelligence officers associated with us during the period, if they had any aerial photographs from those days. I hoped that one of them might turn up something and that my special photograph would be in the lot. At a cocktail party in Toronto in the fall in 1979 I talked with Joan Waddell, the widow of the Wing Commander Flying of 39 Recce Wing of which 430 Squadron was a part during the summer of 1944. In those days Wing Commander R.C.A. 'Bunt' Waddell was the flying boss of all of us, responsible among other things for our briefings and our overall operations, as well as the man with his finger on the pulse of not only my squadron but the other two Canadian units in the Wing, 400 and 414 Squadrons. Did Bunt have a boxful or collection of memorabilia from World War II? The answer was yes. I could go through it any time, which I did about a week later. My idea was that since Bunt had had access to all of the pictures taken by our squadrons, he might have taken a copy of my 17 August photograph and thrown it in with the others he thought worth keeping. There was only an outside chance. But it was worth a try.

I dug into Bunt's huge box of books, maps, bits and pieces of regalia and other personal flying treasures. My hopes rose when I found a rolled up bundle of about thirty air photographs, the very thing I thought I might find. A cursory look through the batch did not produce what I was looking for. Nevertheless, I decided I should ask to take them home with me so I could go over them carefully. Joan very kindly agreed.

That evening, during my third inspection of the bundle, I stopped at a picture which began to ring a bell in my memory. The picture was of a port. There was the shore-line. Beyond it was a town with docks and water in the center. Surely that couldn't be . . . I checked the date and the squadron number printed on the bottom of the photograph, then went to the squadron log book. They matched. It was mine! Even so, it was not the Falaise Gap prize I was seeking. The next run through the bundle caused me to stop at a blurred, indistinct photograph taken almost vertically at low level. There were six or seven tank-like looking objects on the ground. Tanks? I wondered if it was the photograph I had taken on the night I found the batch of tanks that almost caused Bunt Waddell to have me court-martialed. Impossible. It couldn't be. Back to the squadron log. It *was* mine taken on a day that was significant for me, but far more so for General George S. Patton, Jr. It was 1 August 1944, the day that he and his magnificent Third Army became operational.

By this stroke of unexpected good fortune, and through the kindness of Joan Waddell, and the long-ago interest of Wing Commander (later Group Captain) Bunt Waddell DSO, DFC, an outstanding leader, my words describing two events in this book are enriched by those photographs.

The third accidental find was Dirk Bogarde, the international film star, artist and, latterly, best selling author.

During a visit to England in June 1980 I picked up a copy of Bogarde's second autobiography, *Snakes and Ladders.* It covered, among other times, his experiences during World War II. He had joined the British army, was commissioned from the ranks, and, as his story went, trained as an Army Photographic Interpretation officer. He did? Interesting. We had half a dozen of them attached to our 39 Reconnaissance Wing. The APIS (Section) people interpreted the aerial photos we pilots took with the special cameras mounted in our Mustangs. Furthermore, his story recounted that he had joined 39 Recce Wing of the Royal Canadian Air Force at Odiham just before D-Day, and was with us through D-Day, France, Belgium and Holland. He was? I didn't remember him. In those days he wasn't a film star — just a skinny twenty-two-year-old British army officer. No reason to remember him. But perhaps, just maybe there was.

Could Dirk Bogarde have been the man who interpreted that critically important (to me) photograph of tanks I took in the late evening of 1 August 1944? As soon as I returned to Canada I wrote to him at his residence in the south of France. I enclosed a copy of the relevant section of the manuscript of this book and a print of the 1 August photo I'd found in Bunt Waddell's memorabilia box. Was he the APIS officer I'd seen that night?

The day he received my letter he wrote a reply which was later followed up by another. Indeed Bogarde was my APIS interpreter.

"Right off I knew the Sortie-Snap," was his response.

Quite by accident the two of us had reached back across thirty-six years to a French farmyard, to an APIS van of 39

Recce Wing enveloped in the uneasy beachhead battle zone darkness of the night of 1 August 1944. For me it was an uncanny, happy, fortuitous link with that event and with a man who is exceptionally talented.

The fourth research accident relates to the last two pages of this book in which the blame or fault for the creation of the Falaise Gap is for the first time correctly assigned to the responsible Allied general. Over the years since the summer of 1944 a certain general had assumed the blame. But his story, while an honest position from his personal perceptions, never rang true to me. I decided it was worthwhile trying to find whether there were any flaws in his story. Added to this was my knowledge that to this time there has been much controversy over the Falaise Gap among the historians. Its occurrence has even been called a mystery.

I reasoned that perhaps there might be clues in the papers or memoirs of the generals directly involved. All of them had died, with the exception of General of the Army Omar Bradley. He had touched on the subject of the Falaise Gap in his memoirs published in 1951. If I could talk with him, or have access to his papers, I might be able to find the clue I was looking for as to who was the creator of the Gap. I talked with his staff at Fort Benning, Georgia. Could I have a word with the general sometime about the Falaise Gap? No, that wouldn't be possible. The general does not grant interviews any longer — after all, he is over 90 years old. However, his papers are at the U.S. Army Military History Institute at Harrisburg, Pennsylvania. A telephone call to that institution brought a negative response. They did not have Bradley's papers. They had been transferred to the Dwight D. Eisenhower Historical Research Foundation at the Smithsonian in Washington. I should talk there with Dr. Forrest Pogue, the Director of the Research Foundation.

When I reached Dr. Pogue by telephone I told him about the book I was researching, and that I was particularly interested in the Falaise Gap — why it happened and who was responsible. Dr. Pogue's response was immediate.

"General, I think I have some notes about that. I think Dempsey was involved [Lieutenant General Miles Dempsey, Commander of the Second British Army under Montgomery], but I'm not really sure. I'll have to see if I can find my notes."

As it turned out, Dr. Pogue was indeed able to find his notes. He had made them in 1946 and 1947 when he set about to interview a series of Allied generals, admirals, air marshals and others involved in the preparation for D-Day-Operation 'Neptune' as it was called. It was a part of Operation Overlord, the liberation of Europe. Dr. Pogue called me back the next day, his notes in hand. He read me a brief paragraph on each of seven interviews. It was the record of his May 1947 interview of one senior officer that contained the full and complete answer as to who gave the order that created the Falaise Gap.

Dr. Pogue, one of America's most distinguished military historians, has written several military history books about World War II. But in none of them did he use the information about the Falaise Gap contained in those notes.

Quite naturally over the span of thirty-two years he had forgotten the exact details of that interview. It took his notes to refresh his memory. Furthermore, when I wrote to the knowledgeable officer with whom Dr. Pogue had talked in 1947, asking if he could in any way augment or amplify the circumstances he had described in the interview, his response was that it was so long ago he could not remember.

There is no doubt in my mind that in finding Dr. Forrest Pogue I had discovered the only man in the world who had the answer to the question: which of the generals — Eisenhower, Montgomery, Bradley or Patton — was responsible for the creation of the Falaise Gap, one of the most costly Allied blunders in the European theatre of World War II. That answer has never before been published. I am grateful to Dr. Pogue for his kind permission to use his invaluable notes.

PATTON'S
GAP

16

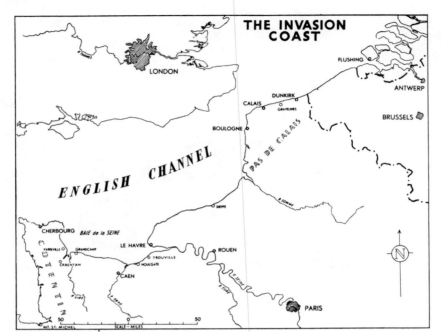

THE INVASION COAST

1

24 April 1944

The time was 18:15 hours. The place: over the German occupied French coast at 5000 feet. The target: two ships reported to be in the harbor at Dieppe.

The sun's unobstructed rays beat down warming its twenty-year-old pilot through the birdcage hood covering the cockpit of the Mustang I fighter aircraft.

Looking intently down past his green brown camouflage-painted port wing, he was frantically scanning the thin layer of flat but lumpy cloud about 2000 feet below, searching for a hole through which he could catch a glimpse of the ground. A landmark had to be quickly found.

The youthful fighter reconnaissance pilot was on his first mission as leader. He had many operational sorties under his belt since he joined his squadron in September 1943. But he had always been a number two, the follower whose task was to guard the leader's and his own tail against attack by enemy fighters. The leader was in command. He had to give all the orders, navigate, carry out the objective and get his section of two, although sometimes four, aircraft safely back to base. He had heavy responsibility.

So it was that the Mustang pilot, with the full weight of his first sortie in the lead, was somewhat nervous. He had a 'bit of a twitch' as the airmen of the day called it. Furthermore, to make matters worse he had to take as his number two a Spitfire IX from another squadron. If he goofed or botched up the operation he and his own squadron would lose face. He'd never hear the end of it. The pressure was really on.

A Mustang and a Spitfire flying an operation together was a most unusual event. Two fighters, recce Mustangs from 430 Squadron of the Royal Canadian Air Force, had been asked to accompany 411 Squadron, a Canadian Spitfire unit, on their bombing operation against two newly discovered freighters in Dieppe Harbor. The attack would be on the inner basin of that heavily defended port where so many Canadian soldiers had been killed, wounded or taken prisoner in August 1942.

From their base at Odiham, southwest of London, the Mustangs had flown south in the late morning of 24 April to Tangmere, the Royal Air Force airfield on the south coast of England that had been turned over to a Canadian wing (three squadrons) of Spitfires.

At Tangmere, the Canadian wing leader, Wing Commander George Keefer, briefed the Spitfire pilots on their operation: dive bomb and destroy the two freighters just arrived at Dieppe. The pair of Mustangs were to use their sideward pointing (oblique) aerial cameras to take glamor photos of the squadron of twelve Spits as they crossed the Channel in tight, close formation, every man in place. Immediately after the last Spit had dropped its bombs the lead Mustang, covered by his number two, would dash across the deadly Dieppe Harbor at next to zero feet to photograph the blazing, exploding enemy vessels devastated by the accurately placed bombs of the diving Spitfires. That was the scenario as briefed.

Unfortunately the engine of the lead Mustang refused to start at the moment designated by the wing commander for 'pressing tits', that is, pulling or pushing all the levers and buttons necessary to start up the engine. A quick on-the-spot series of orders put the pilot of the second camera-equipped Mustang in the lead with a Spit IX from the squadron flying protection for him as his number two. When that adjustment was made the twelve aircraft of 411 Squadron took off followed immediately by the lone Mustang and its single Spitfire protector.

There was only one problem for the Mustang pilot. His radio did not have a common operating frequency with the Spitfire squadron leader. Therefore he could not listen in on the radio instructions or chatter of the squadron. However, he was able to talk to his own Spitfire number two on the emergency frequency. In turn, the Spit pilot could then switch to his squadron's frequency to pass a message if need be.

One thing a fighter recce pilot was never supposed to do was get lost. Ordinary fighter pilots could do so and did so with regularity. But the fighter recce pilot was a highly trained specialist in navigation and map reading. He knew where he was at all times and could find a target in the far corner of a corn field if it was marked on his map by intelligence people before he took off. Well, that was the way it was supposed to be. The young Mustang pilot — he'd been lost once or twice but always found his way home — was full of confidence. He wouldn't get lost. He would perform as if he was an old hand. Besides, all he had to do was follow the Spitfires. The squadron leader would get them to Dieppe. No problem.

The flight across the English channel had been smooth. The late afternoon sky was cloudless. Visibility was unlimited. Some hundred yards off to the right of the squadron the Mustang pilot maneuvered his aircraft to bring the Spits directly into the line of sight of his camera. From that position he took a dozen photographs of the clutch of fighters, all twelve nearly touching, flying together almost as one. Each pilot was doing his utmost to keep his aircraft in its exact tight-formation post so it would appear to be in perfect formation in the pictures. It would cost anyone out of position a round of drinks that night at the local pub!

The photography was finished by the time they were half way across the Channel. The Spits opened up into battle formation, spreading apart to intervals of about fifty yards so each pilot could watch for attacking enemy aircraft.

As the French coast came into view a thin blanket of low cloud could also be seen. It began some three miles offshore producing an apparently solid blanket of cover over the coastal lands where Dieppe was calculated to be.

The inexperienced fighter recce pilot, believing that he was superior in map reading to any Spit pilot, decided that he would try to be the hero by finding Dieppe through whatever cloud holes might miraculously appear in the cloud formation. He would then be able to tell the Spit leader, by this time presumably lost, where to go. After all, Mustang fighter reconnaissance pilots were highly trained in map-reading, whereas Spitfire pilots were famous for their inability to keep track of their own whereabouts! The tantalizing prospect of finding Dieppe first and being 'one up' on the squadron leader filled the young Mustang pilot's mind. Hence, he was frantically searching for a cloud hole below.

There was no hole to be found. He lifted his eyes momentarily to check the position of the Spit squadron that a few seconds before had been about a mile ahead of him.

The squadron had disappeared! The Spits were gone, vanished! Where were they? He *had* to find them.

If he couldn't. . . . It was unbelievable. How could he explain why he had lost and entire squadron! He would never be able to live it down. What a black!

As if by a miracle, about a mile ahead of him down at the level of the cloud about 3,000 feet below, he caught sight of a Spitfire in its dive bombing run hurtling vertically through a small aperture in the cloud. There were no other Spits in sight. It was the last one. That meant the rest of the squadron, all eleven of them, had delivered their bombs and were already heading out across the Channel for England.

Meanwhile, with no direct radio contact with the squadron commander, the Mustang pilot was left behind. Perhaps he could blame his failure on not having the Spit squadron's frequency on his own radio and so was not able to hear them. Any excuse would do.

It was impossible to take photographs through the

cloud or through the hole the Spits had dived through because it was far too small. What to do? With little understanding of the potential dangers, he made his decision.

At the moment he had seen the last diving Spitfire he was heading east. His Spitfire number two was 200 yards to his right in battle formation. The radio instructions to the Spit pilot were terse: "I'm going to do my photo run westbound along the beach. You stay well away out over the water."

The two aircraft, still heading east, began to descend. The Mustang pilot moved his throttle up to full power, putting his machine well ahead of the slower Spitfire. Checking his altitude as he approached the cloud layer, the fighter reconnaissance airman gently pushed the control column over to the left, swinging his huge fighter in an arc north over the cloud, now wispy and thin along the shore. He was still turning and descending. As the beach came into view, he was about three miles east of Dieppe and the towering beach edge cliffs that enclosed the town and its harbor.

Still down he went, the roar of his laboring engine louder than he had ever heard it. He checked his speed. It was higher than he had taken a Mustang before, just over 450 miles an hour. If he leveled out at 300 feet and got in close to the beach he should get at least two or three good photos of the harbor and, with any luck, the ships the Spits had just attacked. At 300 feet and a mile east of the entrance to the harbor, he leveled his Mustang and got set for his run in, ready to activate his camera by pushing the button on the control column. As he rocketed along, he could almost touch the high cliffs. He was ready, but not for what came next.

Suddenly it was as if the whole world had turned into a formidable display of horrifying fireworks. Every antiaircraft gun in Dieppe started firing at him. An almost solid wall of white, burning balls were arcing comet-like toward him, enveloping his hurtling aircraft in a checkerboard of exploding light. Too late he realized that by the time the twelfth Spitfire had bombed the harbor, every German flak gun would be fully manned and red-hot. Petrified and trapped into a situation precipitated by his own inexperience and stupidity, the pilot had no choice but to press on. He just had to get at least one picture.

As the harbor flashed by to his left under the aiming marker painted on the trailing edge of his wing, he pushed the camera button. Now the hail of flak was so heavy and close he involuntarily ducked. He pulled his head down inside the cockpit, the goggles on his leather flying helmet almost touching his right hand which clenched the control column. The instrument panel reflected the kaleidoscope of flashes from the anti-aircraft shells exploding all around him.

The Mustang sped past the harbor through the gauntlet of fire, the pilot expecting at any instant to be blasted out of the sky. He cursed his stupidity and inexperience that had put him in this deadly position. With the innate 'gung ho' attitude of the young, he had seen himself as an invincible fighter-pilot to whom nothing could happen, who could never be hit by flak, who could never be shot down. It couldn't be happening to him!

As quickly as the flak had begun, it stopped. He was beyond it, out of range. With great relief he began climbing northward in the direction of Tangmere, the fighter squadron nest from which he, his number two, and 411 Squadron had departed just a short time before.

After landing at Tangmere and reporting to the commanding officer of the fighter Squadron (a unit which he himelf would command in Canada in 1953, flying Vampire jet aircraft), the Mustang pilot flew back to his own base at RAF Station Odiham. Following a debriefing by an Intelligence officer of 39 Reconnaissance Wing, of which 430 Squadron was a part, he was informed by the unit photographic section that only one photograph of Dieppe harbor had turned out.

Somewhat shaken by his experience the author of the Daily Operations Log of 430 Squadron made this entry about his own trip that day:

F.O.R.H. Rohmer, Yours truly, went out with some Spitfires from 411 Squadron, R.C.A.F. who bombed some shipping at Dieppe. F/L J.H.

Taylor (Can.J.7426) was supposed to have gone as No. 1, but because his engine wouldn't start, F/O Rohmer took a Spitfire along as a No. 2, taking photographs of the Squadron on the way across. The bombing was done through a small hole above Dieppe, but it was too small to photograph through, so F/O Rohmer, the clot, did a run across the mouth of the harbor at 300 feet just after the Spits had bombed. 'Nachully' there was some flak but nothing came of it. One picture of the Basin came out but nothing showed up on it.

A look at that Dieppe photograph of 24 April 1944 will confirm what I wrote that day. But the flak and the two ships, both there, did not show.

Aerial reconnaissance first emerged in World War I as a powerful, important tactical tool used by the army commanders on both sides. Visual reconnaissance by pilots and observers, even spotters in balloons, of the movements of troops, vehicles, tanks, railway trains proved invaluable. For example, heavy movement in any given area would indicate that the enemy was building up for a major attack; or, depending on the direction the movements were going, that he was beating a retreat. Aerial photography enabled the plotting of the location of new trenches and earth work, gun positions, ammunition depots, the location of armored and other vehicles. Artillery spotters were carried in aircraft to direct the fire of long-range guns onto their targets when ground observers could not see them.

In World War II the army had to have the same reconnaissance services available to them: tactical reconnaissance (TAC/R) the visual observation of enemy activity and positions; photographic reconnaissance (Photo/R) low or high to produce, for example, pictures of the enemy fortifications so that they could be hit by our artillery, or when an attack was mounted the troops would know exactly what they were going to be faced with; high level, vertical photography capturing on film such information as the flow of traffic through distant enemy railway yards, the aircraft population on enemy airfields and the like; and artillery reconnaissance (Arty/R) the ranging of heavy guns onto difficult-to-observe or long-range targets.

These were the roles and missions of 430 Squadron and our specially equipped, heavily armed, fighter-reconnaissance, single seater Mustangs, the P51. Before D-Day we were tasked mainly for photographic reconnaissance of targets in France hit by our bombers so that, from our pictures, the photo interpreters could evaluate what damage had been done — also to photograph the potential landing invasion beaches. In addition, we did low level sorties called 'rhubarbs' attacking trains and vehicles carrying German supplies across France.

However, as of D-Day the 6th of June, the fighter reconnaissance Mustangs of 430 and 414 of Royal Canadian Air Force and 168 and 2 of the Royal Air Force were dedicated solely to tactical, photographic and artillery reconnaissance in support of the British and Canadian armies in their assault against the German fortifications on the Normandy coast. We became the eyes of the army, watching and reporting the enemy's every move in the area of the battlefield and the approaches to the front lines. When we found concentrations of tanks or vehicles we would call in squadrons of rocket-firing Typhoons, bomb-carrying Spitfires of the Royal Canadian Air Force and the Royal Air Force, and the Thunderbolts and Lightnings of the United States Air Force. Operating our Mustangs in pairs or fours at low level we were all-seeing hawks scouring the ground for prey. However, the Germans called us not 'hawks' but 'bloodhounds'.

The England I returned to from Dieppe that day was an armed camp. Its verdant countryside was populated by troops of every Allied nation. Hundreds of thousands of them were trained, ready, and waiting for the orders that would direct them to the southern seaports where they would board vessels that would carry them across to France and the invasion beaches, wherever those were to be. Military camps, storage depots, and roadways bristled with guns, tanks, trucks, jeeps, armored personnel carriers, ambulances, and all the weaponry of war that a superbly

Dieppe: 24 April 1944

0013 430/628 15 AUG.44. 14˝ //J. SA/8.4000ʹ

0002 430/536 18 JULY 44. 20˝ //U.SA/12.6000ʹ

430 Squadron's Mustang I's over Normandy

equipped, modern army would have to take into battle. In the large harbors and the estuaries along the much-indented south coast of England sat the hundreds of ships and vessels: battleships, destroyers, landing craft, minesweepers. They would form the invasion armada on D-Day. Squatting in the water to the east of Portsmouth were huge concrete cubes, immense, towering structures, mammoth in size. We fighter-reconnaissance pilots had seen them many times but we had no idea what they were. We would find out soon after D-Day.

In the air hundreds of American, British, and Canadian bombers continued their devastating attacks on targets deep in Germany and, closer to home, in the Pas-de-Calais area of France against Noball targets that we were often tasked to photograph before and after the bomber attacks. As with the concrete structures, we did not know what the Noball targets were or why they had to be destroyed.

What we did know was that the code name Noball had been assigned to a ramp type structure the Germans were building in large numbers in the Pas-de-Calais area near the coast. And we knew that, whatever they were, a massive air effort was being made to wipe them out. Allied medium and fighter bombers, such as those of the Spitfire squadron I had accompanied across to Dieppe, were also constantly hammering radar and wireless installations along the French coast and attacking the German airfields from which the deadly Messerschmitt and Focke-Wulf fighters operated not far inland.

It was a time of strength for the Allied forces. You could feel it in the air. We were strong, well equipped, highly trained, and anxious to get on with it, to invade France, to defeat the Germans, to get the war over with and go home.

Of the host of generals assembled in the United Kingdom to lead us into battle, there were four who were to play dominant roles during the assault on the Normandy beaches on D-Day, 6 June 1944, and through to the final victory in Normandy during the third week of August. They were Eisenhower, Montgomery, Bradley and Patton.

Paramount among them was the Supreme Commander, Dwight D. Eisenhower, the benign military politician and diplomat from Abilene, Kansas.

Eisenhower had commanded the American forces in North Africa during their successful entry into that theater. Both Patton and Bradley had served under him there. An officer with far more experience in mapping strategy and dealing with intra-military politics than in directing armies in the field, Eisenhower was a natural candidate to handle the minefield of international rivalries among the American, British, Canadian, French and other generals, admirals and air-marshals of the Allied forces. He had been nominated by the senior American General of the day, George C. Marshall, to fill the highly sensitive post of Supreme Allied Commander.

At Algiers on 7 December 1943, President Roosevelt had informed Eisenhower that he was going to command Overlord, the invasion of Normandy. This came as a complete surprise to Eisenhower who knew that, at the Quebec Conference in August of that year, it had been decided that General George Marshall was to be the Supreme Allied Commander. However, Roosevelt later felt that he could not afford to let Marshall leave Washington. On the advice of Marshall, the President therefore proposed at the Cairo Conference of early December 1943 that Eisenhower take the high, sensitive post.

It had also been decided at Cairo that Montgomery would be the Commander in Chief of all land forces during the Normandy assault. At the same time he would be the Commander of the British 21st Army Group.

Because the Americans' overpowering number of men and incredible volume of war equipment and material were far greater than those of the long-suffering British and their Commonwealth members such as Canada, Churchill had had no choice but to allow the Americans the ascendent military position in the liberation of Europe — operation Overlord, which would open with Neptune, the invasion of Normandy. In the Allied politics of the day it followed, and Churchill insisted, that if the Supreme Commander was to be an American then the Commander in Chief of the invasion land forces should be a Briton.

This arrangement suited the British very well for they believed themselves to be far superior militarily and intellectually vastly better in strategy, tactics, and combat than any colonials, a category into which all Americans and Canadians unequivocally fell. It thus occurred that General Sir Bernard Law Montgomery, resting on his laurels as the victorious 8th Army Commander against Field Marshal Rommel at El Alamein (and later reluctantly sharing the victory in Sicily with the flamboyant United States general, "Old Blood and Guts" George S. Patton, Jr.,) was appointed Commander of all the Allied Forces that would mount the D-Day assault in Operation Neptune. In this position and also as commander of the British 21st Army Group, Montgomery would have the final responsibility for the planning of Neptune and for its execution, all subject to the approval of Eisenhower and his political masters.

The D-Day army leaders under Montgomery were to be the U.S. First Army commander, Lieutenant General Omar Bradley, and the British Second Army commander, Lieutenant General Miles Dempsey, who would have under his operational control both the 2nd Canadian Corps and the Polish Armored Division as well as his own Second British Army.

Bradley, a one-time school teacher, was an unassuming man. He was quiet, soft spoken, yet extremely intelligent and surprisingly forceful. He had served in North Africa with Eisenhower as the latter's eyes and ears and, like Patton, had gained battle experience there and in Sicily where he had served as a corps commander under Patton. In late 1943 it was a question whether Bradley would be selected as leader of the American land forces on D-Day or whether that distinction would go to Patton. It was General Marshall who made the decision between the two men.

By that time Patton had been through his notorious Sicilian slapping incidents. The first of these two events took place at an evacuation center on 3 August 1943. Patton struck a young private whom he believed to be a malingerer, afraid to fight. Later, on 10 August 1943, the General struck yet another young soldier at an evacuation post after declaring, "I won't have the hospitals cluttered up with these sons-of-bitches who haven't the guts to fight." The subsequent furor and indignation in the United States in the fall of 1943, especially in Congress, over these two affairs put Patton in disgrace and cost him his command of the American

Seventh Army, events finally catching up with him on 1 January 1944 when he was relieved of his post. Even so, his skills as a top battle commander and leader of men were highly visible to his superiors.

In Sicily, he had commanded with huge success the U.S. Seventh Army, hammering rapidly up the western side of the island. Bradley was one of his corps commanders. Patton's British counterpart and equal as an Army commander, Montgomery, and his 8th Army worked slowly up the eastern side of the island. The sharp rivalry that grew between the two generals during the Sicily campaign was spurred by competitiveness deeply embedded in each of them. In Sicily, what was originally a battle to defeat the Germans and Italians and drive them out of the island became a personal foot race between Montgomery and Patton to see who could get to capture Messina first. Patton had won that glory when his 3rd Division with General Lucien Truscott at the head reached the Messina Town Hall at 08:25 on 17 August, 1943. Moments later a tank of the British Eighth Army arrived, but it was too late.

Unfortunately, the shimmering glory from Patton's Sicilian military successes, which had established him in the minds of the American public as a military genius and leader of equal, if not superior, status to Montgomery, would soon be dimmed by the growing black shadow of the 'slapping incidents'. They would cost him not only command of the Seventh Army in Sicily but as well a fighting position at the head of an invading army on D-Day.

On 23 December 1943, Eisenhower prepared the list of general officers he wanted to have as field commanders for the assault on Normandy. His recommendation was the turning point which was to place Bradley ahead of and superior to Patton. In his signal to Marshall in Washington he said:

> "My preference for American Group Commander
> . . . when more than one American Army is operating in 'Overlord,' is General Bradley. One of his Army Commanders should probably be Patton."[1]

Bradley's nomination was later confirmed by Marshall,

who gave as his reason the need for someone, above Patton in rank or command, who could keep in check Patton's often impetuous and overly enthusiastic nature.

What Patton was to be given command of was the Third American Army in the United Kingdom. At the outset its main function was as the spearhead of the fictitious FUSAG, First United States Army Group. This was an imaginary force designed to induce German Intelligence into believing that, even after the invasion of Normandy, Patton would be leading a massive second force against the Pas-de-Calais area. This crucially important deception scheme was called "Fortitude." The Third American Army did in fact have troops at the time Patton was given his United Kingdom assignment in January 1944 but they were far away in the United States of America. The plan was that the presence of Patton, who was highly respected and feared by the Germans, would cause the Germans to hold their forces in the Pas-de-Calais area waiting for his second onslaught. In reality, Patton was not slated to take the field in France until the end of July 1944. He would not participate in operation Neptune, the assault on the Normandy beaches which would mark the beginning of the overall operation, Overlord.

So the Sicily equals of 1943, Montgomery and Patton, found themselves in the spring of 1944 in polarized positions. Montgomery would command the invasion forces while Patton was to cool his heels in England.

Montgomery and Patton were complete opposites. General Sir Bernard Law Montgomery was the battle-seasoned, glorified, victorious leader of the British Eighth Army, vanquisher of Rommel and hero of the British people. The son of an Anglican missionary bishop, he was a man who brought to his adulthood all the bitter experiences of a difficult, unloved childhood, of a mother whom he could never satisfy however much he tried or however good his performance. Small of stature, frail, rejected, he became almost entirely self-reliant. He demanded perfection and obedience from others and dedicated himself to being the best in his military profession. Without doubt he succeeded with his victory at El Alamein. From that time onward he could only be satisfied if all his battles ended in success of his own making and design. His view of his place in history required that he personally, and not his superiors, should plan the battle; and that he, Montgomery, should be the battlefield commander of all Allied armies in the field, be they American, Canadian, Polish or British.

In his book, *The Struggle for Europe,* the experienced correspondent, Chester Wilmot, assessed Montgomery's acceptability to the American generals with whom he would associate or command. Quite apart from Montgomery's possession of the inherent British tendency to regard all North Americans as colonials worthy only to be commanded, Wilmot's view was that to the Americans:

> "His methods were more objectionable because he was so clearly born to command and, even in his most tactful moments, he exercised his authority almost as a matter of right. Moreover, he was not as other men. He revealed no traits of ordinary human frailty, however. He shunned the company of women; he did not smoke or drink or play poker with 'the boys.' He could never be 'slapped on the back.' Because he lived in a small tactical H.Q. with a few aides and liaison officers, he was looked upon as setting himself apart from (and therefore above) his fellows. This impression seems to be confirmed by his practice, resented as much by other British services as it was by the Americans, of sending his Chief of Staff, de Guingand, to represent him at conferences. . . .
> "The American attitude toward Montgomery . . . cannot be accounted for on the ground of national prejudice alone, although this was a contributing factor. His manner and method would have been equally distasteful in an American."[2]

The brilliant, high-strung, inordinately vain Montgomery shared those same attributes with Patton, as well as a distinctiveness, if not eccentricity of dress. Monty's double-badged beret was his trademark as was his cold-weather sheepskin RAF flying jacket. And, as with Patton, Montgomery had a voice quirk: a lisp often affected among British public school boys.

In contrast to the diminutive, bantam rooster image of Montgomery was his arch-competitor from the Sicily days, Lieutenant General George Smith Patton, Jr., commander of the Third United States Army in all its non-existent glory. Born to a wealthy, aristocratic California family of landed gentry, as a child Patton was well loved, even doted upon. Horses, polo, and a consuming interest in the great battles of history and the men who won and lost them were main elements in his early Pasadena days. They led him to the military, West Point and the Cavalry, whose distinctive dress he never abandoned — boots, spurs, breeks and the ever-present ivory-handled revolvers.

Patton was a career soldier, fully dedicated to his profession. He was a flamboyant, hard-hitting, outspoken leader of men with an inspiring speaking ability. His rhetoric was always laced with the most striking four-letter words, those usually reserved for drill sergeants. He was "Old Blood and Guts." Indeed, he was old in combat terms, 58 years of age in the spring of 1944. A sturdy six-foot two-inch man, trim, erect, white haired, he was always immaculately turned out, most often in his cavalry gear. Patton was a compulsive, colorful talker with his peculiar high-pitched voice and immense cuss-word vocabulary. He was the physical antithesis to the casually clothed Montgomery, whom he looked down on as a set-piece general, quite incapable of moving his forces with speed or of seizing opportunities. Of Patton, Wilmot wrote:

> His behavior made him unpopular in high places, but he was not suspect as an autocrat. The "tough guy" pose which he adopted in public (complete with pearl-handled revolvers in open holsters) was worn and familiar in the best tradition of the "Wild West." Although he liked to pretend that he was hard-boiled, he was intensely emotional and soft-hearted. When deeply moved, he readily gave way to tears. Moreover, in all his posturing he conveyed the impression that he was showing off

his personal toughness rather than his professional authority. High-handed though his behavior often was, he commanded in the American manner, debating his plans with his staff in daily conference as a "democratic" general should, and abiding by the principle, "never tell people how to do things, tell them what to do and they will surprise you with their ingenuities."[3]

[Wilmot was wrong. The revolvers were ivory-handled.]

On the day of my Dieppe dalliance, 24 April 1944, each of the stellar generals, Eisenhower, Montgomery, Bradley and Patton, was at his respective headquarters preparing in his own way for the day when the Allied onslaught against Fortress Europe was to begin. At that time it would have been impossible for anyone, especially one at my lowly station in the military scheme of things, to foresee the mammoth battles that were to come. Only our remote, god-like generals and their staffs could envisage the scope and course of events. Of all the Allied generals, it would be this quartet, with their own rivalries, quirks, jealousies, and human strengths and failings, that would transport all of us, more than a million men and women, from the opening victory of D-Day on 6 June through to the closing of the Falaise Gap on 19/20 August 1944, the event that marked the final defeat of the German army in Normandy.

The glory of that victory and the enormous scale of the destruction wrought upon the enemy was, however, to overshadow, obscure, almost obliterate the causes and results of one of the gravest, most costly tactical errors in the history of modern warfare — the creation of the Falaise Gap.

The Falaise Gap was the opening at the eastern end of the enormous pocket in which the German Seventh Army and its supporting Panzer Army were contained as of 12 August 1944. This pocket — or Kessel (kettle) as the Germans called it — was encircled by the Allied armies. Through the gap between Falaise and Argentan, tens of thousands of

Germans were permitted to escape before the Gap was closed on 19/20 August.

Professor Percy Ernst Schramm, The German historian, later wrote of the German escape from the pocket through the Falaise Gap:

> "Although the enemy employed his air force on an unprecedented scale [a total of 8,000 tons of bombs were dropped in but two major air support operations], we succeeded in withdrawing our forces eastward from the *Kessel* . . . A substantial portion of heavy equipment was destroyed by the encircled troops; more of it was lost in the breakout; but more than half of it could be rescued nevertheless. Consequently, the breakout at Falaise, in which the 3rd Parachute Division especially distinguished itself, remains one of the great passages of arms of this campaign. The second opportunity the enemy had during this retreat-operation to cut off and destroy a whole army was thus thwarted."[4]

The first opportunity of which Schramm wrote was at Argentan, where Patton's Third Army was to arrive on 12 August. Had Patton immediately proceeded north a further twelve miles to Falaise and a short distance beyond it to link up with the Canadians and Poles, the entire German force would have been trapped. Patton had reconnaissance parties near Falaise on 13 August, but the order came to pull back to Argentan. The Falaise Gap was thus created. It was to remain open a full week. Through it forged German troops, tanks, artillery, trucks, ambulances — anything that could move.

Who gave the order that kept the American Third Army at Argentan, thereby preventing the final arm of the pocket from being closed on 12/13 August? Was it Patton himself? Was it Montgomery, Bradley or Eisenhower?

The matter of who among those great generals was responsible for the creation of the Falaise Gap and why such an order was given has been described by some historians as a mystery. The memory of that place and moment also carries with it lingering contention and controversy over the results of the existence of the Gap, which brought with it the bitter tang of failure in the presence of what Montgomery called "a victory which was acclaimed as the greatest achievement in military history."

The contention and controversy of the Falaise Gap will never die. But, as will be seen, I have the solution to the mystery.

2

ADMINISTRATION: F/O R. H. Rohmer
(Can. J.24120) returned from Ramsberry
and the Flying Circus today.

430 Squadron Log

What the squadron log did not say was that General Patton
had inspected the Flying Circus that morning, 8 May 1944.
Furthermore, the old boy had words with me!

The log does record that on 28 April I left our base at
Odiham to replace F/O Jack Cox (who was later shot down
on D-Day) as a member of the Flying Circus of fighter aircraft then at Thorney Island, a Royal Air Force fighter
station close to Portsmouth on the south coast of England.

My squadron had been working hard during the spring
of '44, both in operations and training, honing our skills
in aerial photography and in low-level map reading. This
was a special capability that required us to be able to pinpoint the location of trucks, tanks, guns or whatever we
discovered during our reconnaissance and pin it down to an
exact reference point, whether in the corner of a field or the
center of a town.

Another specialty was Arty/R/artillery reconaissance
in which we directed the large guns on to targets. Each

of us had trained on the artillery ranges at Aldershot, learning the art of ranging the guns from the air. After D-Day it would be one of our roles to range the 155 millimeter and other big guns in circumstances where it was impossible for the AirOP's (Air Observation Post) to operate in their tiny light aircraft, the Austers, because of their vulnerability to anti-aircraft fire. The plan was that we would then be called in. Sitting a reasonable distance back from the target at four or five thousand feet and out of range of the enemy anti-aircraft guns, we would be able to direct the fire of the four or six ranging guns; and when the shells were finally locked on to the target all of the guns assigned to the shoot would open up on it.

In addition we had to maintain our proficiency in air-to-air and air-to-ground gunnery so that we could efficiently use the six .5 inch calibre and two 30 calibre machine guns mounted in each Mustang to attack other aircraft or ground targets. Our missions over France during the winter and into the spring period of 1944 mainly consisted of 'rhubarb' operations, carried out at low-level (so low we could cut rhubarb with our own props) across the countryside on pre-determined routes, attacking railway trains or military vehicles; and photographic sorties, using either our vertical or oblique cameras to cover specified objectives such as radar, wireless stations, stretches of beach that might be used for the invasion, and targets that had been selected for bombing attacks or which had already been hit.

We flew these operations in pairs or in fours. On reconnaisannce or photographic operations the leader was the pilot responsible for completing the duty assigned, while the number two, or in the case of formation four, the other three were responsible for covering his tail and keeping an eye out for attacking enemy aircraft. On the rhubarb missions, however, everyone had a chance to attack a choice target such as a railway engine.

430 Squadron was equipped with twelve Mustang I aircraft, the original model of the famous fighting machine, the Mustang IV or P51D, which the Americans eventually developed into the long range escort for their Flying Fortress bombers that smashed Germany by day. Built by North American Aviation of California, our Mustang I's cruised

at about 260 miles per hour. They were equipped with an Allison engine with a cropped blower, that is, the engine's super charger was rendered inoperative with the result that we had difficulty in operating above 10,000 feet. Moreover, the aircraft was large and heavy, making it impossible for us to turn inside a Messerschmitt 109 or a Focke-Wulf in a dogfight. The rule for the Mustang I was: if bounced by an enemy fighter, do not attempt to dogfight because the German is bound to win. Instead, roll over on your back and dive with your engine at maximum emergency power. No German fighter could keep up with us. The Mustang with its weight and superb streamlining would leave any Me 109 or Focke-Wulf far behind at well over 400 miles per hour. That tactical rule was not always followed.

We were happy with our reliable fighters. They had arrived in the early summer of 1943 to replace the less than satisfactory Curtis Tomahawks, 430 squadron's original equipment. About the time I joined the unit at a tactical airstrip near Ashford in Kent in September 1943, the Mustang had satisfied everyone with its ruggedness, reliability and comforting high-speed. The only disappointments were its lack of dogfighting maneuverability and its inability to operate effectively at high altitudes. It was a big, impressive fighter, a much larger machine than the Spitfires of the day. Painted in the dark greens of RAF camouflage and polished with loving care, the Mustang I was a sleek, beautiful airplane.

430 Squadron and its complement of some twenty pilots spent the winter at Gatwick airport just south of London on the London to Brighton railway line. Gatwick was a flying challenge for us and our figher aircraft because the airfield had no runways, only rolling green turf. Taking off was always a series of lurches across the undulating ground of what, in prewar days, had been a racetrack. By remarkably good accidental planning, our standard RAF billets had been placed within a two minute walk of the Gatwick railway station through which the electric trains of the Brighton line either thundered at full speed or, conveniently for us, ground to a halt to take on or disgorge passengers. Happily, there were many trains to carry us to and from London. Victoria Station was only a little over

half an hour away and beyond it, after a short taxi ride, the delights and challenges of Piccadilly Circus, the Regent Palace Hotel and the Chez Moi Club on Denham Street.

The Chez Moi was the privileged hang-out of the RCAF's fighter pilots. Like their RAF colleagues they were easily identified in any crowd of light blue Air Force uniforms by the undone top brass button on their jackets.

The place was no more than a large basement room conveniently converted into a bar. The walls were lined with photographs of jaunty, cocky pilots and their fighting aircraft, predominantly Hurricanes and Spitfires. Any evening my gang and I were in the Chez Moi it was filled with fellow fighter pilots regaling each other with hair-raising flying stories — "there I was at ten thousand feet, upside down, this Jerry in my sights, nothing on the clock but the maker's name!" And other similar traditional 'line-shoots'. For 'line-shoot' substitute bullshit. For 'clock' substitute 'air speed indicator'. For 'Jerry' substitute 'German'. As the evening progressed so did the number of drinks consumed, the density of the cigarette smoke, the volume of the story telling and the recounted bravery of the people who held the floor at the moment. Girls? The odd one could be found in the place. What the members of the Chez Moi club needed in their youthful exuberance (average age probably twenty-two) was convivial comradeship, lots of booze and the excitement of telling and listening to their own stories of outfoxing the Hun. That is: stories about surviving, cheating death. Death was something we never talked about. At least not directly.

It was from Gatwick that I did my first operation over France. It was a photo reconnaissance mission in early December 1943, four long months after I joined the squadron at Ashford. The reason for the delay had nothing to do with my flying ability. It was my appearance. I was slight, thin and had the face of a 16-year-old. I looked so young the squadron commander took a protective, fatherly interest in me and could barely conceive of my being old enough to meet the threat of the deadly Hun. But he finally relented.

I survived my first trip as a nervous number two, ardently protecting the tail of my leader as the pair of us roared across the Channel just above the waves to avoid radar detection, and then pulled up to a lofty 5,000 feet altitude to cross the French coast, find our target, photograph it and hare back to the welcoming shores of Mother England.

If my youthful visage gave pause to my squadron commander, it was to stop General Patton in his tracks, although by the time I met Old Blood and Guts on 8 May 1944 I had many missions under my belt and was rapidly becoming an experienced hand on the squadron. And, of course, having turned twenty the previous January, I was feeling much older and far more confident, even though I still looked sixteen.

After the gray winter at Gatwick, the squadron moved back into tents at the Royal Air Force base at Odiham. There we joined two other Canadian units, 400 Squadron with its Bluebird high-level photography, unarmed reconnaissance Spitfires, and 414 Squadron, which was also a Mustang fighter-reconnaissance unit. Our three Canadian squadrons were the operational arm of the 39 Recce Wing. Once the invasion started, it was designated to work with the British Army as its reconnaissance and photographic eyes. 35 Recce Wing, our Royal Air Force counterpart, was to work with the Canadian Army. This machiavellian twist of cross-ethnic fertilization was attributed to General Montgomery himself, the legendary leader for whom we would be performing all manner of dedicated services.

In the spring of 1944 someone at Supreme Headquarters realized that unless the people fighting the battle on the ground had some opportunity to have a prior look at the close support aircraft that would be working with them in battle, they might well confuse them with the enemy. This was particularly so with the Mustang, which had an uncanny resemblance to the German Me 109. In fact, it was so similar that I can well recall being attacked over Holland in late 1944 by twelve American silver Mustang IV's who must have thought that because we had camouflage paint on our aircraft, and a birdcage hood like the 109's, that we were, in fact, Germans. Probably to this day the American pilots, who descended upon us from above like a group of famished hawks, still grind their teeth when they think of those two Messerschmitts that got away from them by nipping into the nearest cloud. Thank God there was one close by.

In order to show our soldiers what their supporting airplanes looked like, it was decided to form a Flying Circus made up of all of the fighters, fighter bombers, and rocket-carrying Typhoons that were part of the Allied Tactical Air Forces. The Flying Circus, complete with a Dakota transport aircraft, would then travel around the English countryside, appearing on schedule over great gatherings of troops who, faces and eyes turned skyward, would watch each of us fly by at a low level. Every one of the pilots thought it was marvelous to take part in a legalized 'beat-up'.

As the Squadron Log shows, I joined the Flying Circus at Thorney Island, a Royal Air Force base right on the water's edge of the south coast. In my trusty, highly polished Mustang, I landed there on Friday, 28 April, with instructions to stay with the Circus until 8 May. On the tarmac I could see one of every fighter the IX U.S. Air Force and the British 2nd Tactical Air Force had in inventory: the twin-boomed, twin-engined Lightning; the squat, flat nosed Thunderbolt; the Mustang IV of the Americans; the Spitfire and the rocket-carrying Typhoon of the British; and the then not yet venerable U.S. machine, the Douglas DC3, known as the Dakota, which would carry paratroopers and tow gliders across to the invasion area in the dawn of D-Day.

That night there was a get-acquainted bash in the Officers' Mess during which the participating pilots — British, American, and myself, the Canadian — consumed more than enough mild and bitters (the flat British alcohol brew that does indeed taste bitter) and lager beer to make absolutely sure through the resulting haze of booze-enhanced camaraderie that we got to know each other well. We had a grand time that night, particularly with the Americans. They were a happy go-lucky gang having a ball. In fact, during the next few days they adopted me as one of their own to the point that I was allowed to fly their brand new Mustang IV. The rule book said I couldn't. The aircraft was USAF. I was a Canadian. The machine was much different in the cockpit and in handling than my old Mustang I — more power, different engine, less weight. But what the hell! I had the chance, so why not. What a difference between the two.

The morning after our Thorney Island get-together party and a short recovery sleep, we had a briefing by the squadron leader in charge of the organization. After the usual thorough check of our airplanes, which consisted fundamentally of kicking one of the tires, the Flying Circus was airborne. Our ten-day tour took us from airfield to airfield and over massive gatherings of troops clustered in selected fields of English countryside, faces dutifully turned skyward as we roared by one by one, imprinting on their memories an indelible, unforgettable image. At least, that's what we wanted to believe. We were sure that each man would say to himself, "Now I recognize that Thunderbolt and that Spitfire, that Typhoon and Mustang, that Lightning, that Thunderbolt and the Dakota. I swear that on or after D-Day I will not, repeat, will not shoot at them or anything that looks like them."

Without doubt there was great merit in the concept that if the army saw us and were able to recognize us, they would not shoot at us. However, the post D-Day track record of the itchy-fingered, twitchy soldiers in the field clearly demonstrated that they would shoot at anything, no matter what it looked like and no matter what the insignia painted on the fuselage and wings — the American Star, the British Roundel or the Iron Cross. But there was no doubt in our minds that each of us taking part in the Flying Circus was doing something highly beneficial for all our fellow tactical air force pilots who were part of the huge air armada that would sweep the skies of France in support of the liberating Allied armies.

The last stop on our extended tour was at Ramsberry, a Royal Air Force airfield near Liverpool. It was a flying training base and a very 'tiddly' one. After our arrival late in the afternoon of Sunday, 7 May, some officious RAF squadron leader violently objected to my unseemly dress. He thought I should have had on a shirt and tie. Instead, in true fighter form, I was wearing the only clothing I had with me, my airforce blue battledress trousers and jacket, complete with wings and a rescue whistle at the collar, and a dark blue polka-dot scarf around my neck. My trousers were tucked into knee-length, sheepskin-lined flying boots. From the top of the right flying boot the handle of my dagger protruded. My hefty Smith & Wesson revolver was strapped to my right leg just above the boot, readily available should I need to defend myself against the Hun on the soil of France. The distraught squadron leader had no choice but to give up the battle when it was pointed out to him that fighter aircraft do not have baggage compartments and that I really had no choice but to dress as I was.

After that furor had settled down we trooped into dinner, during which it was announced that General Patton was going to inspect us the next morning at 08:00. That news created some excitement. We had not been inspected by a general before. We knew who General Patton was. Old Blood and Guts, the American general who got into trouble slapping a soldier in Sicily. That summed up the extent of our knowledge of Patton.

At the appointed hour the next morning we were ready. Our aircraft were lined up wingtip to wingtip facing west at the west side of the grass-covered airfield. My machine was halfway down the line. Each pilot stood in front of his own aircraft. My Mustang, with its long, high snout, loomed up behind me. It was a clear, bright morning. The sun was at our backs, its light reflecting off the dew on the grass at our feet. A perfect day. At 08:00 sharp a jeep with its top down appeared on the roadway between the buildings in front of us, swung south and pulled round to the southernmost aircraft and stopped. There he was, General Patton himself.

Standing rigidly at attention I turned my head slightly to watch as he climbed out of the vehicle, returning the salute of our squadron leader. Without further ado Patton began to walk down the line of aircraft, passing in front of each pilot. He did not stop to talk to any of my colleagues. But he did stop when he got to me! There he was, right in front of me. I was at stiff, ramrod attention, at my short tallest. My flat officers' cap was squarely on my head, polka-dot scarf neatly in place. The General was elegantly dressed. He had a wedge cap on his white-haired head. The left breast of his khaki battledress jacket was covered with a multitude of ribbons. Light tan riding breeks were above highly

Lieutenant General George Patton Jr.
Spring of 1944

F/O Richard Rohmer: Odiham, May 1944

F/O Richard Rohmer: Gatwick, 1 January 1944

polished riding boots and silver spurs. On each hip was a revolver, the famed ivory-handled guns. He towered over me, all six foot two of him.

General Patton looked down at me, examining the boyish face. Then he looked up at the looming nose of the huge Mustang. Then back down to me again.

"Boy," he demanded, "how old are you?"

"I'm twenty, sir."

His eyes went up to the aircraft again, then back down to me. His right arm lifted as he pointed up to the airplane, but his eyes were still fixed on mine as he asked in his high-pitched voice.

"Do *you* fly that goddam airplane?"

"Yes, sir."

With that he dropped his arm. "Son of a bitch," he said incredulously. With a shake of his head he turned and walked on.

In Palermo on 22 January 1944, Patton, who had already heard the stunning news in a radio report that General Bradley was going to command all the ground troops in England, received his marching orders in vague terms that gave him no clue whatsoever about his next job except that it was to be in the United Kingdom. The action message was:

"Orders issued relieving you from assignment
this theatre and assigning to duty in U.K. Request
you proceed to NATOUSA, Algiers, for orders."[1]

By the time he received that message Patton knew not only that his junior, Bradley, was to be the American Army commander but as well that his Sicily equal and competitor for glory, Montgomery, would command the invasion force. His ego and vanity must have been crushed, but at the same time that brilliant man, poised on the edge of a possible court martial and disgrace, must have recognized that in the seeds of the action message before him the words 'assigning to duty in U.K.' must have meant what they said. The word 'duty' was one of the most significant in George Patton's vocabulary.

Immediately on his arrival in London on 26 January

1944, Patton reported to Eisenhower who told him that he would command the Third Army, an army that Patton knew was still in the United States under General Hodges. Eisenhower was vague about instructions for Patton because plans were still in the making. Basically those plans involved a minuscule, de facto military command of an army that would not become operational until some obscure, distant time after D-Day when the long awaited operation, 'Neptune', the invasion of the Normandy coast, was to begin.

During the period up to D-Day and for some weeks beyond it, Patton's major role was to be as the main decoy in a massive scheme of deception on which would tip the scales of success or failure of Neptune. He would be the main player of operation Fortitude, the purpose of which was to conceal the objectives of Neptune as the main and only point of the invading force.

Fortitude was created at a conference called Rattle held at the Hollywood Hotel at Largs in Scotland, 28 June 1943. It was presided over by Admiral Lord Louis Mountbatten and comprised twenty generals, eleven air marshals and air commodores, eight admirals, and twenty-two brigadiers from the United Kingdom and fifteen Americans and five Canadians, all of comparable rank. Rattle decided the place of the Neptune landings. It would be Normandy. It also decided that during the Normandy assault, in order to keep Hitler's forces dispersed and off balance, and to surprise as well as delay the reaction of the German forces, Hitler and his commanders had to be deceived into believing that other sectors of north-western and northern Europe would be attacked. The Pas-de-Calais region would be the focus of the sham efforts which would carry on long after D-Day, terminating around 20 July 1944. The formal description of Fortitude was:

A broad plan covering deception operations in the European theatre, with the objects (a) to cause the Wehrmacht to make faulty strategic dispositions in northwest Europe before *Neptune* by military threats against Norway, (b) to deceive

the enemy as to the target date and target area of
Neptune, (c) to induce (the enemy to make) faulty
tactical dispositions during and after *Neptune* by
threats against the Pas-de-Calais.[2]

There were two parts to Fortitude. Fortitude North was
a plan for the Scandinavian countries, in particular Norway, whereby a fictional Fourth British Army of 350,000
men, assembling in Scotland, would in concert with the
American 15th Corps — it did exist but was part of another
army and was available — prepare to mount an attack
against Norway either before or after Neptune.

The second, Fortitude South, called for the conceptual
creation of an entire Army Group comprised of a million
men in fifty divisions. The idea was to induce the Germans
into believing that the First United States Army Group
(FUSAG) was being assembled in England to carry out the
main attack in the Pas-de-Calais area: and that the two real
Army Groups, assembling in southern England, Montgomery's 21st and the American First under Bradley, were
merely a diversion.

It was in the Pas-de-Calais that Hitler had lodged his
most powerful Army in the west, the Fifteenth. The function
of Fortitude South was to keep that army in place during
Neptune and for as long a period thereafter as was possible,
ideally at least until 20 July 1944.

If FUSAG was to be credible to the Germans its commanding general had to be both known to and respected
by them. Ideally he would be the counterpart to Rommel,
the one German general whom the Allies admired. Hitler's
High Command was certain that Patton would be at the
forefront of any invasion force. It followed that if he was not
present in the first assult on the Normandy beaches then the
Germans would believe that the attack, whatever its initial
strength, would be only diversionary and that the true
invasion in strength would come later and at a different
place.

Patton was the only American general whom the
Germans respected. They were certain that because of his
success in Sicily he would undoubtedly be in the vanguard

of any fighting force sent across the Channel for the assault on the French beaches. Patton, therefore, was the ideal choice to lead FUSAG

Within a few days after arriving in England, Patton and his experienced Third Army staff were established in headquarters at Peover Hall, an ancient, elegant baronial estate at Knutsford, a small municipality of about 7,000 people approximately ten miles south of Manchester.

As to the name "Peover," it is nowhere recorded what Patton had to say about it when he first heard it. It is, however, recorded that he was pleased with the ancient, timbered manor house that had been the seat of several families over hundreds of years. His living quarters and offices were in Peover Hall, while some of his staff also had offices at Toft Camp, a nearby British military installation that had been made available to the Americans.

By 1 March the organization of his staff was complete, including the acquisition of his closest companion, a white English bull terrier. Patton had found Willie in a kennel in London on one of his many visits to that distant city where all the planning for Neptune and Overlord was taking place, planning he would have given his eyeteeth to get into. Patton had to content himself with working at his own plans for that longed for day when his Third Army was made operational. At that time it was in a transitional stage preparing for the move from Fort Sam Houston near San Antonio, Texas, to the gathering ground of England where its new general and his capable staff would whip it into shape along with other units that would be assigned to the Third Army at the appropriate moment. In the War Room at Peover Hall, Patton conducted daily conferences with his staff as he enunciated policy and made decisions concerning the multitude of logistical and administrative details that are an inherent part of the training and operations of a whole army.

Patton and his team were fully occupied. But the general was unhappy. He was out of the mainstream of Overlord and the Neptune D-Day situation because his Third Army would have to remain in England through and after D-Day as the fictitious Fortitude threat that would continue to pin down the German Fifteenth Army in the

Pas-de-Calais area. London, Overlord, and Neptune belonged to Eisenhower, as well as to Patton's former equal, Montgomery, and to Patton's recent junior, Omar Bradley, preparing to take his First Army ashore at the head of the American D-Day force.

The deception of Fortitude was beginning to take effect. German intelligence agents reported to their controllers that Patton was in England. FHW (Fremde Heere West), that part of the intelligence evaluation of the German general staff responsible for the Western Allies, stated in a 20 March 1944 bulletin that "General Patton, who was formerly employed in North Africa and is highly regarded for his proficiency, is now in England." "Armee Gruppe Patton," the name the Germans gave to his growing fictional force, began to appear regularly in FHW reports.

At Peover Hall Patton was by-passed, although he was called from time to time to higher headquarters in London for briefings.

Thus he was paying penance for his Sicily slappings. However, as events were to develop, the timing, location and circumstances of that penance would serve the ambitions of George S. Patton very well.

On 11 February 1944 he attended his first planning meeting conducted by General Sir Bernard Montgomery and his staff. On the morning of that day Patton had stopped at Bryanston Square in the west end of London to pick up Bradley at his office. The two of them were driven to Montgomery's headquarters at St. Paul's school in West Kensington where Montgomery himself had attended school many decades before.

The American generals were received by the commander of the new British 21st Army Group, the short, diminutive, birdlike General Sir Bernard Montgomery. With him was the commander of the Second British Army, General Sir Miles Christopher Dempsey, who would lead the British and Canadians on D-Day as Bradley would head the Americans. Also there was the ominipresent 'Freddy' de Guingand, Monty's chief-of-staff, the man who often as not represented his chief at the most critical conferences, a practice that, over the months ahead, would be the source of both insult and annoyance to the Army commanders who served Montgomery as well as to the Supreme Commander, Eisenhower.

The meeting was cordial and friendly. Patton chose to be a good listener as Montgomery reviewed in detail the Overlord plan as it had been developed to that moment, including the objective of taking Caen, some eighteen miles inland, on D-Day. It was a plan originally devised by British Lieutenant General Frederick Morgan and his staff but was now in the process of amendment and final establishment at the hands of both Eisenhower and Montgomery. Morgan was also the architect of Bodyguard, of which Fortitude was a main segment with Patton as its key player.

In the next few weeks Patton mulled over the Overlord and Neptune plans and typically came up with a scheme of his own. It was a Third Plan for an actual assault on the Pas-de-Calais area in the event that the Normandy invasion slowed down and the Germans had enough time to mount a strong counterattack. Knowing Monty well from the Sicily campaign, Patton had no faith in the Briton's ability to take Caen on D-Day. He expected that Montgomery would get bogged down. Patton, however, was unable to sell his Third Plan to anyone in the halls of power in London.

His next major exposure to the planning process of Overlord and Neptune was at a Presentation of the Plan exercise conducted in London on 7 April 1944 when, under the aegis of Montgomery, the commanders of the three services — Army, Navy, and Air Force — explained their intentions. They had decided that the object of Operation Overlord was:

> "to mount and carry out an operation, with forces and equipment established in the United Kingdom and with target date 1 May 1944, to secure a lodge-ment on the Continent from which further offen-sive operations could be developed. The lodge-ment area must contain sufficient port facilities to maintain a force of some twenty-six to thirty divisions and enable that force to be augmented by follow-up shipments from the United States or elsewhere of additional divisions and supporting

units at a rate of three to five divisions per month."[3]

The Allied Forces would simultaneously assault beaches on the Normandy coast from the River Orne to the Carentan estuary and an area immediately to the north of it, with the purpose of securing a base area for further operations. The lodgement sector was to include airfield sites, the port of Cherbourg, and the ports of Brittany. The second phase was to be the enlargement of lodgement area.

Montgomery himself explained the objective to the general officers of the field armies and discussed his own role:

> The assault was an operation requiring a single co-ordinated plan of action under one commander; I therefore became the overall land force commander responsible to the Supreme Commander for planning and executing the military aspect of the assault and subsequent capture of the lodgement area.[4]

The troops under his operational control would comprise the British 21st Army Group and First United States Army under General Omar N. Bradley. The 21st Army Group would be made up of 1st Canadian Army under Lieutenant General H.D.G. Crerar, 2nd British Army under Lieutenant General Dempsey, British airborne troops under Lieutenant General Browning and various Allied contingents. The American 82 and 101 Airborne Divisions were attached to First United States Army.

Montgomery explained that General Eisenhower intended "to assume direct command of the land forces on the Continent when the growing build-up of the American forces had led to the deployment of an American Army Group in the field. No definite period was stipulated for this, but headquarters 12 United States Army Group were formed in London and prepared to take command" of Bradley's First Army and Patton's Third Army at the appropriate time.

50

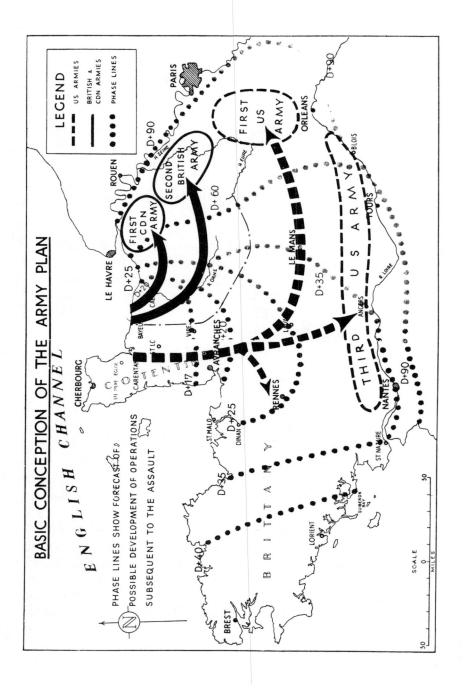

BASIC CONCEPTION OF THE ARMY PLAN

LEGEND

US ARMIES
BRITISH & CDN ARMIES
PHASE LINES

PHASE LINES SHOW FORECAST OF
POSSIBLE DEVELOPMENT OF OPERATIONS
SUBSEQUENT TO THE ASSAULT

E N G L I S H   C H A N N E L

CHERBOURG

LE HAVRE

ROUEN

PARIS

R. SEINE

D+90

FIRST
CDN
ARMY

D+25

SECOND
BRITISH
ARMY

R. EURE

D+90

D+60

FIRST
US
ARMY

ORLEANS

D+90

BLOIS

TOURS

THIRD   US   ARMY

R. LOIRE

LE MANS

D+35

ANGERS

NANTES

D+90

ST NAZAIRE

RENNES

AVRANCHES

D+17

CARENTAN

ST MERE EGLISE

BAYEUX

VIRE

R. ORNE

D+35

ST MALO

DINAN

D+25

B R I T T A N Y

D+35

D+40

LORIENT

QUIBERON
BAY

BREST

SCALE
MILES

50

50

N

Montgomery later stated:

Once ashore and firmly established, my plan was to threaten to break out of the initial bridgehead on the eastern flank — that is, in the Caen sector. I intended by means of this threat to draw the main enemy reserves into that sector to fight them there and keep them there, using the British and Canadian armies for the purpose. Having got the main enemy reserves committed on the eastern flank, my plan was to make the break-out on the western flank, using for this task the American armies under General Bradley, and to pivot the whole front on Caen. The American break-out thrust was to be delivered southwards down to the Loire and then to be developed eastwards in a wide sweep up to the Seine about Paris. This movement was designed to cut off all the enemy forces south of the Seine, over which river the bridges were to be destroyed by air action.[5]

While Montgomery was much later accused of adapting his description of his own plans to match the events as they actually happened in Normandy, it is clear that except for the timings given for reaching certain objectives, which in the actual battle ran late as much as thirty days plus, his master plan was ultimately followed. Monty was to stick with that plan notwithstanding heavy criticism leveled against him in July and August, particularly in regard to his insistence on continuing to "pivot on Caen." De Guingand's summary of the tasks Montgomery gave out to his armies at the Presentation of Plans exercises confirms the general's later description of his intention:

First U.S. Army
(a) To assault.
(b) To capture Cherbourg.
(c) To develop operations towards St. Lô.
(d) After capture of the area Cherbourg-Caumont-Avranches, to advance southwards, capture Rennes and reach out to the Loire.

52

Second British Army
(a) To assault.
(b) To protect First U.S. Army whilst it captured
Cherbourg.
(c) To secure the airfield sites south-east of Caen.
(d) In subsequent operations to pivot on its left
and offer a strong front against enemy movement
toward the lodgement area from the east.[6]

First United States Army was to assault astride the
Carentan estuary with one regimental combat team between
Barreville and the estuary (Utah beach), and two regimental
combat teams between Vierville and Colleville (Omaha
beach). The initial tasks were to capture Cherbourg as
quickly as possible and to develop operations southward
toward St. Lô in conformity with the advance of Second
British Army.

Second British Army assault was to be delivered with
five brigades between Asnelles and Ouistreham (Gold, Juno
and Sword beaches), with the initial task of developing the
bridgehead south of the line St. Lô-Caen and south-east of
Caen, in order to secure airfield sites and to protect the
eastern flank of First United States Army while the latter was
capturing Cherbourg.

The enormity of the initial lift in the assault and
follow-up naval force requirements was staggering: some
130,000 personnel and over 20,000 vehicles, all of which had
to be put ashore on the first three tides.

It was to be an incredible undertaking to which Patton
would be a mere reluctant and distant spectator. His Third
Army was scheduled to be called into operations on D plus
15 with the primary task of capturing the Brittany peninsula
and opening its ports. After that it was to establish itself to
the right of the First U.S. Army and be prepared to operate
to the east either in close conjunction with the First Army or
by swinging south of the Loire if a wider envelopment
appeared to be feasible.

After Montgomery, as commander of all land forces in
Neptune, disclosed his plans to the general officers of the
field armies on 7 April 1944, the most controversial of those,
General Patton, returned to Peover to continue the plan-

ning for the construction of his own Third Army, elements of which had started to arrive from the United States in March.

Between the date of his return to Peover and his inspection of the Flying Circus on 8 May, Patton managed to get into hot water once again. On April 25 he took time out to attend the opening of the Welcoming Club that the people of Knutsford had put together to entertain the growing hordes of American Third Army soldiers arriving at the Toft and Peover camps. Even though he had been cautioned by Eisenhower at a meeting they had held on the same day as the Montgomery planning conference, 7 April, Patton decided to make a speech to the Knutsford group. In it he discussed the "evident destiny of the British and Americans to rule the world." At least that was how the speech was reported in the press. In reality he had included the Russians, but the newspaper reports failed to mention that fact. The result was another furor, this time on an international scale because Patton had allegedly made an affront to the Soviet Union while making what some people considered to be political remarks. Again Congress was in an uproar and Patton was on the mat. Eisenhower advised General Marshall that on all the evidence available he would relieve Patton from command and send him home " 'unless some new and unforeseen information should be developed in the case' " because, as Eisenhower saw it, " 'there was always the possibility that the war might yet develop a situation where Patton, despite lack of balance, should be rushed into the breach.' "[7]

On Monday morning, 1 May, on Eisenhower's orders, Patton reported to the Supreme Commander in his London office at 11:00 hours. Eisenhower told him that he might be forced to send him home. After that meeting Patton wrote in his diary:

"I feel like death, but I am not out yet. . . . If they let me fight, I will; but if not, I will resign so as to be able to talk, and then I will tell the truth, and possibly do my country more good."[8]

However, Eisenhower, a man of deep loyalty and a

general who recognized the military genius of the impetuous Patton, relented, closing the case on 3 May when he
informed General Marshall that " 'the release of Patton
would lose to us his experience as commander of an army in
battle and his demonstrated ability of getting the utmost out
of soldiers in offensive operations." ' In his letter to Patton
advising him of the decision to keep him " 'despite . . .
personal indiscretions" ' he included a one-sentence outline
of his rationale: " 'I do this solely because of my faith in you
as a battle leader and for no other motives." '[9]

When I looked up into the 58-year-old face of General
Patton at 08:02 in the morning of 8 May 1944 and listened to
his incredulous, high-pitched voice, I had no idea that I was
in the presence of a man whose compulsive nature made him
"talk too much," a soldier who was carrying fresh emotional
scars inflicted by his own inability to refrain from acting on
impulse.

No, the man before me was the living, breathing
epitome of a handsome, swashbuckling, straight-as-a-
ramrod, real live leader of men, ready to take on the enemy
anywhere. That's the kind of man I saw and that's the kind
of man Eisenhower and the Germans saw — a man tough as
nails, a military genius whom any intelligent enemy should
fear with reason.

Indeed it was this justifiable fear of Patton that on
D-Day and the critical days immediately thereafter would
cause Hitler to withhold the powerful Panzer reserves that
could have driven the Allies back into the sea.

3

13 May 1944   OPERATIONS: — the weather was fine
                during the day allowing six sorties to be
                flown . . . F/L J.B. Prendergast and F/O
                R.H. Rohmer flew to St. Omer to
                photograph three Noball targets. F/L
                Prendergast camera failed but targets
                were successfully photographed by F/O
                Rohmer.

                                    430 Squadron Log

Our task on 13 May was straightforward. The briefing officer informed us there were three Noball sites at St. Omer that we were to photograph. The targets had been bombed by Bostons earlier in the day. Our photographs would enable the APIS (Army Photographic Interpretation Section) people to assess the damage, if any. As usual there was no word as to what kind of an installation the Noball site was and we didn't ask. The squadron had been doing Noball missions for several weeks and in large number, but at no time were any of us informed what it was the bombers were trying so hard to destroy and we to photograph. However, the pictures we took showed us that at each Noball site there had been built or partially completed what looked like a section of roadway, about 100 yards long and about 20 feet wide. At one end of this roadway there was a slight crook off to the side, making the whole installation look like a hockey stick with a shortened blade.

In addition there were new buildings erected in each construction area.

Another clue was that the Noball targets were concentrated in the Pas-de-Calais area, close to the Channel coastline. If it had been my job to interpret the photographs as well as take them I would also have been able to see that the handle ends of the hockey sticks were pointed toward London. One characteristic all of us were able to observe about the Noball sites was that the Germans built them almost exclusively in wooded areas — in orchards, forests, or copses of trees. It was as if they were trying to hide what they were building without knowing that it was impossible to conceal them from the prying, all-seeing eyes of our cameras and those of our high altitude Bluebird Spitfires.

The routine for these missions was relatively straight forward. Prendergast, as the assigned leader, and I went over the maps on which our route across to France had been plotted. We discussed the direction of his run in on the target. He would fly at 7,000 feet directly over the Noball site. His aircraft would be straight and level so his vertical camera would be pointed at the objective. All three Noballs were close together and caught in one photo. To fly straight and level at the relatively low altitude made one a sitting duck if the area was protected by flak, especially by the deadly accurate German 88mm anti-aircraft gun. The fire direction mechanisms on the 88s were such that the shells invariably exploded at our exact height. Even if they didn't hit you, they would come close enough to scare the hell out of you with their big, black, exploding clouds of lethal metal.

Prendergast's aircraft was rigged with an eight-inch vertical camera. Its small size dictated the height at which he had to take his photographs. My aircraft was equipped with a 14-inch oblique camera, installed just behind the cockpit pointing out to the left and slightly behind the tailing edge of the wing. I would have to be about 200 yards off Prendergast's right so I could keep a protective eye on his tail to make sure we were not taken by surprise by any enemy fighters. Then just as he was completing his run directly over the target I would put my left wing down and

Noball sites

Noball site

fly my aircraft so the oblique camera would be pointed at the target just long enough to get a fast series of pictures.

Our briefing and final discussion as to routes and operating procedures takes place in the large 39 Recce Wing operations tent at our base at RAF Station Odiham. We leave it and walk to our Squadron's Operations tent not far away to collect our helmets, goggles, gloves and parachutes which we drape over our right shoulders to carry them out to the airplanes. Once there, the parachute, helmet and goggles are put on and we climb into our respective aircraft. Prendergast is in Mustang 'N' and I am in 'L'. Those large identification figures are on each side of the fuselage between the cockpit and the tail section. With the assistance of our ground crews we strap ourselves into the bucket seats and start our engines. On go all the switches, including radio. I check its operation by talking with Prendergast whose aircraft is sitting three places away from mine in the line, its prop turning over.

When the engine temperatures are up, another radio check and we taxi out onto the east/west Odiham runway. I follow a few yards behind Prendergast, each of us turning his aircraft from side to side so he can see ahead beyond the big, blinding nose of the Mustang. We stop for a final take-off power run-up check. Take-off clearance comes from the controller's hut. A green Aldis beacon pointed at us, brilliant even in daylight, says 'Go'. We line up on the runway in formation. Prendergast is on the left. I have my left wing tip tucked in just behind his right for a close formation take off, the kind every fighter pilot likes to do. His right hand comes up, palm inward toward his face. He moves it forward and back twice, the signal to begin the take off. We start to roll. In a few seconds we are airborne. An automatic reach with the left hand for the undercarriage level pulls it to the 'up' position. I watch Prendergast's wheels coming up and feel mine lock into place. I wait for the hand signal to lift the 15 degrees of flaps we have put down before take off. It comes. I move the flap selector to 'up.' I can see his flaps lifting until they are flush with the wing and clean. My wing tip is still tucked inside his as we turn west climbing. It is 16:01 in the afternoon.

Prendergast straightens out on his south-southeast

course giving me the hand signal to go into battle formation. Immediately I pull out to the right settling in about 200 yards away from him. I will maintain that station during the entire operation, either 200 yards to the right or 200 yards to the left, depending upon the turns that have to be made. However, on the target run I must be on his right.

At 3,000 feet we level off, heading for Selsey Bill, the great peninsula on the south coast of England toward its eastern end. It is an excellent landmark for departures across the Channel and conversely an ideal low-level landfall on the way back. As we approach Selsey Bill, Prendergast starts to descend. Down to the deck we go as we leave the land and hurtle across the Channel just above the waves to avoid radar detection. I now activate my guns by turning the gun selector switch to 'All'. The two gun charger levers are pulled fully out and I am ready to fire if need be, using the illuminated gun sight just above the instrument panel directly ahead of me.

By this time we have started our watching procedures for we can be attacked by enemy fighters at any moment. I check my station position with Prendergast's aircraft. I sweep my vision behind him, then forward in a clockwise motion ahead and around in an arc back and behind to the right. My eyes search the horizon. Next I turn my head slowly to look directly overhead. My line of sight goes down again to the left rear behind the lead Mustang. And so the procedure is repeated constantly with regular checks into the rear view mirror just above my head. It covers the blind spot that the Mustang I has to the rear because of its enclosed birdcage hood. Nothing is seen.

Radio silence is maintained as an operational necessity.

About five miles from the French coast Prendergast lifts the nose of his aircraft and we begin to climb, planning to cross the coast at 7,000 feet with a landfall at Quand Plage.

What is left of the regularly attacked German radar system will now pick us up on their screens. An alert will be given to the anti-aircraft batteries in our path and the German fighter squadrons in the area will be notified. Whether they elect to respond remains to be seen.

We cross the coast at 5,000 feet still climbing. We are

in the lair of the German Eagle. My head is really swivelling as I read every section of the sky for a sign of enemy fighters. In addition to keeping a sharp lookout, Prendergast is also doing the navigating and map reading. He must get us to the target and back. In a few minutes he is on the radio to me — no need for silence now — letting me know that the target is straight ahead at twelve o'clock. He'll be starting his photo run in about three minutes.

There are no clouds below us and, above, only high scattered cirrus. A beautiful day and therefore a dangerous one for us. We can be easily seen by high flying enemy fighters. At 7,000 feet we're beyond the best operating height of the Mustang so if we are attacked we are at a greater disadvantage than usual.

The next hazard is flak. Will the target be protected by 88s? If so, we're going to be in for a rough ride, especially Prendergast who has to remain absolutely straight and level when he's taking his photographs. But there would be no flinching by Prendergast, whose reputation for coolness and determination has been solidly earned. As for me, I can weave and bob and still maintain my battle formation station and take my oblique photographs.

The moment of truth is at hand. Now the targets are one mile ahead. We are set for the run in.

Because there is no window in the floor you cannot see vertically down in the Mustang, so you must line up your aircraft using predetermined landmarks on each side of the target. Following those you then know without question that you're going to put the camera-carrying vehicle, your airplane, right over the target. So after he is sure he is lined up, Prendergast cannot see the Noball sites, but off to the side I can. There they are in copses of trees, the peculiar hockey stick form, gleaming white in their sheltering woods. The bombs that had been aimed at the sites had carved enormous holes in the countryside all around the copses. At one Noball a string had landed across the stubby blade at the end of the stick. Whether it had been damaged or not I cannot tell at this moment.

Pendergast is into his photographic run. I'm getting set to take my obliques just after he has passed directly over the target. It is now or never for the 88s. Prendergast is over the target. Still no 88s. Now it's my turn. Taking the airplane over on its left side, with top right rudder I bring the Noball sites into the direct line of my camera by matching the targets with the camera-aiming mark on the trailing edge of my left wing. When I'm sure I have them I press the operating button on my control column. In my earphones I hear the electrical clicking each time the camera snaps a photo. After a few seconds, I pull the aircraft level and check my position in relation to Prendergast. I have come a little closer to him, so pull out to the full 200-yard battle formation. No flak. He decides to go back for another run going westbound and so advises me.

After a double cross-over turn of 180 degrees we complete a second run over the targets. Still all is quiet. Nevertheless it is time to get the hell out of there. Rubbernecking for enemy fighters we hightail for the coast, dropping down to wave level as soon as we hit the channel. We double-check our IFF (Identification Friend or Foe) transmitters to make sure they're functioning. We want the radar operators in England to know that we are indeed friendly. As we approach the welcoming contours of Selsey Bill we climb up again to 3,000 feet and go through the procedures of putting our guns on 'Safe'. At Odiham I do a stream — staying well back from Prendergast's aircraft — rather than a formation landing. We're back on the ground at 17:30 hours, one hour and a half to France and back.

As we carry our parachutes and gear back to our squadron operations tent we talk about the trip. It appears to have been completely successful. Naturally we are both relieved that we got away with it without flak or fighters. At the 39 Recce Wing Operations tent we are debriefed by the same intelligence officer who had briefed us. In the middle of the session we are informed that for Prendergast the trip had been for naught. His vertical camera had not functioned as a result of an electrical failure. All that way and at such high risk for nothing — unless my photographs had turned out. They had. So our sortie was successful and well worth the effort.

On the night of 12 June we were to find out just how important the Noball sites really were and why it was so vital that they be destroyed. Our photographic reconnaissance was equally important since it was the only way Intelligence knew whether or not the Noball targets had been destroyed, merely damaged, or completely missed.

Our many flights across the English Channel into the Pas-de-Calais area took us over the powerful German 15th Army which was responsible for the defense of that sector and Flanders. It was part of Army Group 'B' under the command of the much respected Desert Fox, Field Marshal Erwin Rommel. Rommel's command included the 7th Army in Normandy and Brittany and 88 Corps in Holland. In turn, Army Group B and Rommel were subordinate to the German commander in France and the Low Countries, Field Marshal Gert von Rundstedt, whose title was Commander-in-Chief West.

Also under von Rundstedt was Army Group 'G', commanded by General Johannes Baskowitz, which included the 1st Army stationed in the Biscay area and the 19th in the Riviera sector.

Of Army Group status under von Rundstedt was Panzer Group West (PGW) commanded by Leo Baron Geyr von Schweppenburg, who was responsible for the training and administration of the Panzer units although they were under the command of the other Army Groups. The operational control of von Schweppenburg's 1,600 tanks on D-Day and the critical few days thereafter was to be a key factor in the Normandy battle. Hitler personally retained control of von Schweppenburg's Panzer divisions. Only the Fuhrer himself could authorize their movement.

The forces under von Rundstedt amounted to some sixty divisions or roughly one-quarter of the field force of the entire German army.

Von Rundstedt was 68 years of age, the Grand Old Man of the German army. He was his country's most highly respected senior soldier. Tall, thin, gaunt, mustachio'd, balding, the patrician aristocrat was a marked cut above the dynamic, energetic, boisterous Rommel.

Notwithstanding von Rundstedt's position as Commander-in-Chief West, in December 1943 Hitler had personally instructed Rommel to inspect the defenses of the entire European coastline opposite England. Later the Fuhrer gave the Desert Fox command of Army Group B with its new headquarters at La Roche-Guyon. Rommel arrived there on 9 May 1944.

La Roche-Guyon is a tiny, picturesque village on the Seine River between Vernon and Mantes. The Germans had a penchant for selecting opulent châteaux as their command posts and headquarters even when they were close to the front line. So it was relatively easy for us, the recce bloodhounds, and other airmen to find them. The headquarters at La Roche-Guyon was no exception, having been installed in a château that belonged to the La Rochefoucauld family. It was a majestic building which incorporated a partly ruined Norman round tower over 900 years old. Tunnels had been made into the cliff onto which the château backed in order to house some hundred officers and men in Rommel's Army Group staff, providing them with, among other things, protection against air raids. All in all, the La Roche-Guyon headquarters and the surrounding pleasant countryside suited Rommel's tastes.

As time went on it became apparent that Rommel and von Rundstedt did not see eye to eye on the manner in which the invading forces should be met. Von Rundstedt's concept was the "crust-cushion-hammer" plan. This called for a "crust" of infantry along the coastline backed up by a "cushion" of infantry divisions in tactical reserve immediately in the rear. A "hammer" of Panzers would be in strategic reserves farther inland. The purpose of the cushion was to hold enemy forces that penetrated the crust while the hammer was for the decisive counter attack. Rommel's plan, on the other hand, was to totally repulse the invader right on the beaches by concentrating a huge volume of fire on the shore and on its seaward approaches. The beach defenses of the Atlantic Wall would be made as strong and impenetrable as possible. The all-important reserves, including the Panzers, would be stationed near the coast.

The plans of both commanders were compromised. The effect was that most of the infantry divisions were positioned to strengthen the crust while the Panzers were held well back. As Montgomery later wrote:

The result was that, in the event, the Panzer divisions were forced to engage us prematurely and were unable to concentrate to deliver a co-ordinated blow: until it was too late.[1]

From the time he had arrived back in France in December 1943 to inspect the Atlantic Wall defenses and later as commander of Army Group 'B', Rommel had dedicated himself to the fortification of the beaches. For him the main battle line was to be the beach itself. As he roamed the coastline from Holland to the Brest peninsula, he pushed, cajoled, wheedled, ordered his commanders to get on with the building of beach fortifications. Like repulsive prickly weeds, Rommel's obstacle devices began growing on every beach of northwestern Europe. Concrete and steel tetrahedrons, Czech hedgehogs made from steel girders welded at right angles, and countless other crude inventions sprang up to complement the hundreds of thousands of mines that were planted not only in the beaches but in Rommel's Death Zone. This was a six mile deep heavily fortified strip behind the beaches.

Rommel's own idea was to embed heavy timber stakes into the low tide sand using the jet stream of fire hoses. This method allowed each one to be put in position in three minutes as opposed to three-quarters of an hour that the conventional pile driver required. Attached to the stakes were mines, iron spikes and all manner of devices which which would rip open the hulls of landing craft.

To destroy gliders or prevent them from landing in his Normandy Death Zone, Rommel had open fields populated by stakes, poles, and stone cairns.

In Holland Rommel opened the dykes, flooding the rich farmland, making that area a hopeless place against which to launch an invasion. Flooding of the low lying areas in the marshy country around the Carentan estuary in Normandy was also ordered.

Gun positions along the entire coastline were heavily protected by concrete and armor plating against air attack and naval gunfire. The fire of German coastal artillery overlapped along most beaches and was particularly concentrated at the entrances to the Carentan estuary and at Cherbourg. The heavy guns at Le Havre and Cherbourg were capable of reaching areas designated for transport area immediately off the Normandy beaches.

Behind the coast artillery, some two or three miles inland, field and medium artillery units of the divisions occupying the coastal sectors were sited. The task of those guns was to bring shell fire to bear on craft approaching the beaches and on the beaches themselves. In all there were some thirty-two located positions capable of firing on what later became the D-Day assault areas.

But in all these massive, elaborate defenses, the most powerful mobile weapon was the tank, especially the Tiger mounted as it was with the deadly 88 gun. The success or failure of Neptune would hinge largely on whether or how the 600 tanks within the area of Army Group 'B' would be deployed at the time of D-Day and immediately thereafter.

The matter had been settled the day before I met General Patton at Ramsberry. In a German High Command instruction dated 7 May, only three out of the seven Panzer divisions in the West were made available to Rommel. All were first-class organizations: the 2nd Panzer, the 21st Panzer under General Edgar Feuchtinger, positioned at Falaise just south of Caen, and the 116th Panzer north of Paris. The remaining four Panzer divisions were to remain far back from the coast in a strategic reserve under Hitler's sole direct control. In his instructions to Rommel of 7 May, Field Marshal Jodl, Hitler's Chief-of-Staff, wrote:

> "The enemy's intentions are at present so obscure . . . that some capability for strategic command must be maintained by means of keeping a separate, if modest, reserve. These High Command reserves will be released for operations — without further application by yourself — the moment we can be certain about the enemy's intentions and focus of attack."[2]

In other words the reserves would be held back until it was clear that the enemy attack was not simply a diversion. The presence of General Patton and his fictitious First

United States Army Group, with British and Canadian forces threatening to mount the main invasion thrust against the Pas-de-Calais area under the Fortitude scheme, was intended to freeze the strategic Panzer reserve, holding it away from the Normandy beachhead until long after it could have been of value.

The German army command structure was such that its tactical commanders had no license or authority to act unless their immediate commander had given a specific order, as in the case of Hitler being the sole control over the Panzer divisions in the strategic reserve. Even on D-Day, Feuchtinger, sitting with his deadly arsenal of tanks in the Falaise area only 30 miles away from the beachhead, could not get into action until twelve hours after the beginning of the airborne attacks on the Orne because he had been told he was to make no move until he had heard from Rommel's headquarters. It took twelve priceless hours for that permission to arrive.

Even so, Montgomery, his planners, and his commanders faced a formidable, well-organized German force ranged behind the Atlantic Wall.

For Monty it was a special challenge because he was once again matching wits with his arch rival, the legendary Erwin Rommel. It was a scenario rarely provided to field commanders of massive opposing forces, namely a second round, another chance to win a crucial battle in the fight to win the war. Montgomery knew that the fates had once again placed him head-to-head with the most respected, experienced, inventive, perceptive, battle commander in Hitler's arsenal. The world would watch and wait as those two modern-day military titans once again met in the field, stalking each other for the kill.

4

6 June 1944   OPERATIONS: D-Day. The first sorties were airborne before sunrise. This was the start of a very busy day, thirty sorties being flown in all. F/O J. H. Taylor and F/O R. H. Rohmer did a recce of all roads leading into Caen. Photos of transport headed toward Caen were taken.

430 Squadron Log

D-Day! This was the moment we had all been waiting for, preparing for. During the last two weeks of May the pace of our operations had increased. More and more we were tasked for low level photography of miles of beaches along several stretches of French coastline.

Along that same coast German radar installations capable of spotting ships on the English channel were under vigorous air attack. They had to be knocked out. And we had to follow the bombers in with our cameras so the extent of the inflicted damage could be assessed.

Flying past Portsmouth on the way across to France during the last days of May and the beginning of June I could see the multitude of ships large and small gathering there as they were in ports all along the south coast. Troops, tanks, guns, vehicles were at their assembly and marshalling points. For me it was a time of increasing excitement and anticipation. Like all our own pilots and groundcrews I was as keen as mustard. We were on the verge of the promised assault on the enemy, the promised liberation of Europe and the defeat of the German army. We were ready, pawing the ground.

On the night of 5 June, our airfield commander, Group Captain Ernie Moncrieff, held a briefing for all the pilots of the three squadrons that comprised 39 Recce Wing to tell them that the Invasion was on. On a huge map of the Normandy coast he outlined where the landings would take place. The Second British Army was assigned Gold, Juno and Sword beaches stretching from the River Orne on the east to Port-en-Bessin on the west. The American First Army was assigned Omaha and Utah beaches to the west of Gold and part way up the Contentin Peninsula. 39 Recce Wing would therefore be concentrating its efforts in the Gold-Juno-Sword sector. Of particular concern was the area leading from the beachhead up to and including Caen and the roads and railways leading into that city because it was Montgomery's principal objective to reach and take Caen within the first 24 hours.

Every serviceable Royal Air Force and Royal Canadian Air Force heavy bomber would be airborne during the night saturating the area immediately in front of the beaches, knocking out gun emplacements and other fortifications. Paratroopers would be dropped during the night. At first light, troop-carrying gliders would be landing in pre-selected areas well in from the beach. Our primary task would be tactical reconnaissance flights to pick up movements of enemy tanks, troops, or vehicles and to spot the location of guns. All this information would be fed to army headquarters and to the units in the field.

In addition, if we discovered major targets such as concentrations of tanks, we were to radio our Group Control Centre (GCC) and report the location, whereupon GCC would direct in Typhoon rocket-carrying squadrons or Spitfire fighter bombers. Some of the pilots from our sister squadron, 414, would direct the fire of the huge Royal Navy battleships which would be standing offshore. Their targets would be the heavy gun emplacements encased in concrete along the enemy coast.

H-Hour, the time designated for the British and

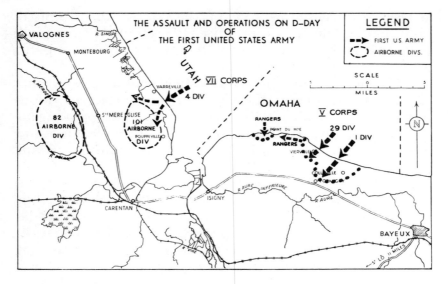

THE ASSAULT AND OPERATIONS ON D–DAY
OF
THE FIRST UNITED STATES ARMY

LEGEND

FIRST U.S. ARMY
AIRBORNE DIVS.

VALOGNES

MONTEBOURG

UTAH

VARREVILLE

VII CORPS

4 DIV

Sᵗᵉ MERE EGLISE

82 AIRBORNE DIV

101 AIRBORNE

POUPPEVILLE DIV

OMAHA

RANGERS

POINT DU HOE

RANGERS

VIERVILLE

COLLEVILLE

V CORPS

29 DIV

I DIV

SCALE

MILES

N

CARENTAN

ISIGNY

R AURE INFERIEURE

R AURE

BAYEUX

Canadian troops to hit the beach, ranged between 07:25 and 07:45 hours. We would be over them.

Actually the Group Captain's news that the Invasion was on did not come as a total surprise. There had been standing orders that immediately before D-Day all our aircraft would be painted at the wing-roots and at the fuselage just ahead of the tail with broad black and white stripes, a further safeguard that the troops on the ground and the crews of ships would recognize us as friendly. On 4 June the order had been given to put on the stripes.

The Group Captain's briefing, the knowledge that D-Day was finally at hand, and the anticipation of taking part in this gigantic effort produced a euphoria probably much like that felt by the members of a professional football team before a championship game. We were 'up'.

After the briefing our squadron's tasking for the morning was issued. I was assigned with F/O Jack Taylor to do a tactical reconnaissance over the beachhead area, south to Caen and for a short distance along the roads leading into that town from the south and southeast. Our takeoff time was to be 06:00 hours. There were to be two sections of two ahead of us, each airborne at 05:00 hours, also tasked to do TAC/R's.

All six of us were quietly wakened in our tents at 03:00.

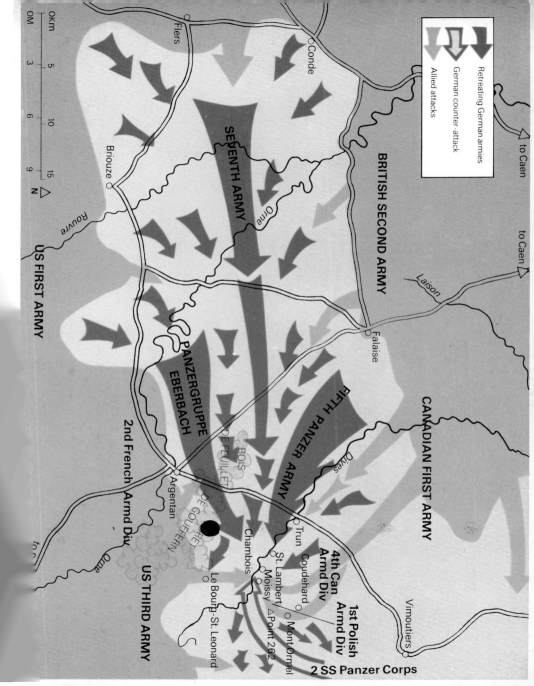

HAWKER TYPHOON 1B

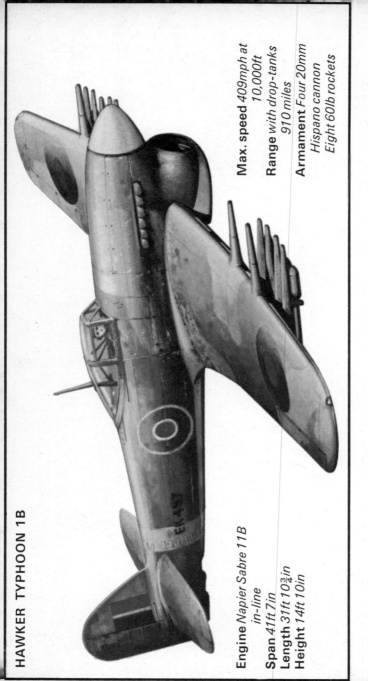

Engine Napier Sabre 11B in-line
Span 41ft 7in
Length 31ft 10¾in
Height 14ft 10in

Max. speed 409mph at 10,000ft
Range with drop-tanks 910 miles
Armament Four 20mm Hispano cannon Eight 60lb rockets

corner. Hausser, the one-eyed ex-Prussian Cadet-school graduate, chose to break out with him. Every man was thoroughly briefed—the paratroops would break out 'Indian fashion'; fire would not be opened till dawn. They had some sleep and a hot meal. Despite their extreme fatigue the spirits of the paratroops rose. In the darkness Meindl led them off at 2230 somewhere near St. Lambert. Across the Dives wild firing greeted them from all sides. They had bumped into soldiers as tough as themselves ... Major David V.

after the shape of the height they had defended.

The wounded Lieutenant General Paul Mahlmann, of 353rd Infantry Division in Meindl's Corps, managed to get many of his men across the Dives at Moissy. Also wounded was Lieutenant General Freiherr Heinrich von Lüttwitz of 2nd *Panzer* Division, who mounting a morning attack with his last 15 tanks, actually found the bridge at St. Lambert still intact and got some troops across unhurt only to be greeted by fire from the Canadians in the village. Here he recalled later: 'The crossing of the Dives bridge was

We dressed quickly, and without taking time to wash or shave, hurried to the mess tent. Our fabulous chef, Stradiotti, personally appeared to produce eggs, bacon and coffee for us. After breakfast it was over to the Wing Operations tent to be briefed on our operations.

The two sections ahead of us took off in the darkness shortly after 05:00. Both returned a few minutes after 07:00. We were airborne at 06:00 just before sun up and, as the record shows, Taylor and I were the only people from 430 Squadron to be over the beaches at H-Hour.

In the semi-darkness we did a stream rather than formation take off. As soon as I was airborne, I began a turn to the left in order to place my aircraft inside of Taylor's banking to port about half a mile ahead of me. That way I could catch up with him quickly as our paths crossed. He was already in a gentle arc in the same direction toward a course that would take us south to exit the coast just to the east of Portsmouth. As I caught up with him, crossed under and moved out to my comfortable battle formation position 200 yards to his right and just slightly behind, the darkness

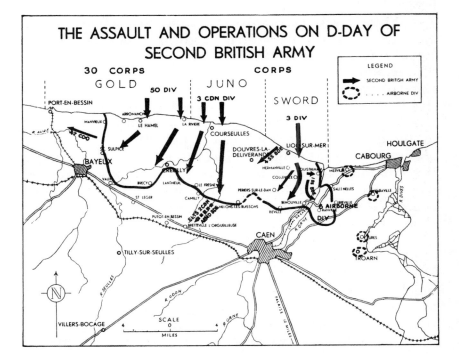

THE ASSAULT AND OPERATIONS ON D-DAY OF SECOND BRITISH ARMY

70

was fast disappearing. But that day the sun was invisible, obliterated by a solid blanket of high, gray cloud that looked to me to be sitting above us at perhaps 10,000 feet. We knew the wind was strong, close to 20 mph from the west. It wouldn't affect us but it would undoubtedly play havoc with the men crossing the Channel in ships big and small.

As we approached the crossing-out point on the south coast the sight that lay before us was awesome. As far as the eye could see the sea was covered with ships in a vast miles-wide unending column reaching south to the horizon, plowing through whitecapped waves toward the Normandy shore. Ships coming in from ports to the east or the west of Portsmouth converged on the column about ten miles south of the coast. Even I could judge that we were flying over the largest armada that had ever sailed on any waters. While we still could not see the French coastline, we knew that the head of this enormous force of ships was sitting off the invasion beaches, its mighty battleships, cruisers, destroyers and other assault craft spewing thousands of shells and rockets onto pre-determined targets in the final minutes before H-Hour.

While I was constantly checking the sky for enemy aircraft and occasionally catching glimpses of Allied fighter squadrons in the distance, it was impossible to keep my eyes off the amazing sight below us. The water was thick with ships rolling in the heavy seas, some of them towing protective barrage balloons to stave off low-level enemy aircraft attacks. From my vantage point everything appeared shaded by the diffused light filtering through the heavy overcast above us. Even the whitecaps had turned gray. The bobbing ships painted in their myriad patterns of dark, blending colors gave off a common grayness only slightly contrasted against the uninviting blackness of the wind-whipped channel waters carrying them.

Then we could see the outline of the Normandy coast dead ahead. Sitting over it was something we had not anticipated. It was a high, towering wall of broken cloud that had built up over the entire sector of Normandy beaches to be assaulted. That unexpected cloud barrier would make it next to impossible for the heavy and medium American daylight bombers to work effectively against the pinpoint targets they had to be able to see. Our fighter squadrons would have great difficulty in catching any marauding enemy aircraft because they could quickly take cover in the clouds. Allied fighter bombers and rocket aircraft would be similarly impeded, for, as we soon discovered, the uneven base of the cloud was only 500 feet above the ground. Anybody flying under it would be highly vulnerable to flak and, for that matter, fire from machine guns and rifles. Furthermore, defending enemy fighters could use the low scud cloud as they maneuvered into firing position on one's vulnerable tail.

Heading straight south for the beach just to the west of Ouistreham and by Lion-sur-Mer off my right wingtip, we dove down below the unwelcome cloud bank to cross the still vacant beach. Our speed was well over 400 miles an hour. Our eyes were completely peeled and our heads on swivels. It was Taylor's job to lead. He had to do the map reading and the reconnaissance. He would note the location of tanks, moving vehicles, and gun emplacements, and whether there was artillery or flak to be seen. If possible, he would photograph with his 14-inch port oblique camera the important items he observed.

Within two minutes we were over Caen where the wall of cloud that sat over the beachhead had dissipated. We were able to climb rapidly to 6,000 feet, a far safer altitude at which to operate. During the less than two minutes it had taken to fly at low level from the coast to Caen we had swept by fields littered with huge Horsa troop and vehicle-carrying gliders. They had gone in in the darkness in the early hours of the morning to attempt to seize the bridges over the Caen Canal and the Orne River. Some of the gliders were still whole, others had wings ripped off or had crashed, totally torn apart.

As Taylor and I made our first run over Caen we could see brilliantly burning light anti-aircraft tracer shells slowly arcing up toward us, behind and on into the clouds above. Those first welcoming barrages were coming fairly close but were nothing to worry about. I always had a feeling of detachment and they'll-never-hit-me attitude to the apparently slow-moving flak I could see on its way. It was no different that morning when I felt particularly fearless and invincible. But in the next weeks, my encounters with the accurate, invisible shells of the deadly German 88 aircraft guns and the high velocity light flak that appeared on the battlefront changed my attitude to one of great respect and on not a few occasions to unadulterated terror.

Thirty minutes were spent checking all the roads leading into Caen. Taylor saw some motor vehicles moving toward Caen on the main highway about five miles southeast of the city. Beyond that little movement was seen.

Then we turned back for the beaches, again diving down to low level to get under that wall of cloud. Arriving at the coast just to the west of Ouistreham, we swung west to follow the beach line about a half mile inland.

It was H-Hour. Below us the terrain was crater-pocked from the thousands of bombs that had rained down during the night. New craters were being made before our eyes as shell after shell from the battleships, cruisers, and destroyers standing offshore smashed down under us. The devastating barrage was now lifting from the shore working inland in an attempt to destroy any enemy forces that might impede the imminent beaching of the first landing craft.

Out to sea we could see them coming, the first lines of landing craft filled with men, tanks, rockets, flak vehicles. Landing craft designed to explode any mine fields were in the vanguard, the swimming Sherman Duplex Drive tanks wallowing behind like rectangular rhinoceros in the surf. They were almost there, almost at the point where bottoms and tracks would touch the sands of Normandy. They bobbed and plowed through the heavy waves about a hundred yards offshore, their gray white wakes marking the growing distance between their sterns and the naval force that had escorted or carried them across the Channel during the stormy night. That mighty armada was now standing about three miles offshore with all its guns trained and firing at the beachhead and us.

From my cockpit I looked out into a horizon filled with the thick cordite smoke from the constant firing of hundreds of huge naval guns. So heavy was the blanket of smoke that it almost totally obscured the massive fleet. Through the heavy black pall, but made more visible and pronounced by it, I could see the flashes of the countless guns, like a long

0078   108/234 7 JUNE 44 F 14/1

Horsa Gliders at Ranville beside the Orne River,
northeast of Caen

168/234 7 JUNE 44 F 14/1

Horsa Gliders at Ranville

unending line of twinkling Christmas lights winking on a dark foggy night. That they were firing directly at us never even crossed my mind.

At Arromanches we turned around and headed back toward Ouistreham, arriving there just as the first landing craft and Duplex Drive tanks hit the beach under heavy fire from German machine guns and 88's. We could see the landing craft disgorging tanks and men into what was rapidly becoming a shambles as enemy fire concentrated on the beaches.

As we turned back once again toward the west the same scenario was developing where the 3rd Canadian Division was coming in on Juno beach at Courseulles. Beyond them and to the west of Arromanches, 30 Corps of the 2nd British Army was beginning its assault.

Back and forth Taylor and I ranged over this incredible, lethal theater of death and destruction. The turning point in World War II was taking place as we watched. We were witnesses to one of the monumental military events in the history of mankind.

So entranced and enthralled was I by the enormity of the scene that I failed to monitor my instrument panel regularly. When finally I did drop my eyes for a split second to run over my engine instruments, temperatures, pressures, and the fuel, I was shocked. The fuel contents gauge on the floor to the right of my seat registered at the empty mark! And there I was, sitting over the Normandy beaches, at least 100 miles from the coast of England. Time to get the hell home. Obviously I had been using a lot more fuel than the lead aircraft, otherwise Taylor would have turned back for England long before.

I radioed a fast call to him with a touch of alarm in my voice. We turned north immediately, climbing up and out over the thundering naval ships, leveling off at 2,000 feet. I did not want to waste any fuel by climbing higher. The next step was to get the propeller into coarse pitch and engine power back for minimum fuel consumption. Then I quickly leaned out the mixture of fuel going to the engine to further minimize fuel consumption. This meant that my airspeed was about 150 miles per hour, roughly 100 less than our normal cruising speed. Taylor stayed with me. He did not cut his speed back but circled and weaved above me to give me protection against any potential enemy fighter attack.

Would I have to bail out? The last thing to do with a Mustang was to ditch it in the sea. It would not skim along the surface. Instead, experience had shown that the aircraft would go straight into the water just like the shark it resembled. The pilot would then ride it to the bottom and that would be the end of the matter. No, if the engine quit I would bail out. At least I wouldn't be alone in the water; below me I could see nothing but ships of every type and kind plowing their way through the sea toward the Normandy coast. You could practically walk on them they were so thick.

The needle of the gas gauge was now on the left edge of the empty mark. Time to run through the bailout check. If the engine quits I will pull back the red emergency handle on the starboard window rail and push straight up on the hood. If it works that will get rid of the hood. Next stage, check on my Mae West and the pull handle that will release the CO_2 to inflate it. Remember to grab the parachute release handle as you step out. Well above the waves, turn the round parachute release handle to release. Bang the handle to get rid of the parachute harness a split second before hitting the water. Make sure the lanyard from the dinghy pack on the parachute I'm sitting on is attached to the Mae West so the pack won't float away. The dinghy will have to be inflated quickly so I can get into it as fast as possible. Everything checks. If I run out of gas I'm ready.

As soon as we left the French coast I sorted out in my mind where I would head. I wanted the closest airport I could find. I knew where it was and told Taylor of my intentions.

When I was about 10 miles from the English coast the needle on the gas gauge was well below the empty mark. Miraculously the engine was still grinding away. I had a few words with the airfield controller at my chosen destination to explain my emergency situation. Immediately he gave me clearance for a straight in landing on the north/south runway. Into the final approach, wheels down, flaps down, approach speed 120, round out, throttle off, touch

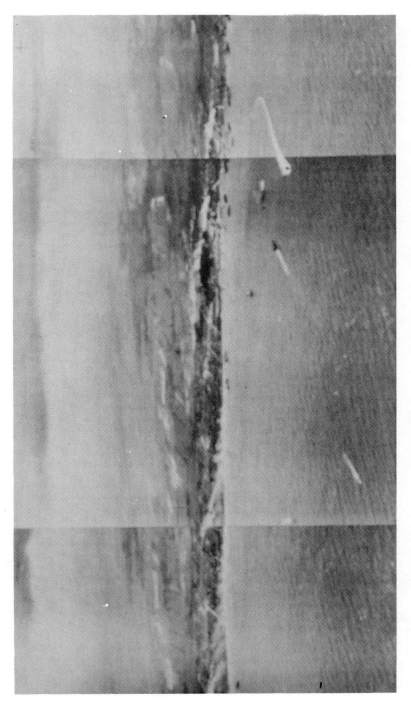

Ouistreham: 10:00 Hours, D-Day

Invasion fleet off beachhead, D-Day+4

down on the button end of the runway. Turn off at the first taxi way on the right. The engine coughs. Coughs again. Then quits.

It is 08:09 hours on D-Day 6 June 1944. The point of touch down was Thorney Island, that happy place where I had joined the Flying Circus six weeks before. Within three and a half hours I would be leading a section across the beachhead for a tactical reconnaissance of the Bayeux area.

The final decision for the D-Day assault was based on weather. Go or no go? That question could be answered only by the Supreme Commander himself, General Dwight D. Eisenhower. It would be an extremely difficult choice.

Eisenhower had arrived at his Portsmouth battle headquarters on 29 May. There at Southwick House he and his high-level staff together with Montgomery and his field commanders — who had already moved their own tactical headquarters into the Portsmouth area preparatory to embarkation — met many times during the week. They dealt with a multitude of last-minute questions that had to be answered at the highest possible level. Judgments were made in an atmosphere of collective decision making under the chairmanship of Eisenhower, by now the experienced military-political diplomat and the acknowledged leader of the highest of the High Command. His senior airman and deputy Supreme Commander was Air Chief Marshal Sir Arthur Tedder. The senior sailor was Admiral Sir Bertram Ramsay. His first soldier was Montgomery. The tactical air force commander was Air Chief Marshal Sir Trafford Leigh-Mallory. All were British save Bradley, the commander of the U.S. First Army. But whatever the opinion of this illustrious, largely British group, the final decision and responsibility would be Eisenhower's.

On 29 May 1944 the weather for the five upcoming days looked good. Accordingly Eisenhower sent to all commanders the signal "Exercise Hornpipe plus six," the code setting D-Day for 5 June 1944. From that moment the intricate, complex jigsaw pieces made up of the massive forces of men and equipment scattered across southern England started to fall into place. Movement began toward assigned embarkation points from as far north as Swansea and Cardiff, as far west as Falmouth and east as Portsmouth and Newhaven.

The great battleships in the Scapa Flow, the sea lochs of western Scotland and Ulster whose enormous guns would be brought to bear on the enemy coast at first light on D-Day, began their preparations to depart for their assigned positions off the beaches of Normandy.

However, by Thursday, 1 June, the meteorological staff of Supreme Command began to receive word of low pressure disturbances forming in the Atlantic far to the west. Worried about the prospects, they warned Eisenhower that the weather outlook was not good for the 4th, 5th, and 6th. During the rest of the week there were several conferences with the meteorologists as concern for the weather picture increased. The forecast for 6 and 7 June was for much cloud and westerly winds in the range of Force 4 or 5. This situation could produce heavy seas that would make beach landings impossible. On Saturday the 3rd the forecast for 4 to 7 June was for cloudy and stormy weather with winds in the range of Force 5. At Eisenhower's 04:15 conference on Sunday, 4 June, the forecast had not changed. The Supreme Commander had little choice. He ordered the postponement of D-Day by 24 hours. The signal went out — "Ripcord plus 24."

At that late moment all the assault force ships were loaded and in position ready to sail. There were some 3,300 British and Canadian vessels and 2,000 American. Behind them in the channels, loughs, and estuaries scattered across the southern coast of England a thousand more ships were being filled. Ripcord allowed Eisenhower to delay the final decision for a day. If he delayed longer, Neptune would have to be postponed until the next period during which the moonlight and tides would again be right. That would be 19 June. The consequences of canceling Neptune and returning the massive force to port and shore would be horrendous. Not only would there be a dampening effect upon morale, the security of the operation of the assault itself and the potential success of the Fortitude deception would be jeopardized.

Finally the moment of decision had arrived. At 21:30 on Sunday, 4 June, the conference room at Southwick House was filled by all the members of the High Command. They listened to the forecaster's briefing with only one question in mind. Should it be go or no go for 6 June? The best meteorological opinion — not unanimous among the team of SHAEF's weathermen — was that there would be a break in the weather after midnight on Monday. The wind would diminish sufficiently to allow the multitude of ships in the Channel to operate effectively. The weather would be tolerable though only marginally. At best the weather would make the operation chancy.

The briefing and questioning were finished. Eisenhower the military diplomat, the Supreme Commander who had to make the final decision knowing that he would not be the battle commander, the man responsible for the assault, turned to Montgomery, the man who did have that onus, and asked the testy Monty his opinion. It was politic, although not necessary. If Monty was to say no, Eisenhower would have to agree. But if Monty said yes, Ike could still have said no.

His land force commander responded immediately and emphatically. "I would say — Go!" That was it. Ike made the decision. "I don't see how we can do anything else."

D-Day would be Tuesday, 6 June. A final review conference was held at Southwick House at 04:15 on Monday morning, 5 June. Nothing had changed. There was no turning back.

As the first minute of 6 June passed, endless columns of skytrains — Dakotas filled with paratroops or towing enormous Horsa gliders loaded with men, jeeps, and guns — headed for the English coastline bound for the shores of Normandy. This air fleet of some 1,100 transports and gliders was the aerial counterpart to the armada of ships plowing through the heavy seas below them, the largest the world had ever seen.

Within an hour, guided by the flares of their Pathfinders who parachuted in ahead of them, the 101st Airborne Division of the Americans and the U.S. 82nd Division and its men jumped into their assigned western sectors of the beaches, suffering heavy losses as they were scattered across the pitch black French countryside.

On the east the British paratroopers and the 1st Canadian Paratroop Batallion, who went in at the same time under parachutes or by Horsa glider, were able to seize most of their River Orne objectives. At 03:00 in the morning when the troops began to embark into heaving pitching assault boats from huge transport ships standing off the Normandy beaches, there had still been no German response either in the American or in the British-Canadian sectors. By then thousands of paratroopers swinging in the blackness of the moonless night under billowing chutes or in whistling, ghost-like gliders were coming to earth in France. Hundreds of bombers were delivering their lethal cargoes along the shores of the bay of the Seine in that night of total darkness. The light of the moon was totally obscured by the thick overcast of cloud that Eisenhower's meteorologists had predicted. An 18 knot wind blew in from the northwest making huge waves that would create havoc among the heavily laden landing craft, not only as they hit the beaches at H-Hour but also when they made their treacherous way inshore from the mother ships.

In the long, agonizing, wind-whipped crossing of the Channel only one of the more than 6,000 ships had been lost to enemy action. In the air not one of the vast skytrain was brought down by the Luftwaffe.

From the bombers that night and early morning some 10,000 tons of explosives rained down on the beaches and their approaches. At first light hundreds of fighters and fighter bombers joined in the assault. Offshore the guns and rockets of more than 600 ships hammered the beaches as thousands of troops poured onto the beaches in the face of a determined defense by an enemy who, astonishingly enough, had been taken totally by surprise.

The assault went in from H-Hour, 06:30 hours at Utah beach on the American western flank through to the later H-Hour, 07:45 at Sword beach of the British, a span of one hour and twenty-five minutes caused by tidal variations.

Tens of thousands of trained men stormed the beaches to fight for their lives. Most of them had never fired a shot in anger. Many were deathly ill from seasickness. Thousands would be lost or injured on that first day when the success or failure of Neptune sat precariously on the knife-edge. Factors of weather, surprise and the unpredictable reaction of the massive Nazi forces facing them could tip the balance either way. Within a short traveling range of the Normandy beaches lurked some 1600 Panzers. If they were galvanized from the 15th Army in the Pas-de-Calais area, the Evreux sector (12 SS Panzer Division) and Chartres (Panzer Lehr Division), they could descend en masse upon the Allied forces during the tenuous, critical D-Day hours and the following three to four days as the Allies were clawing their way ashore and inland.

The only Allied force that could keep those powerful Panzers and the German infantry divisions of the 15th Army away from the beachhead was the fictional First United States Army Group, FUSAG, and its real leader, General George Patton. The question was whether the deception of Fortitude would work. Would Hitler be convinced that Armee Group Patton would carry out a second but main attack against the Calais shores? If so, to meet the true 'Grossinvasion' and hold back his reserve Panzer divisions, the Fuhrer would have to keep his 15th Army in position in the Pas-de-Calais area.

On the eve of D-Day and during that momentous twenty-four hour period a broad range of air and naval operations was conducted to deceive the enemy. In the first few minutes of 6 June, Royal Air Force bombers dropped over 200 half-life-sized dummies of paratroopers, 'dolls', complete with parachutes and accompanied by rifle and machine gun simulators exploding as they fell. Parachute flares and Verey lights lit the black sky in the middle of this scenario designed to create the impression that paratroop landings up to brigade strength were occurring. The idea was to engage identified German anti-paratroop units in tracking down operations in the difficult Norman country-side outside the actual airborne landing areas. Once on the ground small groups of real paratroopers set up record playing and amplifying machines. From these at high volume came the sounds of gunfire, exploding bombs and the voices of soldiers in battle. This was operation Titanic, which took place in the environs of Le Havre and in the areas of the Forêt d'Ecouves, the Forêt de Cerisy (later to accommodate Montgomery's headquarters), Lessay, St. Hilaire-du-Harcourt and Villedieu-les-Poêles. Titanic was highly successful in deceiving the confused German high command for many hours.

At sea throughout the night before H-Hour, eighteen launches of the Royal Navy and RAF sailed in convoy toward the coast of Calais, each flying a twenty-nine-foot Filbert balloon and, from a raft behind, a second one. Attached to each Filbert was a nine-foot reflector that simulated a radar echo of a 10,000 ton vessel. Some fifteen miles off the English coast the group had split in two heading for different destinations in the Pas-de-Calais area.

By 02:00 the ships' cathode ray tubes indicated that the Filbert reflector devices were being interrogated by German radar. About that time two RAF bomber squadrons flew overhead the two mini-fleets to drop bundles of radar-deceiving strips of aluminum foil. All of this was designed to create the impression of the approach of a large invasion fleet. When the vessels were about ten miles offshore, huge sound amplifiers were turned on, carrying the noise that would be generated by an armada of ships approaching. The intent was to lead the Germans to believe that a major attack was being mounted between Le Havre and Calais. This confusing, successful deception took the Germans in completely.

By the end of D-Day the Americans at Omaha Beach had a bloody toehold but not a deep one, perhaps no more than one and a half miles. At Utah a beachhead was secured on a 4,000-yard front with penetrations in depth to up to 10,000 yards.

At Gold Beach in the British sector, 50 Division of 30 Corps, although not achieving the intended goal of Caen, made an advance inland of some five miles. 3 Canadian Division had pushed forward steadily to reach a comparable depth to that reached by 50 Division on its right. On its left at Sword beach, 3 British Division assaulted the beaches just east of Lion-sur-Mer. Their objective was to advance on

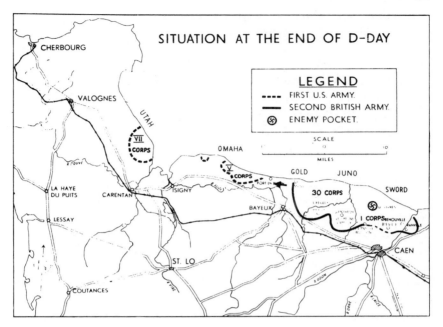

SITUATION AT THE END OF D-DAY

LEGEND
- - - - FIRST U.S. ARMY.
──── SECOND BRITISH ARMY.
🌀 ENEMY POCKET.

Caen and link up with 6 Airborne Division east of the Orne.
Montgomery later wrote:

> By nightfall, the division was well established with
> forward elements on the line Bieville-Benouville,
> where contact was made with 6 Airborne Division.
> Ouistreham had almost been cleared, but the
> Commandos had not succeeded in capturing the
> heavily fortified strong point at Douvres.
> East of the River Orne, 6 Airborne Division
> withstood a number of counter attacks during the
> day; in spite of heavy casualties the airborne troops
> succeeded in frustrating repeated attempts by
> enemy infantry and tanks to capture Ranville and
> to wipe out the Benouville bridgehead . . . . As a
> result of our D-Day operations, we had gained a
> foothold on the Continent of Europe.
> We had achieved surprise, the troops had
> fought magnificently, and our losses had been
> much lower than had ever seemed possible. We had
> breached the Atlantic Wall along the whole 'Nep-

tune' frontage, and all assaulting divisions were ashore.[1]

In the D-Day assault some 12,000 Allied troops were killed, wounded, or reported as missing. Casualties were heavy but not nearly so great as the 75,000 anticipated if Neptune had been carried off without two important ingredients — complete surprise accompanied by successful Fortitude deceptions.

During D-Day the Supreme Commander, Eisenhower, kept abreast of events at SHAEF Headquarters at Southwick House in Portsmouth where he would maintain his headquarters for some weeks. There he and his chiefs-of-staff closely monitored reports on the situation amid enormous anxiety for Bradley's near disaster at Omaha beach where his troops were being badly mauled. The heavy German defenses combined with a surging sea that sank most of the inbound armor and weaponry were threatening to totally destroy the American force at Omaha.

An impatient Montgomery was also at Portsmouth. General de Guingand wrote:

> Montgomery kept to his office most of that day waiting to see when he should move to Normandy. His Tactical Headquarters was now on its way across, and he was champing at the bit to get going himself. As the day progressed it became clear that Bradley and his First U.S. Army were having a very sticky time of it at the Omaha beach . . . otherwise things were going more or less to plan.[2]

At Southwick Park that day Montgomery was seen trimming the roses in the garden outside his headquarters. He left the next morning to take command in Normandy.

Similarly, on D-Day Montgomery's counterpart, Field Marshal Gerd von Rundstedt, the German Commander-in-Chief West, was seen pruning roses in the garden of his headquarters, an enormous three-storey structure on the rue Alexandre Dumas in St. Germain-en-Laye. He had, how-

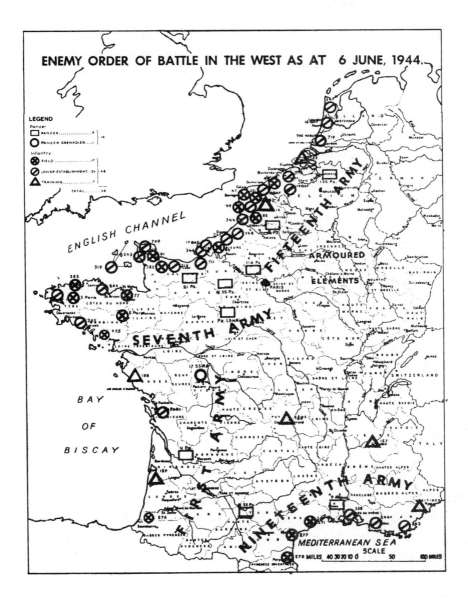

ENEMY ORDER OF BATTLE IN THE WEST AS AT 6 JUNE, 1944.

84

ever, spent most of the hectic morning assessing the situation and getting urgent messages off to Hitler after being
informed at 03:00 hours of ships' engine noises coming from
the Bay of the Seine. That information was quickly followed
with news of the British and American airborne landings.
Von Rundstedt made up his mind immediately that these
reports marked "definitely the opening phase of a landing
to be expected at dawn."

At Rommel's headquarters at Chateau de la Roche-
Guyon, General Hans Speidel did not come to the same
conclusion as von Rundstedt. In the absence of Rommel,
who was on leave at his home in Germany, Speidel, his
chief-of-staff, was in charge of the headquarters. He was
not certain whether they were airborne landings in strength
or only parachutists dropped to provide a link between the
French Resistance and later invasion forces. The German
7th Army log of the day records:

> "Chief-of-Staff of Army Group B believes that for
> the time being this is not to be considered as a large
> operation."[3]

Shortly after 04:30, von Rundstedt took action. He
ordered the Panzer Lehr Division, at that moment between
Orleans and Caen, and the 12th SS Panzer Division (Hitler
Jugend), between Paris and Caen, to move to the invasion
area immediately. He then advised OKW, the German
Supreme Command, of what he had done. His communica-
tion was in the form of a signal which stated in part:

> "OB-West is fully aware that if this is actually a
> large-scale enemy operation it can only be met
> successfully if immediate action is taken. This
> involves the commitment on this day of the avail-
> able strategic reserves ... the 12th SS and the Panzer
> Lehr Divisions. If they assemble quickly and get an
> early start they can enter the battle on the coast
> during the day."[4]

However, employment of the strategic Panzer reserves,

of which the 12th SS and Panzer Lehr Divisions were a part, required the decision of Hitler himself.

By 07:30 OKW informed von Rundstedt that neither division was to be committed without the instructions of Hitler, that Hitler Jugend was to be stopped at Lisieux and the Panzer Lehr was to remain where it was. Von Rundstedt's counterattack on D-Day would therefore be limited to only what he had — the 21st Panzer with 146 tanks and 51 assault guns — instead of the 500 tanks and 100 assault guns the two elite Panzer divisions withheld from him would have provided.

By 10:00 that day, Hitler, having just awakened, was informed of the landings. The question was whether he would believe what Fortitude had been designed to make him believe, that these landings were mainly diversionary and that the Allies intended to make a second but major landing. If he believed in the latter then he could not commit his strategic reserves to Normandy. If he disbelieved Fortitude and was now convinced that the main thrust was in Normandy he would order a signal sent "Initiate Case Three." That message would release all strategic reserves, plus the 15th Army in the Pas-de-Calais area with its Panzer divisions. In addition, infantry and other mobile divisions throughout France would move into the battle.

What would Hitler do? On his decision that day rested the fate of the Allied Invasion.

General Alfred Jodl, Hitler's chief operations officer, advised the Fuhrer that he had personally countermanded von Rundstedt's orders to Hitler Jugend and Panzer Lehr divisions. Hitler assessed the information Jodl presented to him, coming to the conclusion that the Normandy attack was indeed diversionary. A decision to permit von Rundstedt to use the 'Case Three' reserves or any part of them could not be taken until he was certain that the Allies did not intend to attack the Pas-de-Calais area. Accordingly, Jodl's countermanding order to von Rundstedt was approved.

By mid-afternoon Hitler reversed himself on the Hitler Jugend and Panzer Lehr decision. Von Rundstedt could have them. However, he could not have the remainder of the strategic reserves nor the Panzer resources of the 15th Army in the Pas-de-Calais. The final message from von Rundstedt that day asking for the 'Case Three' reserves was not acted upon by Hitler.

Hitler was convinced that Armee Group Patton, led by that most formidable of American generals, would soon be leading the massive forces of his FUSAG across the Channel to assault the Pas-de-Calais area in the true Grossinvasion.

Without the threat of Patton and his ficticious FUSAG Hitler would have thrown into the battle not only the strategic reserves but the entire 15th Army itself. Had these powerful, immediately available, highly trained and well-equipped forces been poured into the beachhead area between D-Day and D + 3, the concentrated weight of their military might would have come crashing down upon the slim Allied forces struggling to stay on the beachhead.

While he was not physically a participant in D-Day or its planning, General George Patton was a major player in the success of D-Day and Neptune. Through Fortitude and the credible concept of the potential FUSAG attack on the Pas-de-Calais area, Patton was a tangible to-be-reckoned-with presence in the mind of the ultimate decision-maker of the Third Reich, Adolph Hitler.

5

12 June 1944　　OPERATIONS: An artillery shoot was
flown by F/L J. Watts with F/O's F.P.
Bryon, T.H. Lambros and R.H. Rohmer
as cover. In French coast Cabourg.
Targets to be engaged were enemy
artillery. Due to our own guns not
being ready, only first target was
engaged, which was southeast of Caen.
Out French coast Cabourg.

430 Squadron Log

That artillery shoot had seen the four of us airborne out of
Odiham at 13:15 and back again at 15:15. After debriefing I
had to hurry to change from my usual battle dress flying
gear into my light blue Royal Canadian Air Force 'walking
out' uniform with shirt, tie, polished brass buttons and the
ever present flat hat; and to pack my smallest bag with a
change of underwear, black socks, and shaving kit — not
really needed except for the toothbrush — before the 5:30
train left for London.

A one-day 'spot of leave' had been granted to three pilots
from each of 39 Wing's three squadrons. We had been
working almost round the clock since D-Day, usually
getting up at 03:00 or 04:00 in the morning for breakfast,
briefing and first-light sorties. Flying was finished late in
the day, debriefings often lasting until after dark. It was a
demanding and dangerous time, although in our squadron
we had been remarkably fortunate in that we had lost only
one pilot, F/O Jack Cox. He was shot down on D-Day when

the formation four that he was in was attacked by four Focke-Wulf 190's.

Our Wingco Operations, Wing Commander RCA (Bunt) Waddell, decided it was time to get a rotational system of one-day leaves going to relieve the high tension under which we had been working.

Naturally it was to London that this first gang headed, all nine of us. Most had made bookings at the Regent Palace Hotel, that renowned gem of British hostelry that sits cramped in on a triangular piece of land on the northern rim of that famous British battleground, Piccadilly Circus. There the aptly named Piccadilly Commandos operated by day and mainly by night, lurking in every cranny and doorway from which they assaulted innocent soliders, sailors, and airmen with salvos of enticements.

On arriving in London, our hard-flying team emerged into the pitch dark of the blackout and leaped into reliable square-box London taxis that were waiting, their hooded headlights dimmed. From the railway station we went straight to the Regent Palace. After a quick registration and throwing of bags in rooms we were off on a tour of our favorite clubs, a handful of nearby places where membership was limited to la crème de la crème, the Canadian and British fighter pilots, those men with the unique, traditional distinction of wearing undone the top brass button on their jackets — the sign of the fighter pilot. All bomber and coastal commander crews and other lesser-like were excluded.

Following a long evening tour, which took us first to the basement bar of our hotel, then to the Chez Moi Club and finally to the Crackers Club, we arrived on foot at the front door of the Regent Palace, much the worse for wear. By now there were only six people in our team, the biggest of whom was Flight Lieutenant Jack 'Sailor' Seaman, a tall, square, quiet hulk of a young man. On the other end of the scale I was by far the smallest, weighing in at 145 pounds, and not as high as Sailor Seaman's left shoulder.

As we approached the front door in the dim shadows of the blackout there came into view a woman standing near the entrance. She was on the west side of the Regent Palace's pieshaped piece of land which came to a point just a few feet south of the door. Ranged behind her was her stable of ladies of the night. Some eight of them were lined up along the curb.

In a flash our team lined up opposite them and loud tongue-in-cheek (on our side) haggling began. Being by nature a fierce fighter, I decided that the best place for me to stand was directly behind the protective big body of Sailor Seaman. From that supposedly safe vantage point I entered the shouting fray from time to time by sticking my head around Sailor's left shoulder to mouth something provocatively rude at the madam, then ducking back behind his large frame.

I had just made one of my brave vocal forays and retreated behind Sailor when he suddenly stepped aside. There facing me, about one and a half feet away, was the madam. With experienced skill she cocked her clenched fist and smashed me full in the mouth. Under the force of the blow I staggered backward. Fortunately for my reputation I did not fall. Astonished and in no little pain I pulled myself together, marched back to where she was standing, planted my feet and returned the right smash. Whereupon she tottered backward, falling into the arms of her charges. That exchange of blows ended the session forthwith.

With the aid of my roommate, Flying Officer Joe 'Splash' Roussel, I made my way up to the room, hand over an extremely painful mouth. When I got into the bathroom to put cold water on my face, the mirror told me the bad news. My lips were swollen like an orangutang's. That wasn't the end of the evening for my friends but it certainly was for me.

Later that night, contemplating my misery of too much booze, compounded by thick lips, my ears picked up the sound of an unusual aircraft engine. Pilots were sensitve to the sounds of the engines of the myriad aircraft that populated our skies in those days. I certainly was. I had never heard this one before but I knew it was an airplane, a low flying one at that. Its noise was deep, gutteral, throbbing and, as it approached, loud, pulsating with such force that it made the windows shake. As the machine came overhead in the darkness I threw open the window to scan the black sky. I could see nothing. The unusual aircraft was out of my line of sight, but its noise was all enveloping, ominous.

Suddenly there was silence. Complete silence, almost as deafening as the noise that had stopped. That was strange. An aircraft low over the center of London and the engine stops? It wasn't that it sputtered and wound down. It stopped abruptly. Most peculiar. In a few seconds the silence was shattered by a powerful explosion which lit up the sky. The first V-1, the infamous flying bomb, had arrived. It was the precursor of hundreds that Hitler was to shower down upon London until the launching sites in the Pas-de-Calais area were overrun by the Allied forces much later.

Now the secret was out. Even we fighter reconnaissance pilots could be told. The Noball sites we had been photographing in France in the last months were launching pads for the V-1. Those hockey sticks were ramps up which the ignited engines of the V-1's drove the pilotless flying bombs in a direct line toward the heart of London. Now there was no doubt in our minds about the importance of the attacks on the Noball sites and our supporting work. Without the confirmed destruction of a vast number of the launching ramps as well as the V-1 assembly and storage locations by USAF, RAF, and RCAF bomber attacks, the devastastion of the V-1 onslaught on London might well have been sufficient to deflect the course of the war.

The order that brought the V-1 Flying Bomb crashing down at Bethnal Green in London, was issued by Hitler himself immediately after he had been informed by his staff that Allied landings were under way in Normandy. He commanded Jodl to pass the code word *Junkroom*, the signal to begin launching the devil's own device, the V-1, against the people of London. In themselves the V-1's were symbols of the extent to which the strategists of World War II were prepared to go in order to bring the enemy to his knees, thereby achieving the ultimate victory.

The V-1 was indeed a flying bomb. It was a pilotless, almost impervious, winged projectile, launched from specially constructed sites scattered around the Pas-de-Calais area within about 100 miles of the center core of

London. It could reach any part of the 692 square miles of Greater London. There its precisely calculated fuel supply would run out. At that instant the thundering, pulsing roar of its paraffin-powered ramjet engine would abruptly stop, filling the air with the silence of the imminent death and devastation that would inevitably occur with its mindless impact.

The V-1 pilotless aircraft had a wingspan of about 17 feet and a length of 25; a range of between 120 and 140 miles with an optimum operating height of 1000-4000 feet. It flew at speeds over 400 miles per hour. In its bulky nose it carried a warhead of one ton of high explosives. In theory its carefully measured fuel load was sufficient to take it from the point of launching in France to the Tower of London, give or take two minutes of flying.

Hitler's original intent for the V-1 was that the first attacks against London would begin as early as October 1943. His plan was that when full production was reached, 2,000 rounds per month would be delivered against the target city. As the Fuhrer planned it, London would soon be turned into a flaming cauldron, an inferno that would bring Great Britain to its knees pleading for peace long before the gathering Allied invasion forces would be in a position to mount their first attack against Fortress Europe.

One of the first clues that the Germans had started on the development of a missile program, one that ultimately produced not only the V-1 but as well the V-2 rockets, came in March 1943. In a bugged conversation between two captured German generals in London, one told the other about the rockets he had seen being tested in Germany and expressed surprise that London was not yet in ruins from a rocket bombardment. From that time intelligence reports began to arrive into the hands of the British from their agents in the field, from aerial reconnaissance, and from Ultra. This last was the code name for intelligence of the highest grade derived from cryptanalysis.

The threat of mass destruction was real and frightening. The urgency of neutralizing the V1 was compelling.

The most significant document that rang the alarm bells in London was a report from a German source that described the V-1 and its program in detail. It came into the hands of the British Intelligence Chief in Lisbon during the early summer of 1943. In part it stated that:

"Hitler and members of his Cabinet recently inspected both weapons [the V1 and V2] at Peenemünde. About 10th June, Hitler told assembled military leaders that the Germans had only to hold out, since by the end of 1943 London will be levelled to the ground and Britain forced to capitulate. October 20th is at present fixed as Zero Day for rocket attacks to begin. Hitler ordered the construction of 30,000 A-4 [the original nomenclature for the V2] projectiles by that day; this is, however, beyond the bounds of possibility. Production of both weapons is to have first priority and 1500 skilled workers have been transferred to this work from anti-aircraft and artillery production."[1]

The first British reaction to this discovery was an all-out bomber attack on Peenemünde led by RAF Pathfinders in their Mosquitos. This was followed by raids on plants where the flying bomb was being manufactured and attacks on launching sites. It was only by a concentrated effort by Bomber Command and the United States Air Force that Hitler's start up date of October, 1943, was avoided.

The bombing of the 'ski' sites, our Noball targets, began on a large scale on 21 December 1943. On Christmas Eve some 1,300 USAF aircraft dropped 1,700 tons of bombs on a series of targets. From that time on, the bombing campaign against 96 identified Noball sites continued. Attacks by both British, Canadian, and American bombers were made in an all-out attempt to destroy each and every one of them. By 11 June 1944, only eight surviving Noball sites were available for use, but 66 'modified sites' were being rushed to operational readiness following Hitler's *Junkroom* order five days before.

Of the first ten V-1's that were launched on the night of 12/13 June, five crashed immediately after the launch, one went missing and the other four (including the one I

V1 Flying Bomb on launching

Noball ramp for V1 launching

heard in London that night) reached England. Notwith-standing this feeble start there was no reason to believe that the battle against the V-1 sites at their manufacturing plants and storage areas had been totally successful. By mid-June the picture was much different. In one 24-hour period commencing at 22:30 hours on 15 June more than two hundred flying bombs were launched from the Noball sites. One hundred and forty-four reached England. Of those seventy-three crashed on Greater London, wreaking enor-mous destruction.

In the end some 8,617 flying bombs were launched from France. Of those approximately 2,340 arrived at the London civil defense region killing 5,500 people, seriously injuring some 16,000 more and destroying thousands of buildings.

As if the V-1 was not enough, the first V-2 rocket fell on London on Friday, 8 September, a frightening projectile that arrived without warning and exploded. The detonation was followed by the sound of the rocket as the noise caught up with the missile which had been travelling well beyond the speed of sound. By 7 April 1945, 1,190 V-2 rockets had been successfully launched against London. The arrival of 1,115 of those was recorded, some five hundred and one falling in the London civil defense region.

As the first flying bombs landed on England on the night of 12 June, Montgomery and his army commanders, Bradley and Dempsey, had their hands full with the counter-attacking Germans. Rommel had concentrated his Panzers and infantry in the area of Caen where Montgomery, true to his original plans, had chosen to pivot. His difficulty was that Caen had proved to be impossible to take. Vicious close-quarter infantry encounters and costly collisions of the Panzers with the British and Canadian armored divisions in that sector allowed little or no forward movement for either side.

Clearly Montgomery had correctly judged how the Germans would react. Rommel and the German High Command put their main force against the experienced British Army they had fought many times. To OKW, the Britons and Canadians were the major threat. The untried, inexperienced Americans who had been severely damaged on Omaha beach on D-Day could be easily held in check by much lighter concentrations of forces. The bulk of the weight of German armor available to Rommel was therefore concentrated in all its brute strength against the British-Canadian forces in a ring around and to the north of Caen. That steel wall had inflicted on the British-Canadian forces such a high loss of personnel, tanks and other armor that by 12 June Montgomery was compelled to stop, lick his wounds, and regroup. He would not use the politically unacceptable words "go on the defensive." What he did say was:

> I therefore ordered a policy of limited offensive operations in furtherance of the plan, which were carried out although they often involved great risks.[2]

When Montgomery had arrived off the beachhead aboard HMS Faulknor on D + 1, 7 June, he located General Bradley aboard the USS Augusta. At that point Bradley was deeply concerned about the operational situation on Omaha beach where his troops were suffering severe losses. They discussed Bradley's problem and agreed on how it could be solved. During the remainder of the day Montgomery cruised around the beachhead waters meeting with, among others, General Eisenhower, Admiral Ramsay and his own General Dempsey.

At 6:30 on 8 June Montgomery left the Faulknor to step on French soil. He immediately proceeded to his tactical headquarters which had been set up in the gardens of the Chateau at Creully, a small village a few miles east of Bayeux. There the diminutive British general, whom Patton considered was "not a man for fast and bold action, but a master of the set battle and more concerned with not losing the battle than with winning one," was installed with his staff. From this tactical headquarters Montgomery did indeed begin to conduct his set piece battle under his master plan.

Briefly, it was so to stage and conduct operations

that we drew the main enemy strength on to the front of the Second British Army on our eastern flank, in order that we might the more easily gain territory in the west and make the ultimate break-out on that flank — using the First American Army for the purpose. If events on the western flank were to proceed rapidly it meant that we must make quick territorial gains there.

On the eastern flank, in the Caen sector, the acquisition of ground was not so pressing; the need *there* was by hard fighting to make the enemy commit his reserves, so that the American forces would meet less opposition in their advances to gain the territory which was vital on the west.[3]

On 7 June, 12 Panzer joined 21 Panzer Division west of Caen; on the 9th, Panzer Lehr was identified south of Bayeux, and on the 12th, 17 SS Panzer Grenadier Division was astride the Aure River. On 9 June, 1 SS Panzer was en route south to Normandy, while 2 SS Panzer, 2 Panzer and 11 Panzer Divisions were either preparing to move or had started toward the front. Hitler, however, still refused to commit his strategic reserves Panzers. He was waiting for Armee Group Patton to strike against the Pas-de-Calais.

Two battle commanders' conferences had taken place on 9 June. One was on the German side and the other on the Allied. Both resulted in offensive attacks that brought about as vicious, destructive, close-quarter armored and infantry battles as any that took place on the Normandy beachhead.

The enemy meeting took place at the headquarters of young SS Colonel Kurt Meyer, commander of the 25 SS Panzer Grenadier Regiment of the 12 SS Panzer Division. Meyer was at Ardenne Abbey just outside Caen, where he was visited by his superior General Geyr von Schweppenburg, commanding the Panzer Group West. This conference decided that there was to be a massive effort to break through to the beaches with three armored divisions. Out of Caen, on the right would be 21 Panzer, in the center 12 SS, and on the left near Bayeux, Panzer Lehr. The attack would begin the next day as soon as Panzer Lehr had arrived.

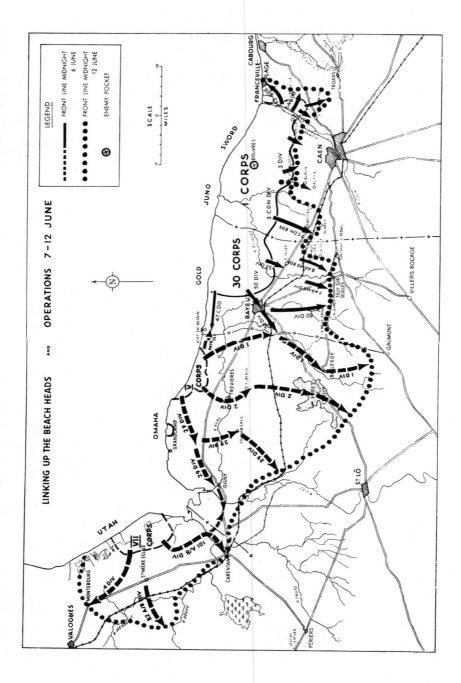

LINKING UP THE BEACH HEADS and OPERATIONS 7–12 JUNE

LEGEND

FRONT LINE MIDNIGHT 6 JUNE
FRONT LINE MIDNIGHT 12 JUNE
ENEMY POCKET

SCALE
MILES

On the same day, 9 June, Montgomery met with Bradley and Dempsey in a field near Port-en-Bessin. He had a plan. Both the 12 SS and 21 Panzer, dug in on the defensive around Caen, would be by-passed and encircled. On the left through the bridgehead held by British and Canadian Airborne troops on the east side of the Orne a thrust would be made by the 4th Armored Brigade and the 51st (Highland) Division. Their goal was Cagny. On the right from Bayeux, 30 Corps, its 7th Armored Division in the vanguard, would move to take Villers Bocage and Evrecy. At the time Cagny and Evrecy were taken, the entire British and Canadian 1st Airborne Division would parachute in between them completing a potentially impregnable ring around Caen in which, according to the set-piece plan, the powerful German forces would be trapped and destroyed or captured.

Collaterally, Bradley's American forces were to attack in the direction of Caumont for the purpose of enlarging the size of the beachhead and at the same time deflecting German concern away from the major assault the Americans were to make on Cherbourg.

The result of the concurrent German and Allied planning conferences was a massive head-on collision of opposing forces, each geared up and mounting an offensive operation. The impact was colossal and devastating in the extreme. Enormous armored destruction was wrought on both sides, with the 3rd Canadian Division in the thick of it.

At the battle's high peak on 11 June several members of the Black Watch Regiment were captured far out on the eastern flank. They were shoved against a wall and shot in cold blood, a repeat of the execution of a group of Canadian prisoners on 8 June by Kurt Meyer's troops. Meyer later claimed that before his conference at Ardenne Abbey on 9 June he had been shown bodies of German prisoners who had been similarly shot by the Canadians.

For two days the battle raged with ferocious intensity, men dying by the hundreds, tanks on both sides being "brewed up" as they burst into flames pierced by the guns of opposing armor; or shells from 25 pounder guns; or projectiles from the infantry-held Piat; or by deadly 88 fire from the legendary Tiger tanks or heavy fire by the American built Shermans and the English Churchills.

On the west, the attempt to encircle Caen took the 7th Armored Division into the battle of Villers Bocage on 12 June, where they met the vaunted Panzer Lehr. Ultimately the British were rebuffed and on 14 June they were forced to fall back some seven miles. This retreat marked the failure of Montgomery's first major attempt to encircle and take Caen.

General Bradley and his American forces to the west of Caumont had reason to be pleased with their own progress. By the evening of June 12th, they had spent one week ashore without a single threatening counterattack on the American beachhead. On the right of British 30 Corps the Americans were sustaining little opposition against their advance on Caumont, some 20 miles inland, quite a different scenario to that in which the British and Canadians found themselves.

On the other hand, Montgomery's pivot thesis, designed to pin down enemy arms and strength, was truly working as the Germans concentrated their massive forces on the Caen sector against the British and Canadians.

Assessing the situation as of 12 June, Montgomery, the commander of all Allied land forces on the beachhead, ordered a policy of limited offensive operations while affirming:

> my immediate objects remained to capture Cherbourg and Caen, and to develop the central sector, the bridgehead to Caumont and Villers Bocage. Examination was made of the possibility of using airborne forces to hasten the capture of Caen, but conditions were found to be unsuitable for their employment.[4]

What Montgomery was saying was that his force had been stopped miles from their objectives of Cagny on the left and Evrecy on the right. Therefore, as to planned use of airborne forces to complete the encirclement of Caen, "conditions were found to be unsuitable for their employment." In other words the gap the airborne was to jump in and seal off was never created. The plan had failed. Caen could not be taken.

Notwithstanding the stand-off in the Caen sector, by 12 June all the beachhead area had been linked together into a continuous front over 50 miles long thrusting inland from 8 to 12 miles. On the eastern flank, the Orne bridgehead across the river and canal was secure.

As yet no German formation from the north of the Seine had made an appearance. Still mesmerized by the potential of Armee Group Patton, the 15th German Army waited its onslaught in the Pas-de-Calais.

On the beachhead and through the two newly built 'instant' Mulberry ports, one in the American Sector and the other in the British area off Arromanches, some 326,000 men, 54,000 tanks, personnel carriers, bulldozers, countless other vehicles together with 104,000 tons of material had been landed.

Meanwhile, back at Peover Hall, an increasingly frustrated George Patton had stuck on the War Room wall his Michelin touring map of France, scale number 1:1,000,000 and on it had followed the battle. He was worried about Montgomery's lack of progress. Patton was convinced that notwithstanding Monty's theoretical recognition of speed and the need to 'crack about' he would and indeed had become bogged down in front of Caen.

Despite the stationary stand-off position achieved by 12 June at substantial cost to the British and Canadians, General Montgomery wrote to the Chief of the Imperial General Staff, General Sir Alan Brooke: "Am very satisfied with progress of operation." Only two days later, even though there was no material change in the situation, he reported to Brooke, "We are in a very reasonable position in Second British Army." However as to Bradley's First Army, he reported at the same time that "the American situation is not so good."

In reality his report ought to have reversed the British-Canadian and American situation descriptions. It is rarely recognized, however, that as Commander-in-Chief of all Allied Land Forces it was Monty's responsibility to fight two wars, one on the ground against the enemy, and the other a war of words in which through voluminous reports, signals and letters he had to daily account to his political and military masters for battlefield successes or failures and for his beloved plans.

Montgomery saw himself as an expert in both kinds of wars. Indeed, when he faltered in one he was usually able to survive by winning kudos in the other. Furthermore he was keenly aware of the nationality of the person to whom he was reporting. The large nationalistic ego of the Americans was sensitive and easily offended. That of the British was no smaller and no less delicate. Monty was a highly skilled massager of both. He had to be.

6

29 June 1944   OPERATIONS: At long last the weather broke sufficiently for the squadron to move to B.8 landing strip, near Bayeux, Normandy. We had been waiting for this for several days. S/L F.H. Chester led the squadron in three sections. Landing was made at B.8 without incident. The Orderly Room and Pilots room was established in three upstairs rooms of abandoned Chateau Magny and the squadron was ready for work. In the afternoon TAC/R's were flown by F/O's J.A. Lowndes and K.K. Charman and by F/O's T.H. Lambros and R.H. Rohmer. Fires were seen in Evreux and M.T. were spotted.

430 Squadron Log

Mobility was the essence of all the airfields in the 2nd Tactical Air Force including ours, 128 Airfield, which accommodated the three squadrons of 39 Recce wing. Everything we had, personal possessions, tents, kitchen equipment, servicing hangars, tools, parts, absolutely everything, had to be capable of fast movement from one operating base to the next one.

Mobility meant moving all of these things, either by truck or in vans, each specially designed and equipped for the particular use assigned to it, such as: a headquarters van, photo processing truck, signals, medical, orderly room, central maintenance for the aircraft and the like. Sleeping accommodation, messes, and supplementary space for the specialized vans was in the standard form of the ubiquitous canvas tent, man's primitive, only partially effective shelter against penetrating rain, piercing cold, and no defense at all against falling shrapnel. Our personal kitbags, sleeping and messing tents were usually carried by a Dakota aircraft so that the pilots could set up shop the same day they arrived at the new base, while the vans and trucks of the rest of the mobile airfield proceeded by road (except for the initial cross-Channel move by ship), usually taking some days in the process.

Pilots had to be able to operate their fighter aircraft from the paved runways that the old RAF stations such as Odiham, Tangmere, and Thorney Island possessed, or from rolling grass turf, as at Gatwick, or from untreated earth strips that the blades of the bulldozers of the Royal Engineers would carve out of a farmer's field or through his orchard. The first experimental tactical airstrip had been bulldozed out on a farm near Ashford in Kent where 430 Squadron was located when I joined it in September 1943. The next strip on which we were to land was our first battle airfield in Normandy named B.8.

The airstrip the Royal Engineers had cut out for us at B.8 lay to the northeast of Bayeux at Magny, about three miles from the outskirts of the lengendary Norman city. B.8 was a single strip running east and west to accommodate the prevailing winds. The surface was a brown, light loam that had been easily leveled by bulldozer blades across about 3,000 feet of flat, cleared agricultural land, planted at the time in grain crop. Close to the edge of the strip and near its west end stood a large gray two-storeyed stone residence, more in the style and size of a manor house than a chateau, as the scribe of the squadron log, an obvious romanticist, had called it. Chateau Magny had not been abandoned. The residents had been given the opportunity to move out all their furniture and possessions before the engineers had finished their construction work.

I was part of the second group to land at B.8 on 25 June. There were three of us, Bill Golden, Danny Lambros and I. We touched down on the new airstrip shortly after noon. The bulldozers were still working around the edges of the strip but no other vehicles were in sight. No tents had been erected, nothing was there except a huge stock of piled jerry cans full of aviation gasoline, the stuff we needed. It was a warm sunny, summer day, with lots of blue sky and just fragments of clouds.

The moment of landing, of touching down in France for the first time, was inspirational. It was the kind of emotion that those who are fortunate enough to arrive at a truly new frontier must have when they enter its threshold. We were there! Being on French soil at last was also tangible evidence that all of us, Army, Navy and Air Force, had succeeded in bringing off at least the initial beachhead conquest. Together we had secured a tenuous foothold inside Fortress Europe and the preserve of the most formidable of Germany's fighting generals, Field Marshal Erwin Rommel.

As soon as our tanks had been topped with gasoline we were airborne again for our tactical reconnaissance into the area of Argentan through to Alençon. We flew south at 5,000 feet crossing over the enemy lines northeast of Caen in battle formation, with about two hundred yards between the lead aircraft and the two of us with him, one on each side. Each of us had begun flying as if we were on a rollercoaster swinging from side to side, then up and down, changing altitude in a range of some five hundred feet. We had learned that without this constant change of line and altitude, those incredible German 88 anti-aircraft guns would be putting their vicious black shells either into our aircraft or close enough that we would hear them explode. The rule was: "If they're close enough that you can hear them explode you're in real trouble." Even so, as we crossed the enemy lines either going out or coming back in that dense, heavily-defended sector, the rollercoaster movement was no guarantee against being hit.

From the 25th to the 29th we continued to operate from our base in England but it became standard squadron practice to land at B.8 to top up with fuel before going on. 128 Airfield and all its personnel, vehicles and equipment finally arrived at B.8 on Thursday 29 June and immediately set up shop to receive and maintain the full complement of 39 Recce Wing's aircraft, some 26 Mustang I's and 12 plus Bluebird Spitfires. By that time most of the Mustang pilots had been into B.8 at least once so we were getting used to its approaches and the characteristics of the airstrip itself.

Therefore, when 430 Squadron arrived at B.8 on Thursday 29 June in a squadron formation of ten, followed by the airlift party in a Dakota escorted by our other three Mustangs, our complement of twenty pilots was delighted to see that trucks, vans, tents and the officers and men of 128 Airfield were already in place.

The incoming aircraft were directed and marshalled to dispersal areas along the south side of the strip stretching from mid-strip to its western boundary. The aircraft were parked near the maintenance vans and tents and the other sub-units of the airfield which were also concentrated on the south side both to the east and west of Chateau Magny.

The Chateau, perhaps a hundred years old or more, was L-shaped with the long arm of the L running north and south and the short arm parallel to the runway, the west and north walls making the 90 degree join. A large bedroom on the second floor at the north end of the building was captured by the pilots as our 'waiting room'.

A pilots' waiting room was a place where we did exactly that — wait. The wait was for a call from 'Ops', the Operations Headquarters of our Wing. When the Wing H.Q. received tasking requirements from 2nd British army (Dempsey's) Headquarters for a TAC/R, Photo/R, Arty/R or whatever, the army liaison officers and our Wingco Flying staff would sort out what had to be done, how and by whom. That sorted out, a telephone call would be made from the Wingco's Op's van to the waiting room where the on-duty pilots would be gathered. There the duty Flight Commander — the same twenty Squadron pilots were divided into two Flights, A and B — would receive the call and designate which of the waiting pilots would carry out the sortie. Those chosen would then trudge off to the Ops van to be briefed. Shortly after that they would be airborne.

The traditional waiting room had perhaps a dozen and a half or more hard, collapsible chairs, (like card table chairs) two or three long portable tables on which to play cards or write. On the walls were a dart board, pictures (Betty Grable legs type) and a notice board complete with flying advice and rude but current jokes. In modern times a pilot's room might be called a lounge. Not in those days. It was a 'waiting room', nothing more, nothing less.

The remainder of the morning of 29 June was spent sorting out the 'issue' tables and chairs that we would need in the pilots' room in the Chateau Magny. We checked the hand-crank telephone from our room to the Operations van from which calls would come telling us who was needed and what time to report to the headquarters for briefing.

Our pilots' room, which was about thirty feet long by twenty, had large shuttered windows which swung open on each side of the fireplace in the north wall and in the west wall. Between them we had an excellent view of the airstrip, the better to watch the comings and goings of our own aircraft and those of the other squadrons. It was particularly nerve-wracking to watch some hapless colleague bring in a Mustang, badly beaten up by flak, to land without flaps or belly-up or with only one leg of its undercarriage down. Then of course, there was the fascination that all airmen have in simply watching aircraft landing and taking off, especially the landings, some of which are a series of bouncing touchdowns, others smooth, three-point perfection. Anyone who made a bad landing certainly heard about it.

We were never quite certain what had happened to it, but apparently at one time there had been another wing attached to our Chateau Magny building on its northern wall. We knew it had been there because attached to the outside of the north wall at ground level immediately below the large window to the east of our fireplace sat a toilet, open for the world to see. A drainpipe followed the wall down from the second floor to the back of this toilet, then into a septic tank. However, because we had no running water the second floor toilet was not serviceable. We would have to use the outside throne. Airmen's ingenuity quickly prevailed. Walls, a flap as a door and a roof, all of canvas, were improvised and the outside toilet quickly came into service. As will later be seen, it was not without its hazards.

At the same time other squadron pilots were milling about in an ancient apple orchard that had been selected as the spot where our sleeping and mess tents would be located. It was behind a stone fence north of the airstrip at its western end, within easy walking distance of our Chateau. Pitching our tents among the trees was a wise decision on someone's part, as we would soon discover.

The milling about was caused by the need for careful selection of one's tent location in the orchard because for the first time we had to pick a spot where we could dig slit trenches, two to a tent. In the trenches we would put our sleeping cots. Then we put our tent up over the pair of trenches.

My own digging session was delayed because I had to fly a tactical reconnaissance operation with Danny Lambros. We went east to Evreux, well beyond the front lines. There we spotted many fires burning in the town and several motor transport on adjacent roads. However, we were back at base shortly after 14:00 hours, so there was plenty of time to get on with the slit trench digging and put up the tent. F/O Ed Geddes, who was to share the tent with me for the rest of our stay at B.8, and I struggled with the erection of our canvas edifice. Finally we had it in place in time for an unappetizing first supper in France.

During that initial night the German bombers were out in force, prowling the beachhead in the darkness, attracting all manner of anti-aircraft firing. Quite apart from this noise we began to hear strange whistlings which some clever soul quickly identified as falling shrapnel. The tons of anti-aircraft shells being lobbed skyward toward the Hun, having exploded, had to come down. Our orchard was getting its fair share and was to receive it every night of the weeks that we were there. While we saw very little of Jerry during the day, he was active under the protective cover of darkness except when bad weather forced him to stay on the ground.

Another happening caused all of us to go back to the shovels the next day to make those slit trenches much deeper. The squadron log entry for 30 June gently deals with the event but it scared the hell out of most of us, making us realize beyond a shadow of a doubt that we were no longer living in comfortable, protected England but in the battle-field.

General: We are quite happy with the general set-up here. Our living tents are pitched under the trees in a very pleasant orchard. There is an abundance of drinking water and the tinned rations are quite good. The first night in France was quite peaceful except in the early hours of the morning when a lone F.W. 190 came screaming across the Airfield followed by Spitfires and bursts of anti-aircraft fire.

While our log-keeper, F/O Ed Winiarz, ignored the night's bomber and anti-aircraft activity when he used the words "quite peaceful," even he was observed digging in deeper the next day.

Far more disturbing for the squadron pilots, now at a grand total of eighteen, was that we lost four people in the previous twelve days. It's a devastating experience to see a close friend perish before your very eyes, or to be told he is missing or shot down and will never be back.

I was fortunate. I lost only one man in my 135 operational sorties. We had just taken off when he reported to me on his radio that he had a glycol (engine coolant) leak. I turned my head to the right to check his aircraft. Sure enough a gray blue cloud of vapour was streaming back from his engine enveloping the cockpit. I shouted at him to go back and land. As he turned toward the airstrip the aircraft never recovered from its bank to the right. Instead it went over on its back and straight into the ground where it exploded in a ball of flame.

When I landed minutes after I was shaking from head to toe. Out of my aircraft, I was in tears, probably as close to a mental collapse as I have ever been. The man who had disappeared from this earth in an inferno was my friend, a pal. Grief, horror, shock combined with an understanding that there but for the grace of God. . . . Would I be next? Of course not. It could never happen to me.

The squadron log tells the story of how we lost our men — enemy fighters and the inability of the Mustang to dogfight:

17 June Operations: Twelve first light sorties were flown. F/O's R. H. Rohmer and T. H. Lambros on a TAC/R of area observed motor transport and tanks. F/L R. B. Moore and F/O P. St. Paul had very exciting and disastrous sorties. On a TAC/R,

eight F. W. 190's attacked them near Condé. F/O
St. Paul gave a short burst on one and headed for
cloud. F/L R. B. Moore was last heard to say that
he was landing at B.8 airstrip but no further news
was heard. Personnel. F/L R. B. Moore was today
posted missing on Air Operations.

Red Moore was never heard from again.

21 June Operations: No sorties were flown until
the early evening. With F/L R. F. Gill, F/O C. P.
St. Paul and F/O H. K. Jones as cover, F/O C. E.
Butchart flew on a TAC/R of roads at Dreux.
F/O's Butchart and H. K. Jones became separated
from the rest and nothing further was seen or heard
of them. A TAC/R also flown by F/O T. H.
Lambros with F/O R. H. Rohmer, F/L J. H.
Taylor and F/O D. A. Whittaker as cover. A few
MT movements were seen.
Personnel: F/L J. R. Manser was made Flight
Commander of 'B' Flight. F/O C. E. Butchart and
F/O H. K. Jones were posted as missing on Air
Operations.

Butchart and Jones were attacked by F.W. 190's.
Butchart, an old bush pilot and a superb airman, shot down
two before he was hit. He crash landed, surviving with a
badly damaged foot which had been hit by a cannon shell.
He was a prisoner of war for the duration. I missed Butch
greatly. He had been a sort of father figure for me, since he
was much older than I, in his early thirties. We had been at
Operational Training Unit (OTU) together, joined 430
Squadron at the same time, and shared the same tent at
Odiham. Jones did not survive.

28 June Operations: Weather in England was very
poor today and no aircraft were airborne. However, F/O F. H. Bryon and F/O D. A. Whittaker,
operating from B.8 Airstrip, flew three tasks. The
first one a TAC/R was successfully completed. An

artillery shoot was done in the afternoon and targets successfully engaged. In the last sortie of the day, both aircraft were intercepted by 6 Me. 109's just before entering their area and F/O Bryon did not return. Personnel: F/O F. H. Bryon was posted as missing as a result of air operations.

The Allied Forces did indeed have air superiority but it was quite obvious to us that it was not complete. By the end of June the enemy's resistance both in the air and on the ground had stiffened considerably around the entire Allied lodgement in Normandy. Caen, which was Montgomery's objective on D-Day, still lay beyond his reach, its environs now thickly populated by crack German troops, their supporting deadly Panzer tanks, and scores of the versatile anti-tank and anti-aircraft 88 mm. gun.

From D-Day through to the end of June, the fighting was bitter, intense, and virtually stalemated. Would the stalemate be broken? Would we break through, break out? Those were questions that we pilots could only speculate on. It was up to General Montgomery to make it happen. He would have to use all the intelligence and forces at his disposal against a determined, highly experienced German army under the brilliant Rommel, whom Montgomery had already defeated once on another continent.

As we settled in at B.8 and Chateau Magny we sensed from what we could see from the air every day that our stay would be long and that the risks ahead would be high. We could also see that the volume of war equipment supplies and material being brought into the beachhead was enormous. Almost all of it was coming in through one Mulberry port the invading force had brought with it.

On 10 June as we crossed over the Normandy beach at Arromanches we had seen the first clues about the use of the huge concrete structures we observed before D-Day sitting in the water in the Portsmouth area. They were pieces of Mulberry, an artificial harbor. There were two of these gigantic, ingenious structures. The one at Arromanches was to serve the British and Canadian armies and the other off the American beaches to the west would provide for Bradley's forces.

As soon as Churchill became Prime Minister on 10 May 1940 he began to push for the design and construction of landing craft and artificial harbors without which the return to France four years later could not be achieved. In 1943, at the Quebec conference of Churchill and Roosevelt and their military staffs, the worrisome matter of supplying the armies across the invasion beaches was settled. There would be two artificial ports, each with a capacity comparable to that of Dover. They would be built in sections, towed across the Channel as quickly as possible after D-Day and sunk in pre-selected sites.

Hitler was convinced the invasion forces would have to seize a large port at the beginning of their attack in order to receive the vast volume of supplies necessary to support an army. Accordingly he had designated all major ports in northwest Europe as 'fortresses' that would be held until the exhaustion of every last possibility of defense. What he was not aware of was that as a result of the Dieppe disaster in the summer of 1942 the Allied tactic was changed to attack ports not frontally but from the rear. In the Dieppe raid Canadian and British troops were sent in directly against the beaches of that port in a frontal assault. They were slaughtered by an alerted German force whose guns commanded the beaches from above.

Nor was Hitler aware that at the outset of the assault the Allies would achieve surprise by bringing their own ports with them. When shown aerial reconnaissance photographs of the enormous concrete caissons sitting in the waters on the south coast of England he recognized that they had to be quays. However, he believed they would be used to replace the dockage his engineers were to destroy in any Channel port that was attacked. If the Fuhrer or his staff had guessed their true purpose, his generals would have been able to narrow down the potential landing sites to those that could receive the Mulberries. That would have taken them to one place. Normandy. There they would have been able to concentrate their defensive forces behind Rommel's Death Zone.

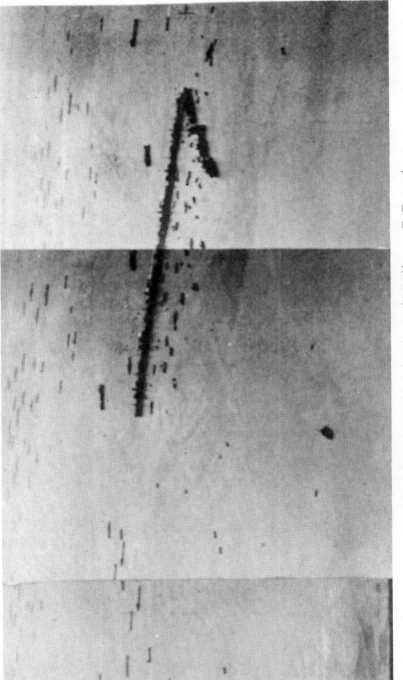

Gooseberry: The beginning of Mulberry D-Day+4

Field Marshal
The Viscount Montgomery
of Alamein
K.G., G.C.B., D.S.O.

The caissons of steel and concrete we pilots had seen were the 'Phoenix' units. To build the two Mulberry ports, 146 of these were required from ten of the smallest at 1,677 tons each through six sizes to the largest, 60 of which were needed at 6,044 tons each. Commencing D+4 some 70 ancient freighters and old warships were towed across the Channel and sunk as breakwaters for the Mulberries. They were Gooseberries. Linking the Phoenix units to shore were floating bridges called 'whales'.

As planned the Mulberries were put in place rapidly and were in operation at both the American and the British-Canadian beaches. However, the weather of the worst summer since 1900 was to play havoc with the supply system. In a severe storm which lasted from 19 June through 22 the American Mulberry harbor was destroyed. At the same time about 800 landing craft, tugs, freighters, and other vessels were either sunk or damaged severely. The devastation was far greater than on D-Day. With the destruction of the American Mulberry most of the burden of supply for all forces ashore, up to 12,000 tons a day, fell on the Mulberry at Arromanches. The nearby tiny fishing harbor of Port-en-Bessin had been cleared and opened but was of little value. With only one major port, which was highly vulnerable not only to the inclement weather but as well to destruction by German forces, it became imperative for the Americans to seize the major port of Cherbourg as quickly as possible.

Accordingly, on 18 June, Montgomery instructed First United States Army to capture Cherbourg and clear the peninsula of enemy. His orders also included bringing ashore XV United States Corps with its three infantry divisions beginning 24 June:

> as soon as additional American troops were available First United States Army was to break away to the south directed on Granville, Avranches, and Vire. The left wing of the army was to maintain the closest touch with Second Army in order to protect the British right flank.[1]

The American general who captured Cherbourg on 26 June in accordance with Montgomery's orders was Major

General Lawton 'Joe' Collins, a hard-hitting commander who had attacked with such energy, drive and tenaciousness that he astonished the German defenders of the Contentin Peninsula. They had expected much less from the inexperienced Americans. Their assessment changed as they realized the American West Pointers were as hard nosed and disciplined as their British counterparts — or so they believed.

Montgomery's orders of 18 June to the British-Canadian Second Army were explicit and optimistic. It was to capture Caen and:

> provide a strong eastern flank for the Army Group:
> continuing the policy of absorbing the enemy
> reserve divisions in its sector.[2]

Again Montgomery would attempt to take Caen using a pincer movement, pushing his forces down on each side of the heavily protected city. He had wanted to get the operation going by 18 June, but because of ammunition supply problems following the massive, destructive storm, his Second Army Commander, Dempsey, was not able to begin the operation until 25 June.

By 29 June, Dempsey's 8 Corps had secured a bridge-head across the Odon some six miles west of Caen in the Grainville-Baron sector against some of the fiercest resistance yet put up by the defending German forces and, in particular, their Panzer divisions. Montgomery recorded that:

> During the day both 1 and 2 SS Panzer Divisions
> were encountered, and 9 SS Panzer Division with
> reconnaissance elements of 10 SS Panzer Division,
> both from the Eastern Front, also made their
> appearance. There were now elements of no fewer
> than eight Panzer divisions on the twenty mile
> stretch of the Second Army front between Caumont
> and Caen.[3]

The 9 and 10 SS Panzer Divisions which Montgomery had identified were under orders from Rommel to cut through the British bridgehead by Bayeux and on into the beach near Arromanches where the Mulberry, the single harbor upon which the entire Allied force now depended, was to be destroyed.

Again the collision of the two offensive forces caused enormous losses to both sides as masses of tanks and men confronted each other at point-blank range. When on 28 June the British seized an intact bridge across the Odon the German 7th Army Commander, General Dollman, ordered the entire 2 SS Panzer Corps into the breach. As Montgomery put it:

> At this stage in the operation the enemy made a determined effort to restore the situation. He put in a strong counter attack from the south-west, with one thrust astride the River Odon and the other astride the Noyers-Caen road; enemy detachments also infiltrated towards Cheux. Heavy fighting went on along the whole right flank of the Corps salient and the southern bridge at Gavrus was lost.[4]

The order given by Dollman to the Commander of 2 SS Panzer Corps, General Hausser, on the morning of 28 June was one of the last he was to make. During the night of 28/29 June, Dollman discovered that Hitler blamed him for the premature loss of Cherbourg. He refuted it in a telegram in which he referred to faulty intervention by others in his own command affairs. That done, he committed suicide at his Normandy command post before dawn on 29 June. In so doing he was to join a long list of German generals who were to forfeit their lives by their own hands after being found guilty of neglect, error, or treason by a malignant Hitler. At the top of this list was to be Rommel himself and von Rundstedt's immediate successor as Commander-in-Chief of the German Army West, Field Marshal Gunther von Kluge. Altogether some 97 German generals were to commit suicide, whereas in the Kaiser's war only three were to take that route.

Rommel was still certain, as was Hitler, that the Normandy landings were a feint to draw away forces from the intended main invasion in the Pas-de-Calais. He remained entranced by the looming shadow of Patton, convinced by the misleading reports of German intelligence agents in England about the massive strength of the fictitious FUSAG. With Patton on his mind, Rommel spent an inordinate amount of time in the Pas-de-Calais area with his 15th Army. On 19 June he inspected the defenses between Le Havre and the River Somme, the spot where he expected the next enemy assault. One 22 June he was again in the Pas-de-Calais area watching the V-1 flying bombs throbbing their way toward London, all the more convinced by the presence of the V-1 sites there that Patton's Armee Group would be lured into that area in order to attempt to neutralize the deadly buzz-bombs.

The premature loss of Cherbourg and the surreptitious withdrawal of the 77th Infantry Division from the Contentin Peninsula provoked Hitler into bringing all his senior commanders from the west to confer at Berchtesgaden. They would meet at the Berghof, his mountain villa, on 29 June. Both Rommel and von Rundstedt arrived on that day but had to wait for six hours before the Fuhrer was prepared to talk to them. Hitler listened to his Field Marshals explaining their positions and the reasons for the problems in Normandy. What they wanted was greater freedom of action for the commanders in the field because they could react promptly and much more surely than commanders at headquarters. Rommel had earlier expressed the opinion that his functions in Normandy were so restricted by Hitler that any sergeant-major could have carried them out; the Fuhrer interfered in everything and turned down every proposal Rommel made. The meeting with Hitler, who was displeased with both von Rundstedt and Rommel, did nothing to change Rommel's view.

When Field Marshal Rommel returned to his headquarters on the 30th his commanders proposed an immediate evacuation of the area around Caen where their tanks were concentrated, and the taking up of a new defensive line out of range of the heavy naval guns that were inflicting enormous casualties on them. In response to Rommel's proposals supporting that proposition, von Rundstedt sent a personal signal to Hitler endorsing the action. Hitler replied:

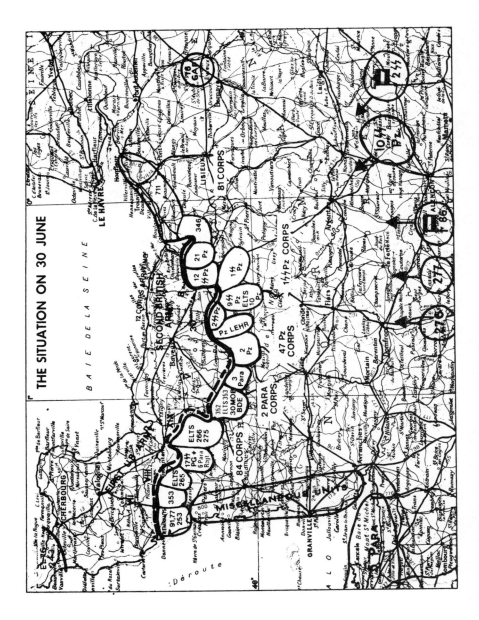

THE SITUATION ON 30 JUNE

"The present positions are to be held. Any further breakthrough by the enemy will be prevented by tenacious defense or by local counter-attacks."[5]

The next day, 2 July, the Fuhrer relieved von Rundstedt of his command, citing ill health as the cause. When he heard the news, Rommel knew he would be next. On 3 July von Rundstedt's successor, Field Marshal von Kluge, arrived at the Chateau de La Roche-Guyon. Two weeks later Field Marshal Erwin Rommel was indeed to be next, although not at the hands of the Fuhrer.

Across the Channel on 30 June Patton had left his Peover Hall headquarters for the last time, moving his headquarters to Braemore House in Hampshire, 19 miles west of Southampton. From there, he would finally be leaving for France, but not at the head of the First United States Army Group which Rommel and Hitler were expecting in the Pas-de-Calais area. Rather, it was the embarkation area of Patton's Third Army.

His movement to France would be carried out in utmost secrecy in order that the Germans should continue to believe that at any moment America's top fighting general would be leading his huge Armee Group (FUSAG) force in an onslaught against the Pas-de-Calais area. Unbeknownst to the enemy, the footprints of General Patton and his real Army would soon begin to leave their indelible marks on the soil and soul of the France he knew so well and loved so dearly.

7

7 July 1944   OPERATIONS: No sorties were flown
until the afternoon when an Artillery
Shoot was done by F/L E.S. Dunn
with F/L J.B. Prendergast, F/O's K.G.
Gillmor and H.L. Wolfe as cover. The first
target, a bridge, was successfully engaged
before engaging the second target. Two
aircraft were hit by flak and damaged. As
F/L Dunn was slightly injured the task
was abandoned. Later, F/O V.C. Dohaney
engaged the second target successfully
after our artillery silenced the flak. F/O's
J.N. McLeod, R.H. Rohmer and D.A.
Whittaker flew as cover. Three sorties
were airborne late in the evening to
observe road movements immediately
after the bombing of Caen by Lancasters.
It became dark before the bombing was
completed and no observations were
made. Caen itself was a mass of flames.
430 Squadron Log

Not recorded in the squadron log that day was one unusual
operation having to do with fire, but not the enemy's.
During the morning Dohaney and other card-playing
friends were at a game of Red Dog in the pilots' room on the
second floor of the Chateau Magny. They were waiting for
the weather to clear and the Ops phone to summon them for
briefings. I watched the Red Dog game for a while, smoking
the occasional cigarette, as did almost all our gang. It was
the practice to throw still lighted butts out the closest
window. Once in a while they were ground out in a grimy,

makeshift ashtray on the long, folding issue table that was the centerpiece of the large room, barren except for eight or ten sturdy chairs. Feeling a strong call of nature I went downstairs and out the north door, pulled back the canvas flap of the Chateau Magny throne room — our canvas-enclosed outside toilet — and proceeded to sit thereon, first having checked to ensure that there were no enemy bees down the hole.

We had discovered their presence a few days before when one of my squadron mates had been hit from below in a sneak bee attack which, fortunately for him, turned out to be his most severe war injury. However, my reconnaissance into the depths of the throne satisfied me that none of the buzzing enemy was present. So, barebottomed I perched, sitting there for a goodly length of time reading some nondescript magazine that was part of the throne room equipment.

Suddenly from above me there were shouts of alarm and panic. Almost at the same instant a torrent of water was poured down on me from the window immediately above by some avid pilot turned fireman. Some idiot had thrown a burning butt out the window. It had landed on the throne room roof and had eventually set it afire, unbeknownst to me. As the smoke curled up, one of my keen-eyed colleagues had either seen or smelled it and leaped into action. Water buckets were stationed at all rooms of the Chateau as a precaution against fire. So, without any warning to me, my savior proceeded to dump the contents on the fire. The water went directly through the hole made by the blaze and landed on me. I was soaked and shocked at the same time. Cursing wildly and showing absolutely no gratitude I pulled my wetted self together, stormed upstairs to the pilots' room, only to find my colleagues in various states of paroxysm, tears in their eyes, doubled up with laughter. I was not amused, even less so when one of those ribald turkeys gasped through his laughter that they all thought I needed a bath anyway.

The artillery shoot undertaken by Pappy Dunn on the late afternoon of 7 July was part of the prelude to a massive ground and air assault upon Caen in order to finally take that stronghold thirty days after the originally scheduled date of capture, 6 June. Montgomery was under tremendous pressure from the British press and from Churchill to get moving, pressure that would still be there and increasing during the first days of August.

Dunn had two targets. The first was at grid reference 029669, a railway bridge across the Orne on the southern outskirts of Caen. The second at grid reference 011610 was a road bridge across the Orne some six miles south of the first objective. Covered by the other three aircraft, the first thing he had to do was make radio contact with the artillery fire control center for the Division of 155 mm guns whose shells he would direct onto the target. The control center would inform him when their four or six ranging guns were ready to fire. Then Dunn would maneuver himself and his protecting three aircraft to a point where he knew he could run in toward the target and be in the best possible place to see the shells fall. They would land within the number of seconds of the shell's time of flight that the control center would give him. Given a time of flight of, say, twenty seconds, Dunn would fly toward the target. When he was in the right position to see the fall of the shells, he would give the order 'Fire!' The radio operator would repeat back in a shout intended so the battery could hear — 'Fire!' At that instant the battery's ranging guns would fire. In twenty seconds the radio operator would say 'Shot' which meant so far as he was concerned the shells were hitting the ground at that instant.

If all went well the first shells would land within 200 or 300 yards of the target. It would then be up to Dunn to begin his ranging procedures to get the shells directly on target.

Ranging the heavy guns could be a long procedure. In Dunn's instance it took him about an hour to get them on target. For the first of his two assigned targets he and his escorting aircraft were able to stay out of range of the flak to the northwest of Caen. They could stay over the guns inside our own lines and still be able to see the target and follow the shot.

However, for the second target it was quite a different matter. Pappy Dunn wanted to go across the enemy lines into the area lying about four to ten miles south-southeast of Caen. He believed that in that sector he would best be able to see the second target. It was about twelve miles south of Caen. At the same time he would be over enemy open ground, expecting a minimal risk of flak. Instead he ran into what he described as continuous, intense, accurate light flak (light flak being 40 mm rather than the heavy 88).

When he was hit Pappy Dunn had to abandon the mission. However, it was imperative that the second bridge be knocked out. Dunn's formation had been airborne at 16:00 hours. They were back on the ground at 17:35. One hour and ten minutes later another section of four was airborne to tackle the second target again. F/O Vince Dohaney was in the lead with Jack McLeod, Dennis Whittaker and myself as cover. As we crossed the enemy lines to the west of Caen the cloud was still 10/10 at 5,000 feet. We would have to stay well below that altitude. As with Dunn's formation we would be within perfect range of the light flak.

However, this time arrangements had been made with our artillery to saturate the flak installations with a massive barrage just before Dohaney began his shoot. If we were going to be successful and survive, that flak had to be neutralized. The Apple Pie treatment was delivered by our artillery on time and on target. The deadly flak was silenced as thousands of rounds cascaded down on the German guns. Dohaney then got busy with his shoot on the bridge. It was successfully completed in half an hour. The bridge was down and we were back on the ground at 19:35, just fifty minutes after we took off.

Fortunately the injury to Pappy Dunn when he was hit by flak that afternoon was not serious. But the increasing amount of flak being thrown at us, 88 mm, 40 mm, and anything else the Germans could find, was beginning to cause concern. F/L Jack Watts' aircraft had been hit by an 88 while he was leading a TAC/R in the Caen area on 4 July. The 88 had hit the hydraulic line. All the fluid had escaped, making his flap system inoperative, with the result that he had to make a no-flap landing, touching down at about 100 miles per hour, a high speed which rapidly ate up the entire length of airstrip, forcing him to ground loop when he ran out of runway.

On 8 July two aircraft in another formation led by

Watts were hit when they encountered intense flak twelve miles southwest of Caen. The Germans called our Mustangs *bluthunde*, or bloodhounds, but we were beginning to feel more like sitting ducks.

The weather also conspired against us throughout the month of July. The bad weather started on 1 July when no tasks at all were flown due to low cloud and rain. From the 3rd through the 6th operations were severely restricted, but when they were possible they had to be conducted at low level because of the height of the cloud ranging from 1000 to 2000 feet. By complete contrast on 6 July there was no cloud and visibility was unlimited. However, on the 7th we were back to overcast 10/10 at 5000 feet. If we were to conduct operations at all the continuing low cloud forced us beneath it, within range of anything that could be fired — rifles, machine guns as well as anti-aircraft guns. Moreover, the accuracy of the enemy at the lower altitudes was greatly improved, except when we were at treetop level. Occasionally we made a run at that height into a specified pinpoint target, but as a rule reconnaissance and photography required us to operate from 5,000 to 7,000 feet. On days when the 10/10 overcast ceiling was about that height we were silhouetted perfectly against the dull gray sky and could be easily tracked by anti-aircraft gunners or readily spotted by any Focke-Wulfe 190 or Me 109 pilot flying at a lower level.

There was no choice. The tactical and photographic reconnaissance operations and the artillery shoots simply had to go on. The British, Canadians, and now the Poles for whom we performed our tasks were slugging it out toe and toe with the Germans in an attempt to reach Caen. Our eyes, our photographs and reports were absolutely essential to them. Or so we believed.

The bombing attack and our artillery shoots that day on the bridges south of Caen were indeed part of Montgomery's plan to finally capture Caen. It was still his strategy to keep pushing against the Germans in the Caen area in order to hold the maximum number of enemy troops, tanks and guns at the eastern end of the bridgehead. He would thereby allow the Americans the fullest opportunity of success when the time arrived for their attempted breakout on the western flank. Montgomery had hoped that these

122

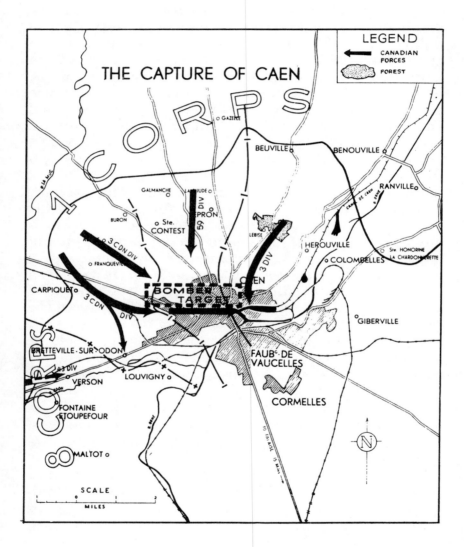

THE CAPTURE OF CAEN

LEGEND
CANADIAN FORCES
FOREST

I CORPS

GAZELLE

BEUVILLE
BENOUVILLE
RANVILLE

GALMANCHE
LA BIJUDE
ÉPRON
59 DIV
BURON
Ste.
CONTEST
FRANQUEVILLE
HEROUVILLE
Ste HONORINE
LA CHARDONNERETTE
LEBISE
3 CDN DIV
3 DIV
COLOMBELLES
CAEN
CARPIQUET
3 CDN DIV
BOMBER TARGET
GIBERVILLE
BRETTEVILLE-SUR-ODON
43 DIV
FAUB^G·DE VAUCELLES
VERSON
LOUVIGNY
CORMELLES
FONTAINE ÉTOUPEFOUR

II CORPS

MALTOT

SCALE
0   1   2
MILES

N

breakout attacks would be under way by 3 July, but General Omar Bradley, the Commander of the American First Army, found his forces still contained in the flooded, marshy country in the Carentan estuary. It was a totally unsuitable area for deployment of the major assault forces necessary for the breakout thrust. As the situation developed, Bradley would not gain such a deployment area until he reached the general line of the Periers-St. Lô Road on 18 July. In fact, he was not able to launch his breakout attack until 25 July.

There was enormous pressure on Montgomery to capture Caen. Thirty days later the objective he was to have captured on D-Day was still not in his grasp. He simply had to wrest that key objective from the Germans. The powerful, experienced enemy was dug in and well organized in mutually supporting positions in a number of small villages which lay in an arc north-northwest of Caen. Because of the strength of the German defenses, Montgomery decided to ask for the first time for the assistance of Bomber Command of the Royal Air Force which contained a large number of Royal Canadian Air Force units. Bomber Command agreed after much negotiating as to the details of the plan for this operation, the first of its kind.

The target area assigned was on the northern outskirts of Caen, a rectangle 4,000 yards wide and 1,500 yards deep. It contained major defensive positions and an enemy headquarters. The intent of the air bombardment was to destroy these positions and the supporting artillery; also to cut off the lines of supply to the enemy's forward troops. The bombardment was to take place between 21:50 and 22:30 hours on 7 July. It would be followed by a ground attack which was to begin at 04:20 hours the next morning. It would be carried out by three divisions, 3 Canadian Division in from the northwest, 59 Division from the north, and 3 Division from the northeast. They were to converge on Caen, clear the main part of the town on the west bank of the Orne and take the river crossings. This was the plan.

The only part of it that we lowly pilots knew about was that there was to be a massive bomber attack on Caen; that our shoots that day had something to do with it; and that the bombers were coming in at ten minutes to ten. So far as we were concerned this was a show we just could not miss. I didn't. I saw it all, not from the air but from the ground. Since B.8 was some miles away from the target area, three of us had decided to get into a jeep and drive east, find a point of high ground where we could see Caen in the distance, sit back and watch the show.

By the time we heard the drone of the first bombers out over the Channel, the 10/10ths cloud cover that had plagued us over Caen just a little more than two hours before had moved out. There was no cloud. This would allow the heavy bombers to come in at a much higher altitude, thereby better able to avoid being hit by the vicious onslaught of the German 88 batteries that ringed the Caen area.

In a few moments the lead Pathfinder aircraft appeared, crossing inland just to the east of us, between Ouistreham and Lion-sur-Mer, the same point of entry Taylor and I had used on D-Day morning one month and one day earlier. Strung out behind and above the Pathfinders, who went in at a much lower level in order to drop their guiding flares on the target rectangle, came a long, seemingly endless column of Lancaster and Halifax bombers, some 460 of them. They were flying not in any formation but separated by altitude and spacing to avoid hitting other aircraft with falling bombs.

The roar of the powerful engines of the enormous air armada was like the roll of incessant drums as the lead aircraft released the first bombs to open the unprecedented, concentrated attack in a sky already turned black by the exploding shells of the German 88s. In the far distance we could see brown black fountains of earth and smoke lifting into the air in the target area as the bombs landed. In a few seconds the noise of the first explosions reached us, a thunderlike sound that would continue for 40 minutes as each attacking bomber released its huge load, approximately five tons of mixed 500 lb. and 1000 lb. bombs. On they came, wave after wave. Many suffered direct hits from the 88s, falling from the sky like great birds brought to ground at the end of a hunter's gun. Running the exploding, black, deadly gauntlet of anti-aircraft shells in broad daylight, a new experience for the British and Canadian bomber pilots who operated at night, must have taken all the courage of every man in every crew. Still they pressed on, delivering their bombs with deadly accuracy, a result which was not always achieved in later tactical bomber operations in support of army attacks in the Caen area. But on the evening of 7 July, with British and Canadian troops held back some 6,000 yards away from the target area, the bombers were right on.

No enemy fighters were seen from where we stood. But midway during the passing of the unfaltering procession of bombers, a Mosquito aircraft, which we guessed to be one of the Pathfinders, came fluttering down from above the bombers. It was spinning slowly, lazily, completely out of control. With an enormous, ground-shaking thump it crashed to earth about a mile south of us. What had hit the Mosquito we had no idea.

Finally the last aircraft of the column delivered its load in the fast gathering darkness, its bombs descending into a flaming cauldron of burning buildings and crater-pocked terrain. The work of the bombers was done.

The air attack had had a devastating effect on the German troops, some of whom were found still stunned long after the event. To the north of the town, enemy troops were cut off and as a result received no ammunition, gasoline, or food while one complete regiment in the eye of the storm of bombs was completely wiped out.

On schedule the next morning, the three divisions, two British and one Canadian, moved in on Caen. After tough fighting for the next two days that part of the town lying to the north and west of the Orne had been taken. The enemy remained in occupation of Faubourg-de-Vaucelles on the south side of the river.

The operation had been a success for Montgomery. He was thirty-four days behind schedule, but he finally held Caen.

Lieutenant General George S. Patton, Jr., was in France. Exactly thirty-two years before, Patton and his wife had done an extensive tour of Normandy while on their way home from the Olympic Games at Stockholm where he had competed in a military contest called Modern Pentathlon. He wound up fifth in a field of thirty-two contestants. Now he was going to participate in another form of physical competition for which he was equally well trained and experienced.

On 6 July, George Patton's own D-Day, he had attended the usual morning briefing at Braemore House, then driven to the nearby airstrip with three members of his staff, his personal luggage, and his constant companion, Willie, the bull terrier. There they climbed into the C-47 transport which was already loaded. Patton's jeep was tied down at the rear of the aircraft.

At 10:25 Patton and his party were airborne. It was almost a year to the minute from the time he had left Algiers for the Sicily that he and his then equal, Montgomery, would conquer. Now he would be simply one of Montgomery's army commanders, taking directions from him. The only trouble was Patton did not have an army in the field. Some of the units of his Third Army were operating under General Omar Bradley in his First Army. Patton would get them back on the day the Third Army became operational. But when that would be was by no means certain at that point.

Escorted by a clutch of P-47 fighters, the C-47 made an uneventful trip across the Channel to a narrow airstrip behind Omaha beach. As soon as the aircraft was on the ground and shut down, Old Blood and Guts stepped out of the aircraft to be greeted by several hundred American soldiers. Naturally it was expected of him that he make a speech. When his jeep was out of the aircraft he mounted it and began, his shrill, high-pitched voice reaching out across the crowd of khaki. Jokingly he told his audience that he was the Allies' secret weapon. In a serious vein he cautioned them that his presence there was indeed secret and they could not tell anyone they had seen him in France.

Then, in typical emotional, blood-firing, stimulating Pattonese he shouted:

> "I'm proud to be here to fight beside you. Now let's cut the guts out of those krauts and get the hell on to Berlin. And when we get to Berlin, I am going to personally shoot that paper-hanging goddammed son-of-a-bitch [Hitler] just like I would a snake."[1]

He then sped off in his jeep down the road with his driver, Sergeant Meeks, at the wheel and his two staff officers and Willie in the back. He was bound for Bradley's head-quarters, a few miles away in a field south of Isigny. But crowded roads made it a slow trip. In his diary Patton wrote:

"We drove along the beach for some miles. . . . It is a terrible sight, with hundreds of wrecked ships. Most of the wrecks are not due to enemy action but to the storm which followed the landing for several days.

"Some of the pill boxes which the Germans had erected are remarkably strong but were all captured, which proves that good American troops can capture anything, and that no beach can be defended if seriously attacked."[2]

His old friend and former junior, Omar Bradley, welcomed him warmly at his command post. Bradley was conferring that day with his Deputy, General Hodges, and Collins, the VII Corps commander. They were discussing the problems confronting Bradley across his entire front in the southward attack which had been launched on 3/4 July with XIX Corps pressing for St. Lô on the left, VII Corps in the center moving toward the Periers-St. Lô road and VIII Corps on the right advancing on La Haye du Puits. Progress for VII Corps had been especially difficult because of the numerous water obstacles and bocage, but by 5 July the southern edge of the flooded area was breached by the Americans only to be met by the counterattacking enemy in strength.

The decision taken that afternoon by Bradley was that Collins should try to outflank the enemy using his 4 Division going south down the Carentan road. But as it turned out that tactic was not successful. Furthermore, the next day brought the first appearance of 2 SS Panzer Division against VII Corps' 83 Division. The German tanks had been moved from the Odon sector, a clear indicator that the enemy was becoming concerned about his western flank. On the east XIX Corps took St. Jean-de-Daye on 7 July and pressed on to within 4 miles of St. Lô amidst intense, bloody fighting.

Bradley's overall objective was to move his main line south out of the marshland floods and the dreadful bocage country into the open, rolling, dry ground where he could assemble his forces in preparation for an attempt to break out. However, Bradley was hampered not only by the terrain, which gave the Germans every advantage, but also by the weather. It severely restricted the mobility of Bradley's armor and transport and caused enormous discomfort to his men. Low cloud and rain also seriously restricted attempts to give them air support. And, because of the destruction of the American Mulberry, Bradley faced shortages of supplies and, in particular, ammunition.

As he listened to Bradley, Collins, and Hodges discuss these and other problems, Patton was closer to the war and its planning than he had been in many months. Even so he was concerned " 'that the war would end before I got into it. I was also certain that, by pushing harder, we could advance faster.' "[3]

Patton stayed overnight at Bradley's command post. First thing in the morning he bumped off in his jeep eastward to pay his respects to General Montgomery, the commander of all the Allied land forces on the beachhead. Montgomery's headquarters were still in the Chateau de Creullet at the village of Creully, eight miles east of Bayeux and just a stone's throw away from our airfield in the Sommervieu-Magny area.

Montgomery did not reside in the chateau. His own personal living van, one that he had acquired from the enemy in Africa, was isolated, well away from the remainder of the vans that comprised his command post. That of his chief-of-staff, Freddy deGuingand, later to be knighted in the field, stood at a respectful distance.

On arriving at Creully, Patton found that Montgomery was not at his headquarters. In fact he had gone to visit Bradley to discuss First U.S. Army's mounting problems. So Patton followed him back there to pay his respects as protocol required. The meeting was cordial and brief. Montgomery and Bradley had urgent business to discuss. Furthermore Montgomery had to get back to his headquarters as rapidly as possible to supervise the opening of his next major onslaught on Caen. It was to begin that night

Patton tracks down Montgomery at Bradley's HQ
7 July 1944

General George Patton Jr.

with the massive attack he had negotiated with Bomber Command.

From that meeting Patton went directly to his secret Third Army headquarters in a picturesque apple orchard at Néhou near the Douve River in the Contentin Peninsula. Néhou was in an area that had been captured on 16 June by men of his own nonoperational Third Army attached to Collins' VII Corps in the attack on Cherbourg.

Even though the battle area was far away, Patton's headquarters, waiting and ready to become operational, had all the gear, equipment, staff and infrastructure of what it really was, a major headquarters. There was accomodation for three of the four army corps that would become part of his organization when the time came. All Patton needed were the men and the orders that would make his army operational. The men were still in units in the United Kingdom waiting to be ferried across the Channel or in VIII Corps, at that moment an essential cog in the right flank of Bradley's First Army. And his orders were still weeks from arriving. In the meantime George Patton would just have to wait. Hodges and Collins were experiencing real trouble in mounting their offensive. Their discussion in his presence had been frank. Indeed he could sense that even Montgomery was in substantial difficulty.

Montgomery, on the other hand, faced the opposite problem to that of Patton. He was in the center arena, under full glare of the lights, but he was unable to move. Montgomery was being pressured from all sides. The war correspondents and editorial writers in the United Kingdom were criticizing him severely. But more seriously the Supreme Allied Commander and surprisingly, three of Eisenhower's British senior staff — Tedder, Coningham, and Morgan — were dissatisfied with his progress. Eisenhower diplomatically stated the developing situation when he wrote:

> As the days wore on after the initial landing the particular dissatisfaction of the press was directed toward the lack of progress on our left. Naturally I and all of my service commanders and staff were greatly concerned about this static situation near Caen. Every possible means of breaking the dead-

lock was considered and I repeatedly urged Montgomery to speed up and intensify his efforts to the
limit. Montgomery threw in attack after attack,
gallantly conducted and heavily supported by
artillery and air, but German resistance was not
crushed.[4]

Nor was it crushed by the air bombardment on the night
of 7 July. While Montgomery was delighted to be able to
report the capture of Caen on 9 July, the fact was that his
bloodied, brave British and Canadian troops had still not
been able to cross the Orne at Caen, an event that would have
to await his next major thrust, again bomber supported,
which was to begin 18 July.

By that time Montgomery, still not able to move, still
pivoting, would be engaged in another fight, one to save his
own position as commander of the 21st Army Group, and,
more important, to keep his post as commander-in-chief of
all Allied land forces in France. To be removed would be the
ultimate disgrace for the proud, willful, wily Montgomery,
still the hero of the British people.

8

18 July 1944   GENERAL: This afternoon "brown type"
                  pilots began to make their appearance.
                  Reason: all pilots were being issued
                  with Khaki battledress to be worn when
                  flying for purposes of identification.
                                    430 Squadron Log

Fortunately for us the khaki battledress was American, light weight, comfortably cut summer shirt and trousers and a zippered jacket. However, they were not issued gratuitously. We had to go to the nearest American unit and buy them. The alternative was to purchase the heavy British battledress which no one did. Although the use of khaki was optional and not mandatory, most people made the switch for the summer season at least, and for good reason.

At a distance it was quite easy to confuse the Air Force blue of the Canadian and British battledress with the field gray of the German uniform. Many pilots and other aircrew who had bailed out or survived a crash landing in enemy territory attempted to escape by walking through the front lines at points where the concentration of fighting was not as heavy as it was in the Caen area. Unfortunately, some of them had been mistaken for Germans and were fired upon by our troops. They would not have been shot at if their clothing had been khaki colored, either British or American.

To minimize this obvious risk, some practical Air Force officer at higher headquarters issued permission to wear khaki with appropriate rank badges. I was one of the first to make the switch. As it happened, I never had the opportunity to try to make my way back through the enemy lines but if I had there would have been no question that I was, at least for the moment, "a brown job."

As it was I looked like an American officer, except for my blue Royal Canadian Air Force flat-hat, which, of course, I didn't wear while I was flying. If I had bailed out or crash landed in enemy territory I would have appeared as an American.

I wore khaki U.S. summer weight trousers, shirt complete with a lieutenant's bar (my RCAF rank of Flying Officer was equivalent) on the collar front and a zippered jacket with the rank bars on the shoulder. That was my flying ensemble until September when we arrived in Belgium and cold, wet weather.

One of my closest 'near misses', which had occurred only a week before on Thursday, 13 July, put me in the frame of mind to take up the khaki option as soon as it was offered. The terse remarks in the squadron log are:

13 July 1944 OPERATIONS: — Weather was still unfavorable until mid-afternoon when an area search was flown by F/O's R.H. Rohmer and J.N. McLeod. Small numbers of MT* were seen at various points and photos were taken. Heavy, accurate, intense flak was encountered at Evercy and F/O Rohmer's was hit in several places, damage Category 'B'.

With Jack McLeod as my number two, I was airborne a few minutes after 15:00, again having to work below a solid cloud base sitting at 6,000 feet. Our assigned route took us southwest of Caen, where I checked predetermined roads and areas immediately adjacent to them for trucks or tanks or anything military I could find. Two miles south of Villiers I found some unusual objects which I could not

*motor transport

identify. I took some shots with my oblique camera that the photographic interpreter could puzzle over later. In addition, small numbers of motor transport were seen and recorded at various points.

Proceeding westbound over Evrecy, only sixteen miles south of our base at B.8, I had my aircraft straight and level for a few seconds. After all, I was well clear of the dreadful concentration of 88's in the Caen area and in a sector where little flak had been reported. There was no evidence of any flak coming at me or at McLeod. No warning of any kind.

My confidence was shattered by a tremendous blast accompanied by the instant appearance before my eyes of a jagged hole in my left wing. It was about a foot in diameter. I was impressed.

Without waiting for the arrival of the next shell which I was sure would be on its way to where I would be in the next one or two seconds, I hauled sharply over to the right on the control column and pulled back on it. I didn't bother to look over my shoulder to see how close the next round had come. Now there was only one place to go — straight back to base, but roller-coastering all the way until I was over our own territory.

Once I was safely behind our lines I did a complete check on my controls. They were still operating. Had the shell or piece of it that had ripped the big hole through the wing hit the spar? Evidently not because there was no indication of any buckling of the surface of the wing's skin. It hadn't hit the gasoline tank from what I could see. The only question left was was there any damage to the hydraulic system that would prevent me from getting the flaps down or, for that matter, the wheels? I asked McLeod to slip underneath me to check over my underside for any damage to the fuselage or the bottom of the wings. He took a look and reported back to me that apart from the big hole everything looked good.

Calling ahead to our airfield traffic controller, Squadron Leader Harold Day, ensconced in his little shack at the edge of the airstrip, I declared an emergency, asking for straight-in clearance from the west. It was immediately granted. I approached our strip from the south swinging out to the west, getting my air speed back to 120 miles an hour.

The moment had come. Would the undercarriage work? If it didn't it would mean a wheels-up, belly landing, uncomfortable, rough and dangerous at best.

With my left hand I selected 'down' on the undercarriage lever, shoving it toward the floor. The hydraulic pressure looked okay but I wasn't sure. In a moment I felt the undercarriage unlock. In a few seconds I felt the legs lock down one after the other. As they did the green undercarriage lights switched from red to green. My wheels were okay, down and locked.

The final uncertainty was the flaps. Speed back to 110. Again with my left hand moving out from my left hip I reached for the flap lever, moving it to the 'down' selection. Instantly I could see the flaps moving. The aircraft's nose tipped slightly down as the lowering flaps took hold. No problem.

I touched down and completed my landing normally, swinging off the strip to the south and taxiing my Mustang directly to the tents of the maintenance section. The aircraft would be in their hands for some time, if indeed it could be repaired. As I was marshalled into their parking area I could see people emerging from all directions. There was always enormous interest in the type, location and amount of damage when an aircraft was hit, and, of course, in how close the pilot had come to 'buying it'. In this instance, as the pilot, I too was interested in how close.

Close enough. In addition to the big hole in the wing there were twelve other hits by fragments, a total of 13 on the 13th of July. I've regarded 13 as a lucky number ever since. The piece that had come closest to me had gone through my plexiglass canopy, entering on the left side, passing about an inch over my head, and exiting out the top right — justification for my being short and having to use two pillows behind me in the bucket seat of the Mustang in order to reach the rudder pedals.

My battered aircraft, AP18 carrying the letter 'O', was repairable. After extensive work it was back in operation 13 days later on 26 July when F/O Ed Winiarz flew it on a successful photo reconnaissance mission. Personally, I needed no repairs. My clash with the flak had occurred at about 15:10 hours. By 17:05 I was back in the air on a TAC/R operation from Caen to Alençon. Two of our aircraft went unserviceable, one with a malfunctioning radio and in the other the generator packed up. So did we. The operation was abandoned over Caen. 13 July 1944 was that kind of day.

On 13 July, the day before our khaki conversion, Montgomery again called in the bombers to assist his troops in getting across the Orne River to the east and south of Caen. In that area and west along the entire British and Canadian front as far as Caumont, the Germans were holding with fierce intensity, reacting sharply to attacks, counterattacking with vigor, refusing to budge. In Montgomery's scheme of things the role of the 2nd British Army and the Canadians was to contain the main enemy strength and to wear it down by sustained offensive action:

> Thereby I was creating the opportunity to launch the breakout by First United States Army under the best possible conditions. Second Army was succeeding in its role because the enemy was determined to ensure that we were prevented from exploiting our armoured resources and superior mobility in the better country south-east of Caen.[1]

It was Montgomery's thesis that the key to retaining strong enemy forces on the eastern flank and drawing them away from the Americans on the west was the establishment of strong forces in the area southeast of Caen. He considered that the violence of the enemy's reaction to the operations of the British 2nd Army and the Canadians in the Caen sector had amply shown the extent of the German determination to prevent the progress in that direction. Montgomery was therefore satisfied that he was achieving his immediate objective. The Orne had to be crossed at all costs. When Montgomery called upon the bombers it was for good reason. Without them the possibility of a bloody, costly failure to cross the Orne was extremely high.

At first light on 18 July about 1,100 heavy bombers of Bomber Command and 600 of VIII United States Air Force attacked the target area to the east and south of the Orne from Colombelles southwest to Faubourg de Vaucelles, dropping delayed fused bombs on the flanks of the frontage of attack and on strong points and concentration areas in the rear. They were followed by about 400 medium bombers of the IX United States Air Force which came in from 07:00 to 07:45 hours. They dropped fragmentation bombs with instantaneous fuses in order to avoid cratering. Their target was the area directly facing the frontage of the 8 Corps assault at Colombelles. The ground attack began at 07:45 hours.

By the evening of 20 July, a day of heavy rain which turned the battlefield from a dustbowl into a sea of mud, the eastern suburbs of Caen had been cleared, and the Orne bridgehead had been more than doubled in size. The new front line ran from the Orne near St. Andres to Bourguebus, Cagny, and the outskirts of Troarn.

But there had been no breakthrough. The fight for every yard of ground had been tense and costly. On 18 July alone 150 tanks were out of action in Montgomery's 3 Armored Division as the Germans effectively used their numerous 88 mm dual-purpose guns, which had originally belonged to the flak defenses of Caen, against the oncoming armor.

Omar Bradley, in the bloodiest fighting his army had experienced since D-Day on the Omaha beach, on 18 July took St. Lô and, west of the River Vire, the ground necessary for mounting the major breakout assault operation to the south. The Battle of the Hedgerows which had started on 3 July brought the First Army into St. Lô at enormous cost. The final thrust began on 16 July when XIX Corps with two divisions converged on the town from the east and north, engaging in heavy fighting that was to continue for three days. Accurate tactical close support bombing from American Flying Fortresses was instrumental in driving back a strong German infantry and armored counterattack. By evening of the 18th, 29 Division of XIX Corps had stormed its way into St. Lô.

To the west VII Corps, advancing only eight miles in 12 days of bitter battle, had halted on 15 July and was still some 12 miles from the high ground of Coutances, its objective. In the end, the Battle of the Hedgerows, while successful in opening up the necessary staging area, was a

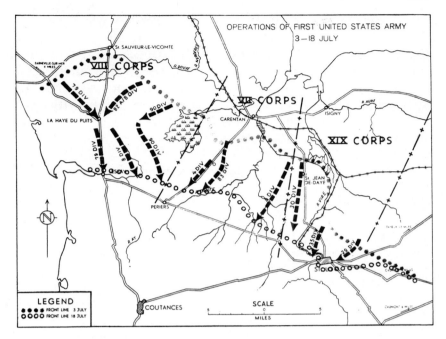

OPERATIONS OF FIRST UNITED STATES ARMY
3—18 JULY

LEGEND
●●●● FRONT LINE 3 JULY
OOOO FRONT LINE 18 JULY

SCALE
MILES

slow and brutal fight in which Bradley's army of twelve divisions progressed only seven miles in 15 days, losing in the process some 40,000 men, thereby seriously impairing the capability of his force.

Bradley called for reinforcements of 25,000 infantry as quickly as possible, but they were not in England and would have to be brought in from the United States. His ammunition supply was extremely short and his force momentarily spent in what General Dietrich von Choltitz, German Corps Commander at St. Lô, would describe as "the most monstrous blood bath, the likes of which I have not seen in eleven years of war."

In the British sector Montgomery, too, was in difficulty. He was still pivoting, still unable to move effectively. He was under constant criticism and presssure. While the attacks by his British and Canadian troops and the counter-attacks by the Panzers and other German forces resulted in a stand-off by 18 July, Montgomery was nevertheless able to say, "above all we were attaining our object by pulling the enemy armor into the line."

Later he was able to produce a chart which showed the enemy strength opposite the American First Army and the enemy strength opposite the British Second Army and the Canadians. This was for the purpose of demonstrating that his pivot plan had worked. The chart shows that on 15 July opposite the First U.S. Army there were only two Panzer divisions with 190 tanks, but opposite the Second British Army and the Canadians there were six Panzer divisions with 630 tanks.

Lest there be any mistake as to who was the commander of all ground forces in France one need only refer to Montgomery's words when he recounted the status of the situation of 9 July 1944. There was no confusion in Montgomery's mind:

I therefore ordered Second Army to operate immediately in strength towards the south . . . There were no changes in my orders for First United States Army. I emphasized again the need for speed. We required to get going before the enemy found the means to increase his forces on the western flank, and to take advantage of the situation I was creating on the eastern flank in the renewed Second Army offensives.[2]

As Montgomery saw it, his forces were ready to break out at the bridgehead. The breakout as he planned it would not be at the eastern pivot through Caen, as Eisenhower and his SHAEF headquarters people thought it would and should. Rather it would be on the western flank. Furthermore it would be accomplished by the Americans, just as Montgomery always planned:

I have said how important it was to my plans that, once started, the breakout operation should maintain its momentum. It was therefore essential to ensure that the assault would make a clean break through the enemy defenses facing the Americans, and that a corridor would be speedily opened through which armoured forces could be passed into the open country. To make sure of this, it was decided to seek heavy bomber assistance; but because of the weather the operation had to be progressively postponed until 25 July in order to obtain favourable flying conditions.[3]

The breakout operation of which Montgomery wrote was code-named Cobra. It was to be based on a plan originally architected by Patton in a solitary all-night session at Braemore House on the night of 30 June - 1 July using a Michelin map. It was a plan Patton had been attempting to sell to Bradley ever since he, Patton, arrived in France. Bradley eventually produced the plan as his own. It certainly was not Montgomery's.

On the eastern flank at Caen, Montgomery had to move or, at least, be seen to move. Therefore he gave instructions to General Dempsey to "step on the gas."

The gas was operation Goodwood. At first light, 18 July, hundreds of Royal Air Force and Royal Canadian Air Force aircraft of Bomber Command and those of the VIII and IX United States Air Forces began an operation designed to "open up the southeastern exits from Caen and to mop up the enemy in that area."

In Goodwood Montgomery struck forward with 1,500 tanks and 250,000 men against the German defenses around Caen. The American, British and Canadian aircraft unloaded more than 7,000 tons of bombs in advance of the oncoming army in a area of little more than 20 square miles. Then three tank divisions and three armored brigades moved out behind an advancing barrage laid down by all of the available, serviceable artillery. In a few hours they launched more than 45,000 shells in the area of 2 SS Panzer Corps alone. More than 800 fighter bomber missions provided close support to the army while over 1800 missions were flown by RAF and RCAF Typhoon squadrons against German tanks, vehicles and gun emplacements. It was and was seen to be the most violent, intense, concentrated, assault made by the Allies during the Second World War in Western Europe.

In press conferences on 18 July Montgomery fell into the trap of using terminology that misled the war correspondents, and therefore the public, into believing that he

was expecting this operation to result in a breakout. Of this
event he was to write:

> Then came operation *Goodwood* in the Caen
> section and the Press regarded this as an attempt
> to break out on the eastern flank; and, as such, that
> operation, too, appeared to have failed. This was
> partly my own fault, for I was too exultant at the
> Press conference I gave during the *Goodwood*
> battle. I realise that now — in fact, I realised it
> pretty quickly afterwards.[4]

Within two days Goodwood had been called off.
Montgomery's forces had penetrated six of the seven heavy
lines of defense the Germans had placed south of Caen. But
it was the seventh last line that held — a deadly, anti-tank
barrier of 88's guarding the entrance to the plains that led
to the Seine. Because of that:

> and also because heavy rain turned the whole area
> into a sea of mud, I decided to abandon that thrust.
> Many people thought that when Operation
> *Goodwood* was staged, it was the beginning of the
> plan to break out from the eastern flank towards
> Paris, and that, *because* I did not do so, the battle
> had been a failure. But let me make the point again
> at the risk of being wearisome. There was never *at
> any time* any intention of making the breakout
> from the bridgehead on the eastern flank. Mis-
> understandings about this simple and basic
> conception were responsible for much trouble
> between British and American personalities.[5]

Regardless of Montgomery's retrospective view of the
situation, the generals and air marshals at Eisenhower's
headquarters in London considered Goodwood to be a total
failure. Before the attack Air Chief Marshal Sir Arthur
Tedder received a telegram from Montgomery on 14 July in
which it was stated about the prospects for Goodwood that
"if successful, the plan promises to be decisive." At 16:30
hours on 18 July Montgomery sent a message to Field

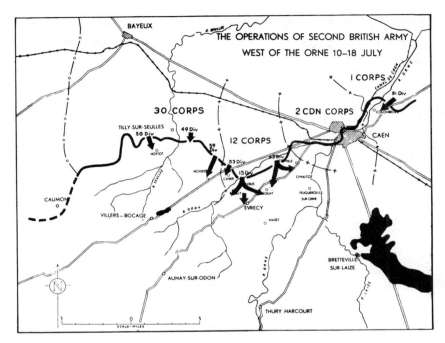

Marshal Brooke, the Chief of the Imperial Staff: "Operations this morning a complete success." That evening he made a special announcement to the press in which he in effect claimed to have broken out. But by the 20th he had been stopped dead.

At SHAEF those who were concerned about the leadership of Montgomery had their worst fears confirmed. In the vanguard was Tedder, who on 20 July wrote that he and Marshal of the Royal Air Force Sir Charles Portal, who was Chief of the British Air Staff, "were agreed in regarding Montgomery as the cause." When Eisenhower then went to Normandy to assess the situation Tedder wrote to him there saying, "all the evidence available to me indicated a serious lack of fighting leadership in the high direction of the British Armies in Normandy." On 25 July, the day Bradley launched Cobra, Tedder wrote that "we have been had for suckers. I do not believe there was the slightest intention to make a clean breakthrough."

Notwithstanding his precarious position, Montgomery survived a visit of General Marshall on 24 July when the powerful top American military man was apparently quite prepared to move to unseat him because of the slow progress. In addition, Monty had a long and satisfactory session with Churchill that same day, and he was able to assure the great man of his mastery of the situation and that his plan of pivoting on Caen while breaking out on the western flank was in fact being followed. However, he was disturbed by the appointment by the government of a War Cabinet Liaison Officer posted to his headquarters for the purpose of sending back "true" status reports rather than the selfserving messages that came from Montgomery.

Writing about the 'cufuffle', as Montgomery described it, that arose out of Goodwood, he was to say:

> All through the fierce fighting which took place in Normandy, there was never any intention of breaking out on the eastern flank towards the Seine; reference to all the orders and instructions which I issued makes that abundantly clear. This false conception existed only at Supreme Headquarters . . . . The misconception led to much controversy and those at Supreme Headquarters who were not very fond of me took advantage of it to create trouble as the campaign developed.
>
> One of the reasons for this in my belief was that the original *Cossac* plan had been, in fact, to break out from the Caen-Falaise area, on our eastern flank. I had refused to accept this plan and had changed it. General Morgan who had made the *Cossac* plan was now at Supreme Headquarters as Deputy Chief of Staff. He considered Eisenhower was a god; since I had discarded many of his plans, he placed me at the other end of the celestial ladder. So here were the seeds of discord. Morgan and those around him (the displaced strategists) lost no opportunity of trying to persuade Eisenhower that I was defensively minded and that we were unlikely to break out anywhere![6]

This 'cufuffle' made a deep, searing impression on this intense lonely man whose pride and ego were the match of any of the self-confident Allied generals. He had become deeply sensitive to and irritated by what he considered to be unfair, unjustified, unwarranted press criticisms about his inability to advance and to the unkind cuts of the British generals and air marshals in their SHAEF ivory tower. There were more to come.

The background of animosity was now in the process of being established against which several critical decisions would be made by the Allied generals, including one that would unquestionably have a profound impact on the course of the war. That decision would be taken on 12 August. Its result was the creation of the infamous Falaise Gap.

9

25 July 1944   OPERATIONS: A record day today, 50
sorties being flown.
430 Squadron Log.

After those few words the log was filled with capsule comments on the individual sorties of the day. No question about it. We were operating at a record level. The pace of activity was increasing on the ground as well as in the air, but bad weather was still plaguing us. On 21, 22 and 23 July no sorties were flown because of extremely bad weather. The next day we were able to mount only five sorties. On the 25th, the cloud cover was 9 to 10/10 at 4500' but we were able to start to make up for lost time doing TAC/R's, Photo/R's, and artillery shoots on railway junctions and heavy gun batteries.

Of the four operations I was able to get in that day between 06:20 and 18:25 hours, the TAC/R flown in mid-afternoon provides the best sense of the increasing scale of daylight activity on the German side during that period. F/L W.M. Iverson was with me on this one, a reconnaissance in the Bretteville area, nine miles south of Caen just beyond the front line. My report was:

10/10ths cloud at 8-9,000 feet 2.-3. M.T. moving
north and south. All roads showed scattered movement. Two possible tanks seen. Flak battery at
995532 [9 miles due west of Falaise] intense,
inaccurate, mixed flak from Bretteville area.

Other reports during the day confirmed an unusual
amount of movement on the part of the enemy. If he was
prepared to take to the roads openly, knowing full well
that the bloodhounds would call in the Spitfires and
Typhoons on choice moving targets, it could be deduced
that reinforcements were being moved in to bolster defenses
or that a counterattack was being prepared.

However, it was not our function to interpret what we
had seen. Our job was to find vehicles, tanks, guns, headquarters and other targets, pinpoint their positions and, if
moving, their direction. By this time Montgomery had
issued an order forbidding tactical reconnaissance pilots
from carrying out any attacks on "targets of opportunity"
such as trucks or tanks. The advertised rationale was that
we were so highly skilled in our map reading, photography,
and artillery shooting that we should not take the additional
risks inherent in attacking ground targets. That work would
be left to the Thunderbolts, Lightnings, Spitfires, and
Typhoons. This order was highly unpopular, but we were
told it had been given by Montgomery himself and we had
no choice but to abide by it.

Far from the battlefield an event occurred that would
have an impact on the conduct and outcome of the war.

This was the abortive attempt to assassinate Hitler at
the Fuhrerhauptquartier at Rastenburg on 20 July. Hitler
had moved there only six days before, pulling his headquarters back from the menacing Red Army, then only a
hundred miles away to the east. The attempt to kill Hitler
was a result of a plot widespread throughout the German
High Command.

From that moment, Hitler trusted no one. His new
Chief of the General Staff, Guderian, later wrote of Hitler:

"the deep distrust [Hitler] already felt for mankind
in general and for General Staff Corps officers and

146

generals in particular, now became profound hatred. A by-product of the sickness from which he suffered is that it imperceptibly destroys the powers of moral judgement; in his case what had been hardness became cruelty, while a tendency to bluff became plain dishonesty. He often lied without hesitation and assumed that others lied to him. He believed no one any more. It had already been difficult enough dealing with him; it now became a torture that grew steadily worse from month to month. He frequently lost all self-control and his language grew increasingly violent."[1]

From the moment of the attempt on his life, Hitler appeared close to insanity. Therefore, the abortive assassination effort worked to assist the cause of the Allies. They made no direct or indirect try to kill him, either by participating in a plot, or by an attack on his headquarters or residence, an operation that would have been relatively easy. Perhaps it was because the view of Churchill prevailed, namely that while Hitler remained in power the Allies could not lose the war.

On the other hand, it would take the diabolical single-mindedness of one madman to keep on fighting when disaster confronted him on all fronts. Hitler's Army Group South was encircled in the Ukraine. There was a revolution in Rumania resulting in the loss of its invaluable oil fields, followed by a revolution in Bulgaria. More ominously, the Soviets were only 100 miles to the east of Rastenburg and advancing. And in Normandy, the left wing of the Seventh Army had given up Cherbourg and St. Lô. Since D-Day, Rommel had lost over 97,000 men, including 2,360 officers on that front, but Hitler had given him only 6,000 replacements. Of the 225 tanks that had been lost, only 17 were replaced. Hitler had refused to weaken the Fifteenth Army sector by transfering urgently needed forces to Normandy for he still believed that the ficticious First United States Army Group was about to attack the Pas-de-Calais.

If Hitler had died on 20 July at Rastenburg, the prospects for peace after the defeat of German Seventh Army in Normandy on 19/20 August with the Americans, the British and their Commonwealth Allies would have been high although probably not so with the Soviets. The peace might have been by negotiated armistice or by unconditional surrender. Either way, it could well have happened.

However, Hitler survived, carrying with him a perpetual flame of the hope of victory. It would not be extinguished until Hitler was indeed dead some months later. The assassination attempt solidified his determination that there would be no surrender. Out from Rastenburg went the general order that anyone who gave up ground would be shot. As to negotiations with the enemy, Hitler stated:

> "Anyone who speaks to me of peace without victory will lose his head, no matter who he is or what his position."[2]

On the Allied side the decision was equally unequivocal. It was for unconditional surrender.

Behind Montgomery's plans in this period was the belief that his British, American, and Canadian forces were on the threshold of great events, ready to break out of the bridgehead. Execution of the ill-fated Goodwood operation, which he had begun on 18 July and had to shut down on 20 July, was both a reflection of that attitude and a reaction to the external pressures at SHAEF and the criticisms of the press and British politicans.

Monty had to be optimistic. Furthermore, he had to appear to be always preparing for the next battle even while the one he was currently fighting on the British-Canadian front was being stopped. He was later to put it succinctly when he wrote about the situation as it existed on 21 July:

> At this stage I appreciated that I should have to be ready to launch a major attack by Second Army on Falaise early in August . . .[3]

In that statement about the Second British Army Montgomery typically failed to include the soldiers who would in fact carry the Falaise brunt, the First Canadian Army and the Polish Armored Division.

This proposed operation toward Falaise would be

another action designed to draw the enemy's armored attention and in particular his Panzers to the eastern flank, while Bradley in the west was mounting his long anticipated breakout operation, Cobra, scheduled to begin on 24 July. To ensure that the enemy opposite the British and Canadian forces had no respite between 20 July and the time of start of Cobra, Montgomery had ordered 2 Canadian Corps under Lieutenant-General Guy Simonds to commence the supporting attack toward Falaise on 25 July. At the same time he ordered that limited operations be carried out on the British front.

On 23 July the First Canadian Army became operational in Normandy under its commander, General H.D.G. Crerar. At that time Crerar also took over 1 British Corps and responsibility for the extreme eastern area of the Allied front. By 31 July, Lieutenant-General Simonds' 2 Canadian Corps also came under his command.

The launch date for Cobra was initially set for 18 July. However, it had to be postponed because of bad weather, whereupon Montgomery rescheduled the 24th for the second try.

At this stage both Eisenhower and Montgomery were anxious to encourage Bradley, whose forces had taken a severe mauling during the St. Lô offensive. On 24 July Eisenhower sent Bradley a message which said that he, Eisenhower, in " 'the largest ground assault yet staged in this war by American troops exclusively,' "would accept full personal responsibility for the " 'necessary price of victory,' " reminding him that the British forces were concurrently to mount a vigorous attack on the east flank. The Supreme Commander stated that this assistance would allow Bradley " 'to push every advantage with an ardor verging on recklessness.' " If the British Second Army should break through simultaneously with American forces the results would be " 'incalculable.' "[4]

With the avowed support of the Supreme Commander and with the encouraging attitude of Montgomery, his immediate American superior, Bradley began to lift the lid of the Cobra basket as scheduled on 24 July. But he found himself again plagued by bad weather, which caused the cancellation of the massive aerial bombardment that had

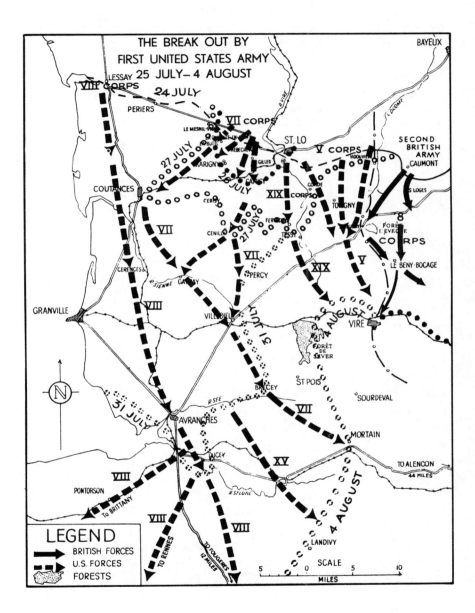

THE BREAK OUT BY
FIRST UNITED STATES ARMY
25 JULY– 4 AUGUST

BAYEUX

LESSAY
VIII CORPS
24 JULY
PERIERS

VII CORPS

LE MESNIL
BUTTE
HEBECRE
MARIGNY
ST. LO
V CORPS
VIDOUVIL
SECOND
BRITISH
ARMY
CAUMONT

27 JULY
GILLES
27 JULY
CANISY
CONDE
XIX CORPS
TOURGNY
S LOGES

COUTANCES
CERISY
CENILL
27 JULY
FERTE
TESS
FORET
L'EVEQUE
CORPS

VII
CERENCES
R. SIENNE GAVRAY
VII
PERCY
XIX
Y
LE BENY-BOCAGE

GRANVILLE
VIII
VILLEDIEU
FORÊT
DE
SEVER
VIRE

N

31 JULY
BRECEY
ST POIS
SOURDEVAL

R SEE
VII
AVRANCHES
VIII
DUCEY
XV
MORTAIN
TO ALENCON
44 MILES

PONTORSON
VIII
R SELUNE
4 AUGUST

TO BRITTANY
VIII
TO RENNES
12 MILES
VIII
TO FOUGERES
12 MILES
LANDIVY

LEGEND
BRITISH FORCES
U.S. FORCES
FORESTS

SCALE
5   0   5   10
MILES

been designed to cut a path through the dug-in, powerful German troops, armor, and anti-tank weapons facing the Americans. The scheduled noon bombardment was stopped by a visitor to Bradley's command post, Air Chief Marshal Sir Trafford Leigh-Mallory. With his keen airman's eye he judged that there was no way for the American bombers, who would require a clear view of their target, to carry out their mission. Unfortunately, his order did not arrive in time to hold off the first wave of bombers. The result proved him right in cancelling.

With cloud partially obscuring the target area, some 300 Flying Fortresses of the Eighth and Ninth Air Forces unloaded 685 tons of high explosive and fragmentation bombs, some of which landed among the 30th Infantry Division killing 25 men and wounding 131. Quite naturally, the morale of the American front line troops was badly shaken.

Bradley was concerned that the premature bombing without any follow-up might give his opposing German generals a clue that some sort of large-scale attack was forthcoming. Indeed, that was von Kluge's analysis when he heard the news of the St. Lô sector bombing. But the magnet of Caen and Montgomery pulled him to the east. In his judgment, that was where the new, heavy enemy offensive would occur. So the German Commander-in-Chief West elected to be at the Caen front on 25 July. The combined air and ground assault along the Periers-St. Lô road that day, together with the death by suicide of von Kluge himself, heralded the rout and defeat of the German army in France.

On 25 July, the lid came right off the Cobra basket as the operation emerged in its full height to strike first from the air and then along the undulating ground to rip through and destroy the enemy.

On cue at 09:40 hours, 350 American fighter bombers of Major-General Elwood Quesada's IX Tactical Air Command began a 20 minute all-out attack against the enemy in a narrow path on each side of the Periers-St. Lô road to the west of St. Lô. Then followed the intense bombing of an area some 2,500 by 7,000 yards containing German concentrations in the Marigny-LaChapelle-LaMesnil area.

Over 1,800 heavy and medium bombers and more than 500 fighter bombers returning for a second assault unleashed their lethal cargoes of bombs, this time augmented by napalm canisters. All told over 4,000 tons of explosives hammered the target area that morning. Concurrently American artillery with their huge guns pumped in more than 140,000 shells.

The devastation was beyond belief. In the inferno of the assault thousands of German troops were killed, tanks obliterated, command posts consumed, a parachute regiment disappeared. The ground shuddered and shook incessantly as towering cascades of earth, explosives, and metal soared high in the air, filling the atmosphere with dust. Unfortunately for the American infantry, another short drop occurred when, by error of a lead bomber, an entire formation of 35 heavy and 42 medium bombers unleashed its cargo at the wrong place. Tragically, it was the same ill-fated 30th Infantry Division that received the full force of the short drop. This time 111 were killed and 490 wounded. Also killed in that bombing was the man who had replaced Patton as the head of the fictitious FUSAG. General Lesley J. McNair had left his post in England to visit Montgomery and Bradley. That day he had gone forward to the 30th Infantry's forward observation points to watch the bombardment and the assault. (To keep Fortitude alive, General John L. deWitt was appointed to succeed McNair.)

At 11:00 in the morning of 25 July, American armor and infantry of VII Corps under Collins moved out against the smashed German sector to the west. Under and behind one of the heaviest onslaughts of artillery, his four infantry and two armored divisions engaged the enemy in a ferocious battle. On 28 July the Germans began to fall back, retreating southward through the coastal towns. It was the intention of the German commanders to form a new line far to the south. All resistance seemed to have disappeared while the American army charged after them under an expanding arc of operations of their ever-present Tactical Air Force's supportive fighter bombers.

On 28 July, Coutances, a key objective on the right, had been taken by the Americans. With its fall the long hoped-for breakout was a reality. Finally there was cause for optimism. Bradley, who felt that he and his men had reason to be 'pretty cocky' told Eisenhower:

"we are taking every calculated risk and we believe we have the Germans out of the ditches and in complete demoralization and expect to take full advantage of them."[5]

The American First Army was truly on the move. It was Bradley's great victory. The time had arrived to consider taking Avranches, the access point to Brittany. The time was also now at hand to look to George Patton. Despite misgivings Bradley needed him. As he said:

My own feelings on George were mixed. He had not been my choice for Army commander and I was still wary of the grace with which he would accept our reversal in roles. For George was six years my senior and had been my Army commander when I fought II Corps in the Sicilian campaign. I was apprehensive in having George join my command, for I feared that too much of my time would probably be spent in curbing his impetuous habits. But at the same time I knew that with Patton there would be no need for my whipping Third Army to keep it on the move. We had only to keep him pointed in the direction we wanted to go.

George soon caused me to repent these uncharitable reservations, for he not only bore me no ill will but he trooped for 12th Army Group with unbounded loyalty and eagerness.[6]

Of Patton's keenness to get into battle there was no doubt. When the news of the attempt on 20 July on Hitler's life reached Patton at his headquarters in Néhou, Patton was electrified by the event. Bradley recalled that "He bounded down to our C.P. [Command Post] at Colombières. 'For God's sake, Brad,' George pleaded, 'you've got to get me into this fight before the war is over. I'm in the dog house now and I'm apt to die there unless I pull something spectacular to get me out.' " Bradley did not budge at that time but Patton's plea caused him to speculate later, "I've often wondered how much this nothing-to-lose attitude prodded Patton in his spectacular race across the face of France. For certainly no other commander could have matched him in reckless haste and boldness."

After the capture of Coutances, Bradley ordered his four U.S. corps commanders to press their attack southward.

By this time it had been agreed that, with Eisenhower's approval, the Third Army would finally become operational at 12:00 noon, 1 August. However, Bradley would need 'Georgie' in the field before that day.

At a pre-Cobra conference on 23 July, Bradley had promised Patton that he would make the Third Army operational as soon as Cobra had achieved its objective. Patton was itching to go. Not only was he concerned that the war might be over before he had a chance to get into it, he was also afraid that Monty, fearful that Patton would steal his show, would keep him out.

Patton had also believed that in order to extend his own tenure, Montgomery wanted to delay the entry of the Third Army into the operational field. But it was Bradley, not Montgomery, who had delayed making the Third Army operational. He did so not only because of his mixed feelings about Patton, but primarily because there would not be sufficient maneuvering room for a second army in the field until the major objectives of the Cobra were achieved.

With the capture of Coutances on 28 July Cobra's objectives were met. The maneuvering room was available.

Thus, on that day, Bradley put in a call to the Third Army headquarters at Néhou where he talked not to Patton, who was out inspecting the 101st Evacuation Hospital and other close-by facilities, but to Major General Hugh Gaffey, Patton's chief of staff. Bradley told him that he wanted Patton to take control of VIII Corps; that the decision for the Third Army to become operational had been taken with Eisenhower's approval and that would be at noon, 1 August; that, until then, Patton was unofficially to control Middleton's VIII Corps; and that he was to direct its move toward the entrance into Brittany.

Gaffey sent a young captain out to find his General.

He located him at 15:30 hours at the gas dump and, as Patton wrote in his diary, he:

> "told me to get back to headquarters at once. I arrived at 16:45 and learned that we are to take over the VIII Corps and put in the XV Corps at the left . . . . I felt much happier over the war. May get in it yet."[7]

In effect, Bradley wanted Patton to do more than direct Middleton's Corps:

> While the Third Army did not become operational until 12:00 on the first of August, General Bradley appointed me to command it by word of mouth on the twenty-eighth of July and explained the plans of the initial use of two corps, the VIII (Middleton) on the right and the XV (Haislip) on the left.[8]

Patton was finally back in the war, but in the interest of the continuity of the Fortitude cover and deception plans his presence at the head of the Third Army in France was to be kept absolutely secret. Any war correspondent's story about Patton would be censored. There would be no mention of his being on the battlefield. Now Lieutenant General George S. Patton Jr. was in the war in three capacities. He was the commanding general of the Third Army, but it was not yet operational; he was also the Deputy Commander of Bradley's Army, the First, but over it he had no control; and he had verbal control of VIII Corps, but its actual commander was General Middleton.

Middleton knew what the situation was. As of the 28th, Patton was his de facto boss and he took his orders accordingly. Immediately Bradley had made Patton "operational," the new Deputy Commander collected General Haislip, General Gaffey, his own G3, Colonel Maddox, and the Third Army headquarters signal officer Colonel Hammond, and drove directly to VIII Corps headquarters to take charge. Patton's first objective beyond Coutances, which had been taken that day, was Avranches, the crucial gateway to Brittany and linchpin to the east.

Over on the eastern flank, the collateral attack to the Cobra operations was started by 2 Canadian Corps on the Falaise Road at 03:30 hours on 25 July under Lieutenant General Simonds. Again, the dense German defenses, comprised of large numbers of infantry, 88 millimeter guns and the full weight of the armored force of 1 SS, 9 SS, 12 SS, and 21 Panzer divisions, brought the thrust to an abrupt halt during the night of 25/26 July. But again the attack retained the German Panzer forces at Caen, keeping them away from the highly mobile American forces now beginning to move rapidly as the head and neck of Cobra venomously struck through and shattered the Fuhrer's forces.

However, the appearance was that once more Montgomery had been unable to move, that he was still pivoting. Criticism of him now moved to the highest level.

During a luncheon with Churchill at 10 Downing Street on 26 July, Eisenhower spoke disparagingly of Montgomery, who was furious when he heard what had happened.

> Exactly what was said at that lunch party I don't know. But Eisenhower wrote to me that evening and one sentence in his letter caused me misgivings, knowing the feeling that existed against me among his staff at Supreme Headquarters. That sentence read: "He [the PM] repeated over and over again that he knew you understood the necessity for 'keeping the front aflame,' while major attacks were in progress."
>
> It seemed to me that Eisenhower had complained to the Prime Minister that I did not understand what I was doing. Actually, as I heard later, he had told the Prime Minister he was worried at the outlook taken by the American Press that the British were not taking their share of the fighting and of the casualties. He gave the Prime Minister to understand that in his view the British forces on the eastern flank could and should be more offensive; they were not fighting as they should, and he quoted the casualty figures to prove his case. This

sparked off quite a lot of trouble. The next night, the 27th July, the Prime Minister summoned a few responsible persons to meet Eisenhower at dinner. I very soon heard what had taken place.

Eisenhower complained that Dempsey was leaving all the fighting to the Americans. His attention was drawn to my basic strategy, i.e. to fight hard on my left and draw Germans on to that flank whilst I pushed with my right. It was pointed out that he had approved this strategy and that it was being carried out; the bulk of the German armour had continuously been kept on the British front. Eisenhower could not refute these arguments. . . .

It was then pointed out to Eisenhower that if he had any feelings that I was not running the battle as he wished, he should most certainly tell me so in no uncertain voice; it was for him to order what he wanted, and to put all his cards on the table and tell me exactly what he thought. Eisenhower was clearly shy of doing this.[9]

Indeed he was. The Supreme Commander's inability to confront him face to face thoroughly rankled the bristling Montgomery. The criticism expressed by the Supreme Commander was to create a growing wedge of vituperative animosity between Montgomery on the one hand and Eisenhower and Bradley on the other. It was bad enough that Tedder, Coningham and Morgan, the British members of Eisenhower's High Command, had been ready to do Montgomery in. Monty was angry, bitter and on the defensive. What had been said on 26/27 July would undoubtedly affect his judgment in important decisions that he would have to make in the following three weeks.

That Churchill was concerned about what he had heard from the mouth of Eisenhower at lunch is clear from the following message he sent to Montgomery on 27 July and Montgomery's immediate response. Churchill was able to rely on Monty's reply during the critical dinner that night.

Prime Minister to General Montgomery
27 July 1944

It was announced from S.H.A.E.F. last night that the British had sustained "quite a serious setback." I am not aware of any facts that justify such a statement. It seems to me that only minor retirements of, say, a mile have taken place on the right wing of your recent attack, and that there is no justification for using such an expression. Naturally this has created a great deal of talk here. I should like to know exactly what the position is, in order to maintain confidence among wobblers or critics in high places.
(2) For my own most secret information, I should like to know whether the attacks you spoke of to me, or variants of them, are going to come off. It certainly seems very important for the British Army to strike hard and win through; otherwise there will grow comparisons between the two armies which all lead to dangerous recrimination and affect the fighting value of the Allied organisation. As you know, I have the fullest confidence in you and you may count on me.

General Montgomery to Prime Minister
27 July 1944

I know of no "serious setback." Enemy has massed great strength in area south of Caen to oppose our advance in that quarter. Very heavy fighting took place yesterday and the day before, and as a result the troops of Canadian Corps were forced back 1000 yards from the farthest positions they had reached. . . .

My policy since the beginning has been to draw the main enemy armoured strength on to my eastern flank and to fight it there, so that our affairs on western flank could proceed the easier. In this policy I have succeeded; the main enemy armoured strength is now deployed on my eastern flank, to east of the River Odon, and my affairs in the west are proceeding the easier and the Americans are going great guns.

As regards my future plans. The enemy strength south of Caen astride the Falaise road is now very great, and greater than anywhere else on the whole Allied front. I therefore do not intend to attack him there. Instead I am planning to keep the enemy forces tied to that area and to put in a very heavy blow with six divisions from Caumont area, where the enemy is weaker. This blow will tend to make the American progress quicker.[10]

Montgomery could indeed count on Churchill, ever his loyal supporter in the teeth of the growing SHAEF and American criticism. Never would the old bulldog forsake Britain's heroic commander in the field. Furthermore it was clear that Monty intended to continue to pivot on Caen.

The vicious behind-the-back criticism from the 'armchair' generals and air marshals at SHAEF would permanently taint the relationship between the Americans and Montgomery. It was a situation that would be exacerbated over the next few days as the open wound made by Eisenhower on Monty's soul and ego festered. Monty lamented:

In a few days' time, we were to gain a victory which was to be acclaimed as the greatest achievement in military history. The British had had the unspectacular role in the battle, and in the end it would be made to appear in the American press as an American victory. . . . The strategy of the Normandy campaign was British, and it succeeded because of first class team-work on the part of all the forces engaged — British and American. But just when final victory was in sight, whispers went round the British forces that the Supreme Commander had complained that we were not doing our fair share of the fighting. . . . From that time onwards there were always "feelings" between the British and American forces till the war ended.[11]

While the troops fight it out with the enemy on the ground, in the air and at sea, losing their lives, spilling blood, suffering total fear for their lives, enduring horrible, treacherous risks, living in privation, the generals also have their private wars usually well away from, safely out of range of any guns. Nevertheless they are capable and quite proficient at blasting, cutting and hacking away at each other, their minds filled with prejudices, biases, and jealousies. There are really two sides of a man that can bear upon the making of a military decision. The human, visceral emotions can have an equal and sometimes over-riding effect on the purely military factors, strategies and tactics that impinge on that same decision.

The Churchill-Eisenhower meetings of 26/27 July and Montgomery's hostile reactions would, perforce, be a powerful future consideration in the minds of Bradley, who knew of Montgomery's reaction by that time, of Eisenhower, who certainly did, and, of course, of Montgomery himself, now completely soured on the Americans. Indeed, the Cobra breakout and the spectacular results that were to be won by the U.S. First Army, and particularly by Patton's Third in its race eastward, would only sharpen Montgomery's concern that the victory would be made to appear in the American press as an American success and, for that matter, in the British press as well. Montgomery knew full well that his continuing inability to 'move' south from the Caen area was attracting escalating criticism from the British press, let alone from his enemies at SHAEF headquarters.

In the monastic isolation of his caravan at Creully and later in the Forêt de Cerisy where he kept himself apart from his staff, Montgomery would have ample time to chew upon the bitter, rancid bone of critcism, jealousy and distrust that had been thrown at his feet by his Supreme Commander, a man who did not have the guts to hand it to him, a man whom Montgomery regarded as an inexperienced military inferior. "It was always very clear to me that Ike and I were poles apart when it came to the conduct of the war."

Eisenhower's inability to confront his British land commander directly, but rather to choose what Montgomery perceived to be the coward's route, created a huge reservoir of long-lasting bitterness, antagonism and resentment within the English General.

10

1 August 1944   OPERATIONS: Haze, mist and poor
visibility prevented any flying until
late afternoon. The last TAC/R,
Photo/R of the day was flown by F/O
R. H. Rohmer with F/O C. P. St. Paul.
No cloud. 50 tanks in Bois du
Homme. 20 M.T. at 7446. Miscellan-
eous MET at scattered points. General
appearance of movements. Enemy
reaction Nil.

430 Squadron Log

Clem St. Paul and I were airborne out of B.8 at 20:40 on a
tactical reconnaissance covering assigned points between
Le Beny Bocage and Aunay-sur-Odon, about 25 miles due
south of our Bayeux base. The area contained a great deal of
high ground in a region where some of the hills were over a
thousand feet high.

A map on which the 'bombline' was drawn was handed
to me during our pre-flight briefing in the Ops van. The
bomb line was put on by our Army intelligence people.
Anything we saw beyond the bomb line we could assume
was enemy and could be reported on the air to Group
Control Center for attack by our aircraft. On the contrary,
anything seen inside the bomb line was deemed to be Allied
and could not be reported on the air (because the Germans
monitored our broadcasts) and could not be attacked. That
was the firm order. The bombline went through Le Beny
Bocage swinging to the north and then easterly to the north
of Aunay-sur-Odon. The sector I was to reconnoiter was in a

pocket or bulge in the bomb line. Therefore I knew I was working close to the front line but no information was given to me about the structure of the battle that was going on at the time.

Still pivoting with 2 Canadian Corps at Caen, now as far south as Bourguébus, Montgomery had determined to push the Second British Army line on the west, and the 1st U.S. Army abutting it, south from the Caumont area. The objective was to reach the general area of Le Beny Bocage. The main attack of the British force would be mounted by 30 Corps on the left and 8 Corps on the right. The area I operated over that night was fronted by 43 Division on the right and 7 Armored Division on the left to the southwest of Villers-Bocage. My bombline was drawn through that town curving to the west and swinging south to Le Beny Bocage.

The attack had started on the 30 Corps front at 06:00 hours on 30 July. By 1 August Le Beny Bocage had been cleared by 8 Corps. Its 125 Division on the left had repulsed several counterattacks. 7 Armored Division of 30 Corps was moving on the left flank heading toward Aunay-sur-Odon.

When St. Paul and I arrived over the assigned area in our Mustangs the battle was raging below us. Unfortunately I knew next to nothing about the tactical situation on the ground.

What I did know was that it was rapidly getting dark. I would have to get my recce done and get home as quickly as possible. We did not have landing lights on our airstrips. They would have attracted the enemy.

There were nine specific points assigned to me. As soon as they were covered I headed for home. Flying north over Montigny at about 2000 feet the flash of a gun in the darkening ground mist ahead of me and to my right caught my attention. I went into a gentle bank to see what was firing. To my astonishment I found I was sitting over dozens of tanks, probably the greatest number I had ever seen in one place in a battle situation. Some were moving, some were sitting, many were firing their guns. It was an incredible sight, one extremely exciting for a young bloodhound. The long guns hanging way out over the front of the tanks signaled only one thing to me. They were German Tigers!

Perhaps if there was a Typhoon squadron airborne nearby, even at that late hour, they could come in and have at them. There was only one problem. The horde of tanks was well inside and to the north of the bombline. The bombline told me that anything to the north of it was ours and could not be reported on the radio or attacked. That was the rule.

But those were Tiger tanks down there!

I made the decision. I called Group Control Center on my VHF radio. GCC responded immediately. My report of the tanks and the pinpoint of their location was delivered somewhat excitedly and acknowledged calmly. They were in Bois du Homme about one and a quarter miles southwest of the main intersection at Evrecy highway. That done I again turned for home in the closing darkness, but not before doing one final thing. I circled, tipped the airplane over on its side, and pointed my oblique camera at a clutch of the tanks moving northward. My right thumb pressed the camera button on the control column to snap a few pictures. I knew it was unlikely that they would turn out because it was so dark, but I did it anyway — then high-tailed it for B.8 with St. Paul still faithfully covering my tail in battle formation.

It was dark when I entered the Ops van to be confronted by our Wingco Flying, "Bunt" Waddell. He did not mince words. Those tanks I reported to Group Control Center were *our* tanks. Army intelligence had no knowledge of any German tanks in the area but knew ours were there in strength getting ready to attack. By talking on the radio to Group Control Center and reporting the tank location I had given vital secret information to the German intelligence people. They monitored all of our broadcasts. On top of it all, the tanks were inside, repeat inside, our bombline and didn't I know the rule was that anything inside the bomb-line was ours! I had compounded the situation by breaking that rule. Surely with my experience I ought to have known better. Monty's headquarters and Dempsey's people at Second British Army HQ were furious. I could expect severe disciplinary action.

God, was I in trouble! Being shot at by the enemy was far less frightening than to be descended upon by one's own Wingco Flying and the entire British Army.

When I protested that I was sure the tanks were German Tigers Bunt Waddell simply waved that off saying it was not possible. There just weren't any in the area. The British Army intelligence people were absolutely sure. That was the end of the matter. I was to report to him first thing in the morning. Would I be court-martialed? There was no doubt he was thinking about it.

Now there was only one thing that could save me. The photographs. But I was positive they wouldn't turn out. It had been far too dark and hazy when I took them. They were my only chance for salvation. Tail between my legs I left the Ops van and hurried through the darkness to the photo developing unit just a few steps away. By this time they would have the film out of the camera and would be processing it. I burst in, breathlessly telling the NCO in charge of the unit about the predicament I was in. He calmed me down saying that he had already started the developing process.

I impatiently waited, practically hanging over his shoulder as the prints emerged. They were still wet as we looked at them. My spirits lifted. We could see tanks, six or seven of them. Not clearly, mind you, but we could see them. I couldn't tell what they were, Tigers or our Shermans or whatever. But, by some miracle I at least had photographs with something on them.

Off again I went into the darkness, the wet prints in my hand. This time I headed for the Army Photographic Interpretation Section van close by. Bursting in on the startled APIS duty officer, who was unaccustomed to seeing a pilot in his place of business at that time of night, I quickly explained the situation, produced my photographs and asked him to make a judgment. What were those tanks?

With no great haste he took the films, put them together in front of him, picked up the main tool of his trade, a pair of stereo lenses which when placed over two in-line photographs gave him a third dimensional view of the objects in the photographs. By this time I was in a terrible state of anxiety. But still he was in no hurry. Studying the images below him he emitted two or three contemplative grunts. Then, laconically, and without even looking up he said, "They're Tigers."

Artillery shoot, 8 August 1944 (F/O Richard Rohmer)

430/581.1AUG44.14"/M SA II.2,000

Tiger Tanks, 1 August 1944. Photo interpreted by
Dirk Bogarde.

Dirk Bogarde at B.8 Airfield near Bayeux, July 1944

Thank Christ! I could have kissed him but I had only one thing in my mind. Thanking him profusely I gathered up the prints and was out the door heading back through the black night to the Ops van just as quickly as my legs could carry me. It was about ten to eleven, but Wing Commander Waddell was still there. With triumphant relief I placed my Tiger treasures in front of him, repeating the judgment of the APIS officer. Bunt Waddell was pleased and I believe he was just as relieved as I was. He would get on to Dempsey's headquarters as quickly as possible. However, he reminded me sternly, do not let it happen again. The bombline is the bombline is the bombline! I got the message.

The APIS officer who gave me the Tiger interpretation was a young British lieutenant, Dirk Bogarde, who later became an international film star, an excellent author and a talented painter. In correspondence we exchanged in the fall of 1980, he wrote, "I . . . remember the tremendous 'flap' that happened the moment we discovered that there were Tigers in the blasted bombing line! Naturally we hadn't seen them because no one expected them to be there anyway. And if *you* had not seen one burst of fire we might never have known until far too late. As it was, and as you know, the road to Falaise was the road of death . . . and very unpleasant it was too: from the ground!"

That day, 1 August 1944, was one of the most important in the life of Lieutenant General George Smith Patton, Jr. At high noon his Third United States Army became operational. Once again Patton was his own man.

In the four days from Patton's verbal appointment by Bradley as Deputy Commander and, as Patton understood it, his appointment to command the Third, Patton had been here, there, and everywhere.

As soon as he had entered the fray on the 28th, Patton directed that his armor should lead the advances ahead of the infantry, a reverse in the traditional tactics of the infantry generals. Patton's plan called for scattered tank units leading the way for infantry to advance against the enemy. As soon as enemy resistance was encountered, tanks and other armored vehicles would be moved rapidly to each flank of the resistance pocket to attack and then move on quickly. The idea was that the enemy would be continually thrown off balance and have no time to re-organize his lines or to counterattack. In the presence of the rapidly dissolving German capability to stand and fight, the Patton concept was ideal.

Patton's first objective after Coutances was Avranches, almost thirty miles to the south, the hinge to Brittany. On Sunday, 30 July, his tanks pushed into Avranches. The next afternoon the city was permanently secured and threats of counterattack had been extinguished. On the same day, Granville was also taken. V Corps succeeded in capturing Toringny on the eastern flank next to the British Second Army, while XIX Corps on the right was thrusting further south toward the Avranches-Caen road. By 1 August, XIX Corps had moved rapidly to the line of Percy-Tessy. Meanwhile, V Corps was moving quickly toward the River Vire and the Forêt de Sever.

On 31 July Patton moved out of Néhou to a new command post position north of the Granville-St. Sever-Lendelin Road. There his dog Willy "contracted a violent love affair with a French lady-dog and also exhumed a recently buried German, to the shame and disgrace of the military service." At high noon on 1 August Patton and his deputy chief of staff, Colonel Paul Harkins, "decided to celebrate the birthday of the Third Army with a drink. The only thing we could find was a bottle of alleged brandy . . . we tried to drink this, but gagged."[1]

On the day the Third Army became operational, Patton's two Army Corps, VIII under Middleton, and XV under Collins, had to pass through Avranches. In Patton's words the movement of such a mass of men and equipment was:

> one of those things which cannot be done, but was. It was only made possible by extremely effective use of veteran staff officers and by the active part taken in it by corps and division commanders who, on occasion, personally directed traffic.[2]

One of the commanders Patton was talking about was

himself. On 8 August his Staff Officer, Colonel Charles Codman, recorded in his diary:

A few days ago in Avranches itself, we were blocked by a hopeless snarl of trucks. The General leaped from the peep [a type of Jeep], sprang into the abandoned umbrella-covered police box in the center of the square, and for an hour and a half directed traffic. Believe me, those trucks got going fast and the amazed expressions on the faces of their drivers as recognition dawned were something.[3]

The Avranches pass-through of the two corps of the Third Army, both now under Patton's clear-cut, dynamic command, signaled on 1 August that the breakout of the masterfully executed Cobra was now turning into a breakthrough. Patton's VIII Corps swung west into Brittany and south toward Rennes while his XV Corps under Haislip turned east as did VII Corps of the First Army heading toward Mortain, the spot which would soon be the focal point of a massive Hitler-ordered Panzer conterattack.

On the eastern British-Canadian flank where the Canadian thrust on the Falaise road had been halted 25/26 July, Montgomery had regrouped his forces. Hastily and under cover of darkness he moved six divisions westerly in order to deliver a strong offensive in the area between Toringny and Caumont. At the same time he required First Canadian Army and the remainder of the Second British Army to keep up a maximum of offensive activity on the rest of the front "in order to pin the enemy opposition and wear it down." On 30 July, the British 30 Corps attack commenced at 06:00 hours, moving toward Villers-Bocage on the Avranches-Caen road, while on its right VIII Corps commenced its attacked one hour later, thrusting toward the same road and beyond it to Le Beny-Bocage. By 1 August Le Beny-Bocage had been cleared while 30 Corps was moving toward Aunay-sur-Audon and the intensely defended Villers-Bocage. In the distance, the heights of Mont Pinçon could be seen beckoning. Montgomery, writing about the enemy, pointed out:

there were signs of his being reinforced in the area south of Mont Pinçon. The Air Force found good targets amongst tanks and vehicles moving west in the Condé area.[4]

All along the British front, fighting continued to be intense as armor and infantry hit head-on in huge masses. The enemy was doing everything in his power to deny the British breakout, continuing to concentrate his Panzer divisions in the Caen-Caumont section just as Montgomery had anticipated. Once again, the same story emerged from the British front:

> Progress was slow in both 8 and 30 Corps owing to enemy counter attacks and the great difficulty of the country.[5]

There was little change.

But in the American sector change, action, motion, advance and by-pass, particularly in Patton's area, were the orders of the day. The desperate commander of the German forces, Field Marshal von Kluge, informed Hitler:

> "Whether the enemy can still be stopped at this point is questionable. The enemy air superiority is terrific, and smothers almost every one of our movements. . . . Losses in men and equipment are extraordinary. The morale of the troops has suffered very heavily under constant murderous enemy fire, especially since all infantry units consist only of haphazard groups which do not form a strongly coordinated force any longer. In the rear areas of the front, terrorists, feeling the end approaching, grow steadily bolder. This fact, and the loss of numerous signal installations, makes an orderly command extremely difficult."[6]

The rout of the German Seventh army in Normandy had begun.

Other changes took place on 1 August that heightened the pervasive atmosphere of nationalistic sensitivity. The

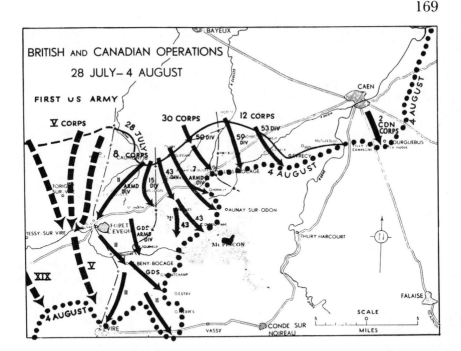

competitiveness that had grown among the Allied nations and their armies was felt most strongly by the generals. They needed to maintain face, not only in the presence of their subordinates and troops, but also among their peers in the military and in the eyes of the press and their countrymen. The man who stood to lose most by the planned personnel shifts on 1 August was the man most sensitive and already bitter, General Bernard Montgomery.

Bradley wrote that in early July, the Supreme Commander had given him:

> authority to split our U.S. forces on the Continent into two field Armies whenever I thought it desirable. I would then relinquish First Army to Hodges and step up to full-time command of the 12th U.S. Army Group. With this shuffle, Monty would surrender his temporary role as Allied ground commander and revert to 21st Group as commander of the British Armies. Thereafter, as dual Army Group commanders, we would report on equal footing to SHAEF.[7]

However, that arrangement was changed before 1 August. Bradley, a considerate man, sympathetic to Montgomery's increasing personal difficulties, admitted that he:

> had not asked to be freed from Montgomery's British Group command. He had neither limited our authority nor had he given us directives that might have caused us to chafe. As long as Montgomery permitted this latitude in U.S. operations, we were content to remain under his command until the tactical situation necessitated a change.[8]

When, on 1 August, the Third Army became operational under Patton, the 12th U.S. Army Group also became operational and Bradley finally became an Army Group Commander with control of both the First U.S. Army under Hodges and Patton's Third. Bradley was thereby theoretically the equal of Montgomery, who still commanded the 21st Army Group, comprised of the Second British Army commanded by Lieutenant General Miles C. Dempsey and Lieutenant General H.D.G. Crerar in command of the First Canadian Army. It was decided by SHAEF, however, that Montgomery would still remain the commander of the ground forces in France. One of the main reasons given was that a city of suitable size to accommodate Eisenhower and his SHAEF staff had not yet been taken in Normandy. When such a place had been secured and the move to France made, Eisenhower would become commander of the ground forces and assume direct responsibility for coordination between the British and American Army Groups. As Bradley explained:

> Therefore, until SHAEF was permanently established in France, Eisenhower directed that Monty would act as his agent, exercising *temporary* operational control over the U.S. Army Group. The Briton's authority would be limited primarily to coordination and the settlement of boundaries between our Groups. Despite this delegation of powers to Monty, Eisenhower would captain the team.[9]

Montgomery's view of his continuing command was similar to but not quite so limited as Bradley's understanding of it:

> There was no change in the roles for First and Third United States Armies; it should be noted, however, that as soon as Third United States Army became operational, Headquarters Twelfth United States Army Group were also to become operational, under the command of General Omar Bradley, in order to control the two American Armies. This Army Group was to remain under my operation control.[10]

The public was not to know of the changeover in Allied command until 14 August because SHAEF had blacked out all news of the change, especially the entry of Patton into the field. However, during this period it was clear from Montgomery's remarks to his chief-of-staff, Major General Freddy deGuingand, and from his communications to the Chief of the Imperial Staff, Field Marshal Brooke, that Monty had a high regard for Patton's tactics and freewheeling success. However, that personal admiration was not to override the embattled Monty's growing animosity and antagonism toward the Americans, SHAEF and, for that matter, the press.

It was part of deGuingand's job to agonize with his military master over the unjustified press onslaughts. The press were preying on him, Montgomery, just as were Eisenhower and Tedder and that lot. The only person in the world whom Monty could and did confide in at the insulated 21 Army Group Headquarters in Normandy was his faithful Freddie, who was to write:

> My Chief undoubtedly suffered a lot from the criticism that appeared in the Press and elsewhere about the slowness of progress in the bridgehead. "Had we reached a stalemate?" "Had Montgomery failed?" These were typical expressions used. I agree that a Commander in that position should be unaffected by such things, but on the other hand,

172

there were considerable dangers that these outspoken comments might have had an effect upon
the fighting qualities of the troops. Unlike in the
Middle East, the troops now read the Press from
England, often delivered the same day. If they
continually read articles criticising Montgomery,
or at any rate suggesting that all was not well,
they might lose faith in their Commander-in-
Chief. Here then was the danger.[11]

Danger indeed. However, quite a different danger than
the physical kind to which Montgomery's troops were
exposed to 24 hours a day.

The radical command changes that occurred on 1
August had little direct effect upon the Allied troops
slugging it out with the enemy in the field. But for the
principal actors at the top of the Allied pyramid in France,
the new responsibilities and postures were of the utmost
personal importance. It was a matter of face, power,
prestige, and influence not only for themselves but equally
for their nations and their national pride.

The cracks in the British-American solidarity that first
appeared on 26/27 July were widening rapidly.

Furthermore, the contrasts in the press between the
American grand breakout in the west and Montgomery's
apparent inability to move south of Caen were enormous
divisive pressures in the widening of the split of misunder-
standing.

11

8 August 1944   OPERATIONS: In spite of the haze and general poor visibility, thirteen TAC/R's were flown today, all successful. Information gleaned from these TAC/R's was quite considerable. The largest concentration was twenty plus tanks observed by F/O Rohmer in his morning TAC/R. Possible tanks among houses and trees at 812425. 1 in flames at 863441.

430 Squadron Log

The area I worked that morning was just to the south of Mont Pinçon, almost to Flérs. The reported burning tank was at the front line of the advancing 43 Division of the British 30 Corps stretching east from Mont Pinçon to Thury Harcourt. While at that moment there was no way I could identify the enemy tanks I saw, I later learned that they were of 12 SS Panzer Division, that day engaged in strong counterattacks against 59 Division attempting to take Thury-Harcourt from the northeast.

As we ranged around enemy territory with our eyes glued to the ground it was becoming increasingly obvious to us fighter recce pilots that the enemy forces were being compressed. The Americans were swinging around toward LeMans some ninety miles southeast of Caen completing their left hook easterly across and under the German Army.

As the compression of German forces accelerated, so did their need to move tanks, vehicles, guns and equipment in the full light of day. Thus forced to expose themselves to the American, British and Canadian Tactical Air Forces, they became increasingly vulnerable to the crushing power of the Allied fighter bombers and rocket firing aircraft.

The massive German counterattack at Mortain in the U.S. sector which was started on 7 August was outside the assigned front of the Second British Army which our Canadian 39 Recce Wing supported. Nevertheless our two fighter reconnaissance squadrons made substantial finds of German tanks and equipment enroute to the Mortain area which were then immediately attacked by Typhoons and Spitfires. An outstanding example was a recce operation carried out by our own 430 Squadron.

In mid-afternoon on 2 August F/O Danny Lambros accompanied by F/O Clem St. Paul took photographs in the Condé area some 15 miles west of Falaise. Lambros' naked eye had not seen what his oblique camera had picked up and the interpreters were able to see when they took a good look at his photographs. What they found were about 60 Panzers and 20 motor transport. Within a half hour of Lambros' landing at B.8 at 16:20 hours, word had gone out of the discovery. The Typhoons with their armor-penetrating rockets were immediately sent in. The result was that 37 of the tanks were destroyed and most of the German vehicles. Quite an achievement for the bloodhounds working as a team with our gutsy Typhoon pilots.

Shortly after three in the afternoon of 3 August F/O Vince Dohaney and I made an airborne decision which, probably to our good fortune, we were not able to execute. With Dohaney leading, Jack McLeod as number two and myself leading the cover section with F/L Iverson, we were off at 14:40 hours to do a TAC/R on roads from Tinchebray to Mayenne to Domfront to Vire. The weather was good with no cloud. Dohaney saw three possible Sherman tanks about five miles northeast of Vire and six motor transport on the road just to the north of Mortain. As we were about to turn northward to return to base we spotted a huge gaggle of German fighters — Focke-Wulfs and Me 109s. They were flying eastbound about two miles to the southeast of us and slightly higher. We deduced instantly that they were going home. They were a long way from their bases in the Seine area so we knew they were flying with no fuel to spare. When they crossed in front of our path we would still be about a mile north of them. Therefore, if we wanted to attack them, we would have to swing in behind them and try to catch up.

Four Mustang I's attack some forty German fighters flying their peculiar, loose, all-over-the-sky gaggle formation? Why not? Clearly they were short of fuel. The last thing they would want to do is dog-fight. Perhaps we could pick off some stragglers. Dohaney's voice came over the radio asking me tersely, "Should we?" My response was immediate. "Let's go." Dohaney called for close-in battle formation, put his power up to 45 inches of boost and 3,000 RPM which all of us copied. We were off, blood racing, guns cocked and at the ready.

As we turned onto an arc intercept course the huge mass of fighters gave no indication they were aware of our presence. Or if they did know we were there, they could probably assess what we were just beginning to realize. There was no way we could catch them. When we did get into line directly behind them we were still about a mile back and below — and they were pulling away.

Well, we tried and it would make a good 'line shoot' when we got back to Chateau Magny.

Our wing's main reconnaissance tasking required us to concentrate on the area immediately to the south of the Second British Army where the beginnings of the pocket were clearly visible as the Americans continued their thrust toward the east. In that pocket was the entire German army in Normandy with reinforcements pouring in from north of the Seine as Hitler prepared for his Mortain attack. To monitor the flow of incoming troops and material the Army also had us carry out an occasional reconnaissance to see what was going on as far distant as the area of the Seine. On 7 August, our 430 Squadron commander, Squadron Leader Frank Chesters, with Flight Lieutenant Jim Prendergast as cover, flew a TAC/R mission to Mantes-Gassicourt on the Seine, the key crossing point of the Germans for the movement of reinforcements. It lay only seven miles south of La Roche-Guyon, still the headquarters of the German Army Group B, now under the command of Field Marshal von Kluge, the Commander-in-Chief West, who had been tasked directly by Hitler, against von Kluge's own judgment, to mount the attack on Mortain near Avranches that had started that morning.

Airborne at 12:25 hours they flew due east, then turned slightly south to pick up the course directly to their far-off target over 100 miles away, a deep penetration for two unescorted Mustang I's. It was a cloudless day but with much haze, a condition we had become used to, with visibility cut down to between five and eight miles. Approaching Mantes-Gassicourt it became quickly apparent that traffic was heavy across the Seine and westbound through the city. Reinforcements were on the move. Along one stretch of road to the southeast of the city, Chesters saw 20 to 25 open and closed trucks. On railway sidings, again to the east along the edge of the Seine, between 80 and 100 freight cars; and in the marshalling yards of the city itself a hundred plus. Without doubt the German umbilical supply cord which had to reach as far west as Mortain was throbbing with activity, filled with food, fuel, shells, spare parts, engines, all the paraphernalia necessary to support the ravenous appetite of a fighting, beleaguered, proud army.

It was an army just days away from an almost complete encirclement, a trap which, if closed, could have brought the surrender of all of the German forces from the Caen-Argentan line to the west. As well, it might have brought the surrender of the Third Reich whose senior generals were now desperately concerned about the ominous shadow of the great Russian Bear rising on the eastern horizon of the Fatherland.

The pocket that was forming around the German forces had been developing through the first week of August. Patton's VIII Corps had turned into the Brittany Peninsula and was approaching Brest. Hinged at Mortain, Patton's XV Corps was galloping through Laval heading for LeMans, while the First Army's VIII Corps, to the north of XV Corps, was swinging toward Domfront. At Mortain and to the north of it was XIX Corps and beyond it to the Vire area was V Corps. Haislip's XV Corps was pressing eastward, well beyond a line running due south of Caen.

In the British-Canadian sector, Aunay-sur-Odon had

been taken on 5 August. 12 Corps troops were along the River Orne for a frontage of seven miles northeast from Grimbosq. All along the line, the fighting was severe, counterattacks intense, and movement limited. Throughout 5 and 6 August, on Montgomery's orders, First Canadian Army was gearing up for another attack southward in the direction of Falaise. This would be Operation Totalize.

That Montgomery still considered himself to be in command of all the Allied ground forces, whether temporarily (as Bradley understood it) or otherwise was perfectly clear in Montgomery's mind. "On 6 August, I issued orders for the advance to the Seine." At that moment the Germans were holding their ground south of Caen. But Montgomery was mystified as to the manner in which von Kluge would try to withdraw. Nevertheless:

> I ordered that we should continue relentlessly with our plans to drive him against the Seine, denying him escape routes through the Orleans Gap. . . . I instructed First Canadian Army to make every effort to reach Falaise itself in the forthcoming attack. . . . Twelfth United States Army Group [Bradley] was to approach the Seine on a wide front with its main weight on the right flank, which was to swing up toward Paris.[1]

To add further to Montgomery's mystification, 116 Panzer Division, 84, 89 and 363 Infantry Divisions and elements of 6 Parachute Division arrived from the Fifteenth Army north of the Seine amid reports of other units on their way from that direction. It was the need for confirmation of such reports that would cause the tasking of the Chesters-Prendergast recce to Mantes-Gassicourt on 7 August.

Even though the enemy had reached the point where withdrawal to and beyond the Seine was, in Montgomery's opinion, the only way he could save his armies, Monty was astonished and pleased that not only had the Germans not tried to do so but in fact at this late date were sending even more troops and equipment into Normandy.

While Montgomery was to write that he could not figure out why, the theoretical answer was given in a secret

Ultra report of a pending counterattack. This information was passed to Montgomery and Bradley earlier. The all-out Panzer assault against Mortain on 7 August had been personally ordered by Hitler contrary to the advice of his commander in the west, von Kluge and his generals in the Normandy field. The first indication of Hitler's Operation Lüttich (the counterattack at Mortain) came through Ultra which had picked up an order to von Kluge directly from Hitler himself. That message, which was monitored on 2 August 1944 at Bletchley in England, was:

> "The decision in the Battle of France depends on the success of (Lüttich). . . . The C-in-C West has a unique opportunity, which will never return, to drive into an extremely exposed enemy area and thereby to change the situation completely."[2]

The main body of some eight armored divisions were to drive through Mortain and retake Avranches, thereby cutting off Patton's army from its sources of supply as well as its reinforcing American reserves. Only elements of a single U.S. tank division and one infantry division faced the Lüttich operation which was to launch at midnight 6/7 August.

Von Kluge perceived the grave dangers inherent in Lüttich operations and immediately sent a signal to the High Command in which he in effect challenged Hitler's judgment:

> "An attack, if not immediately successful, will lay open the whole attacking force to be cut off in the west."[3]

He would have to move his Panzer units away from Caen in order to mount the attack. Furthermore, he could easily envisage the increasing possibility of a complete encirclement by the rampaging Americans once all the remaining German strength was concentrated in the Mortain area. However, the adamant Hitler would not budge. From that time on, Lüttich went forward. When he was challenged by his own generals as to why Lüttich was being undertaken, von Kluge responded with a single-word reply, "Führerbefehl" — it is Hitler's command.

Evidently Bradley passed Ultra's Mortain information on to Patton who recorded in his diary of 7 August:

> "We got a rumor last night from a secret source that several panzer divisions will attack west from . . . Mortain . . . on Avranches. Personally, I think it is a German bluff to cover a withdrawal, but I stopped the 80th, French 2d Armored, and 35th [Divisions] in the vicinity of St. Hilaire just in case something might happen."[4]

It did.

On 6 August Eisenhower was in Bradley's command post. Having been alerted by Ultra to the forthcoming attack the Supreme Commander wanted to be on site when it happened: "Bradley and I, aware that the German counterattack was under preparation, carefully surveyed the situation."[5]

Bradley's Short Hook Plan

After being assured by Eisenhower that the Air Transport Service (ATS) could deliver up to 2,000 tons of supply per day to any of the American forces that might be temporarily cut off by the German counterthrust, Bradley decided to take a major gamble. He would retain only minimum forces at Mortain and push to the southeast with Patton's and the other divisions that had already passed through Avranches. As Bradley recorded his decision:

> In betting his life on the success of von Kluge's panzer attack, Hitler had exposed his whole broad flank to attack and encirclement from the south. If we could only plunge eastward in force while the enemy attacked at Mortain, we might thereafter swing north in a pincer movement to cut off his entire army. I resolved to take the plunge and strike for annihilation of the German army in the west.
>
> Within a week, this decision brought on the Argentan-Falaise pocket.[6]

Having Eisenhower's encouragement and approval was one thing, but in the chain of command Bradley was directly responsible to Montgomery. In the Supreme Commander's presence, Bradley telephoned Montgomery to explain the plan. The response contained a degree of concern, but, agreeing that the opportunities were great, Monty left the responsibility in the hands of his capable 12th U.S. Army Group commander:

> Montgomery quickly issued orders requiring the whole force to conform to this plan, and he, Bradley, and Lieutenant General Miles Dempsey, commanding the British Second Army, met to coordinate the details of the action.[7]

As a result of that meeting and Bradley's proposal, Montgomery's plan to drive to the Seine for a long encirclement of the German forces was substantially changed. Bradley's summary of the situation contains a significant description of Montgomery's boundary responsibility:

> He would join with us in an effort to clamp von Kluge's Seventh Army in the jaws of a double pincer movement. While the American forces drove up from the south, Montgomery would drive down from the north through Falaise to cut off the enemy west of that north-south line and destroy his Seventh Army. As field arbiter on boundaries for Ike, Monty became responsible for coordinating the maneuvers of all four Allied Armies.
> Haislip's XV Corps was to form our U.S. pincer on the south, closing north to Argentan. That final objective lay 12 miles inside the British boundary. But because it contained the strategic road junction where our pincers were to converge, Monty happily forgave us our trespasses and welcomed the penetration.
> "We'll go as far as Argentan and hold there," I told Patton. "We've got to be careful we don't run into Monty coming down from Falaise."

In closing his half of the jaw from the north, Monty was to rush his attack down the Caen road through Falaise and 12 miles farther beyond to Argentan. Once Monty had closed that gap from Falaise to Argentan, we would have blocked the enemy's last escape route from Mortain.[8]

Of the twelve divisions that had been passed through Avranches to the south, Bradley had four that were not yet committed. He would hold those south of Mortain in readiness as reinforcements if needed to contain the German counterattack.

The German Mortain Counterattack

The commander of the German Seventh Army, Hausser, believing his preparations for the Mortain attack had been conducted in the utmost secrecy and that surprise would be one of his major advantages, issued the following order to his Corps and Divisional Commanders as H-hour approached:

The Fuehrer has ordered the execution of a breakthrough to the coast to create the basis for the decisive operation against the Allied invasion front. For this purpose, further forces are being brought up to the Army.

On the successful execution of the operation the Fuehrer has ordered depends the decision of the War in the West, and with it perhaps the decision of the war itself. Commanders of all ranks must be absolutely clear about the enormous significance of this fact. I expect all corps and divisional commanders to take good care that all officers are aware of the unique significance of the whole situation. Only one thing counts, unceasing effort and determined will to victory.

For Fuehrer, Volk and Reich
Hausser

At 00:01 hours of 7 August, Lüttich was launched against Mortain, just 28 miles east of the Bay of Mont St. Michel. Von Kluge used five Panzer divisions as the spearhead of the assault, drawing on armor from the Caen front and fresh infantry from the Pas-de-Calais area. At the time of the opening lunge, only one American division stood between von Kluge's Panzers and the sea. However, by noon the reinforcements from the U.S. First Army had arrived.

Mortain was taken in the opening minutes of the attack. The Panzers fanned out through the defenses of the American 30th Infantry Division. By dawn, German forces had reached a point within ten miles of the main coastal highway running south from Avranches.

But dawn also brought squadrons of USAF, RAF and RCAF fighter bombers. In the vanguard were the Typhoon aircraft armed with deadly, armor-piercing rockets. They descended upon the Panzers like locusts shortly after 08:00 hours as the huge tanks tried to make their way through the impeding bocage. That difficult Normandy terrain which the German Tanks had often used to their own advantage against Allied forces was now working against them.

'Bocage' country is claustrophobic; it consists of small fields split off by massive banked-up hedgerows. Vision is restricted from one hedgerow to the next — usually about one hundred yards. Tanks often found it impossible to break through the hedgerows, and once they got into the narrow sunken lanes they were often unable to manoeuvre out of them. In such, country and armor had to work hand-in-glove. Time and time again tanks found themselves confronted by enemy tanks or anti-tank guns at point-blank range, for beyond the next hedge anything might be hidden.

In addition, American artillery fire was pumping down on selected targets easily seen from Hill 317. This was a 1,030-foot peak that dominated the Mortain countryside. From that vantage point American artillery spotters could survey the entire oncoming attack. The air and artillery attacks on the advancing German forces continued unceasingly and with great power during the entire day, rapidly undermining the morale of the Panzer crews.

Even though the Germans failed to do more than recapture Mortain where their drive had been blunted the first day, they kept reinforcements coming in. Some Panzers arrived the next day, 8 August, from as far away as the Mediterranean coast. From the opening of the battle of Mortain through to its last gasps some days later, a strong inward flow of reserves from the 15th Army in the Pas-de-Calais area was maintained. The fictitious FUSAG no longer deceived Hitler and kept the 15th Army north of the Seine. The Fortitude deception was at an end.

In taking his decision to attack Mortain, Hitler was compelled to throw into that sector all his remaining reserves from wherever he could collect them. In doing so he ran the tactical risk of having those vital forces encircled by the Americans, especially Patton's Third Army already swinging eastward out of Avranches. Hitler took the chance. Bradley seized the advantage by planning his short hook, with which Montgomery not only agreed but also was committed in a course of action.

Monty's Prelude to the Falaise Gap

It was now Montgomery's responsibility to drive through from Falaise to Argentan in a rush.

On the night of 7 August a new assault was mounted against Falaise. Under the brilliant, innovative Canadian Corps commander General Guy Simonds, the Canadians opened Phase I of their assault known as Operation Totalize at 23:00 hours, Monday, 7 August. Phase II was scheduled for 14:00 hours on 8 August.

Totalize preparations had been in the making since 6 August, in advance of and quite independently of the tactics Bradley and Montgomery had agreed upon, which called for Montgomery mounting a 'rush' down the Falaise road to Argentan as approved by Eisenhower. Nevertheless, it would fit into Monty's new commitment.

Totalize was opened by the attack of 1,020 aircraft of Bomber Command dropping 3,462 tons of bombs on the villages in the path of the attack. In Phase I, not one bomb fell among the waiting troops in their armored vehicles. Simonds had devised a unique assault in which he placed his infantry in armored vehicles in columns four abreast, each led by a 'gapping force' comprised of Sherman tanks

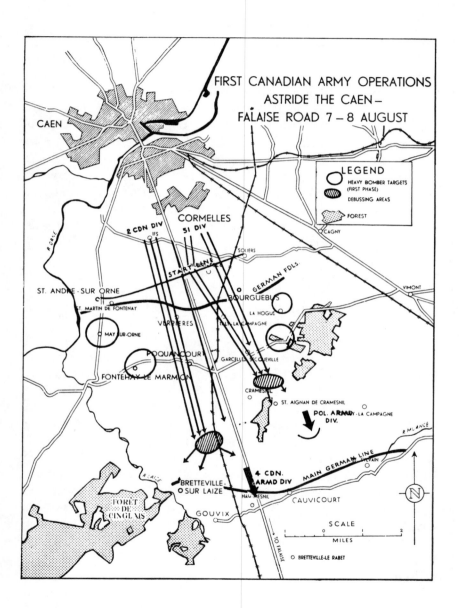

equipped with flails to detonate land mines in their paths; and engineers who had the job of marking the route with lights and tapes. Behind this initial assault force came the main body with the infantry battalion in armored carriers and supporting anti-tank weapons on their own carriers.

At the very rear was a 'fortress force' — also of tanks responsible for making secure the area where the troops disembarked. Navigational aids for the attack under cover of darkness were directional wireless, guns firing tracers, and searchlights that provided "artificial moonlight" pointed southward at a low angle. Even so, units were to stray in the heat of battle.

Ranged opposite the Canadian force were about 60 tanks and self-propelled guns dug in, plus about 90 of the 88 mm. flack guns positioned as anti-tank weapons. The main defense positions were manned by 12 SS Panzer Division with 89 Infantry Division, which had just arrived from the 15th Army north of the Seine, and 272 Infantry Division.

At the time first light arrived, the Canadian infantry dismounted after a four-mile drive straight through the enemy lines. They then took their assigned objectives successfully.

Phase II of operation Totalize went in after a bombardment by 492 American Flying Fortresses dropping 1,487 tons. Unfortunately, some short bombing occurred through a series of errors. Once more lethal loads of high explosives landed in areas packed with Canadian troops waiting to move up and also among the Polish Armored Division which suffered 65 killed and 250 wounded. Over 100 Canadians were lost, mainly from the North Shore (New Brunswick) Regiment, the 2nd Canadian and 9th British Army Group Royal Artillery. Major General R. F. L. Keller, Commander of the Third Canadian Division, was wounded.

When the ground attack did go in, 4 Canadian Armored Division on the right was eventually held up by the stiff anti-tank screen of 88s. On the left the Polish Armored Division similarly was not able to make much headway.

In all, Totalize saw an advance down the Falaise road of about six miles by the end of 8 August. By midnight 10/11 August, the advance had carried another three miles

south in the Quesnay area with Canadian troops astride the
highway. There were still another seven miles to go to get to
Falaise, let alone to Argentan, 12 miles beyond.

It had taken three full days of tough, bloody, fighting to
advance ten miles against a determined, powerful, concentrated enemy force. Totalize was at an end, heavy casualties
having been sustained on both sides. It was apparent that in
order to penetrate to Falaise, let alone beyond, the First
Canadian Army would have to regroup and mount yet
another large-scale, smashing attack.

On the other hand, by 8 August Montgomery could see
that XV Corps of Third United States Army was sweeping
all before it and was admirably placed at Le Mans to swing
north toward the Canadian forces coming southward to
Falaise and Argentan:

> On 8 August, therefore, I ordered Twelfth United
> States Army Group to swing its right flank due
> north on Alençon at full strength and with all
> speed. At the same time I urged all possible speed
> on First Canadian and Second British Armies in
> the movements which were converging on
> Falaise.[9]

Not only was Montgomery by now entirely committed
to Bradley's plan to trap the entire German Seventh Army.
He had even taken to claiming it as his own:

> In view of the Mortain counterstroke, I decided to
> attempt *concurrently* a shorter envelopment with
> the object of bottling up the bulk of the German
> forces deployed between Falaise and Mortain. It
> was obvious that if we could bring off both these
> movements we would virtually annihilate the
> enemy in Normandy.[10]

Inexplicably it was not until 10 August, three days after
operation Totalize had started, that Montgomery belatedly
instructed Crerar, the commander of the Canadian Army, to
"swing to the east around Falaise and then south towards
Argentan, at which point it is proposed to link up with the

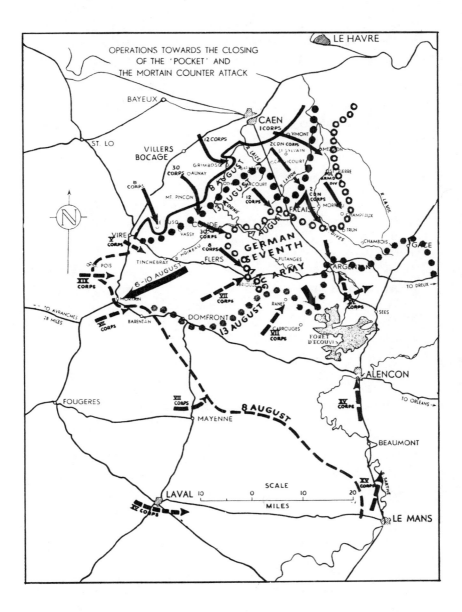

OPERATIONS TOWARDS THE CLOSING
OF THE 'POCKET' AND
THE MORTAIN COUNTER ATTACK

188

Third U.S. Army." Those were three lost days during which the entire thrust toward Falaise and then Argentan could have been remounted, using the maximum resources available from Dempsey's Second British Army to reinforce those of Crerar and Simonds' Canadian forces, complemented by the tough Polish Armored Division. However, this was not ordered by Montgomery, nor was it done.

On 10 August, Totalize was stopped. By that time Montgomery should have known that it would be impossible for his forces to reach even Falaise before Patton arrived at Argentan twelve miles beyond that town.

Patton's Prelude to the Falaise Gap

Meanwhile, General Patton was having the time of his life. He was reveling in the bold chaos his Third Army had wrought. As James Wellard, an experienced war correspondent traveling with Patton's Army described it:

Patton had broken through and the entire German front was collapsing on the western sector covering Brittany. For a few days, nobody knew what had happened or what would happen next. Those of us who were not in the fighting vanguard were carried along on a tide of emotion and champagne. We had lost contact with headquarters and the press camp. But everybody had lost contact with everybody else. This was how Patton wanted it. His armor was still driving and slashing across the German rear. The German defeat was becoming a rout, and the rout a collapse. General Patton had effected the greatest movement of armor and infantry in history.[11]

In a letter to his wife dated 5 August, Patton wrote:

"now we are in the biggest battle I have ever fought and it is going fine except at one town we have failed to take . . . I am going there in a minute to kick some ones [sic] ass."[12]

Colonel Charles R. Codman, Patton's long-time aide, right-hand man and confidante, a well-to-do Bostonian with a background of culture and sophistication that Patton missed, and who was everywhere with his general, described the scene on 8 August:

> The Old Man has been like one possessed, rushing back and forth up and down that incredible bottle-neck, where for days and nights the spearheading Armored divisions, followed by motorized Infantry, have been moving bumper to bumper. More marching in ranks, the General occasionally darting out to haul an officer out of a ditch in which he has taken refuge from a German plane, or excoriating another for taping over the insignia on his helmet. "Inexcusable,' he yells. "Do you want to give your men the idea that the enemy is danger-ous?" Pushing, pulling, exhorting, cajoling, rais-ing merry hell, he is having the time of his life. Our headquarters moves daily, in a series of one-night stands, and we are for the moment located in a tree-covered building near Avranches. . . .
>
> We have been bombed, strafed, mortared, and shelled. The General thrives on it. Yesterday on the way back to our headquarters we were speeding along through choking dust under a high blue heaven crisscrossed with the vapor contrails of our tactical planes. It was a bad stretch of road from which our bulldozers had recently pushed to either side the reeking mass of smashed half-tracks, supply trucks, ambulances, and blackened German corpses. Encompassing with a sweep of his arm the rubbled farms and bordering fields scarred with grass fires, smoldering ruins, and the swollen carcasses of stiff-legged cattle, the General half turned in his seat. "Just look at that, Codman," he shouted. "Could anything be more magnificent?" As we passed a clump of bushes, one of our con-cealed batteries let go with a shattering salvo. The General cupped both hands. I leaned forward to

catch his words. "Compared to war, all other forms of human endeavor shrink to insignificance." His voice shook with emotion. "God, how I love it!"[13]

The Final Steps to the Falaise Gap

Far to the north of Patton and some twenty miles back from the front lines at his own headquarters in the Forêt de Cerisy was another general who loved war — but from a different perspective. Montgomery, the commander of all Allied land forces, was watching his operations map, and issuing the orders that directed the on-rushing Patton and his Army toward Argentan.

The way Patton's forces were moving, the Canadian Army would have to be in Argentan to meet them on 12 or 13 August. Even on the 8th, Montgomery should have realized that objective was virtually impossible to meet. On the 10th, when Totalize had to be shut down, he must have been certain of it. It was completely beyond the capability of the First Canadian Army — even when combined with the Second British Army — to overcome the stubborn German defenders north of Falaise and 'rush' 20 miles south down the road to Argentan to arrive there on the 12th or 13th.

Nevertheless, on 10 August Montgomery issued orders from his van in the Forêt de Cerisy. They went to Crerar, the commander of the First Canadian Army. He was instructed to do the impossible. His troops were to swing east of Falaise, then south to Argentan to link up there with Patton's armored divisions, expected to be there in two or three days.

What would happen if the Canadians could not break through the determined enemy barrier? If Patton reached Argentan would he press on north toward Falaise, attack the German's from the rear and close the pocket?

As the shape and reality of the pocket took form with the thrust of Patton's Third Army eastward, then north toward Argentan during 10 and 11 August, the answers to those questions were not apparent. They were on the night of the 12th and early morning of the 13th.

12

12 August 1944   OPERATIONS: in spite of hazy conditions thirteen TAC/R's and one photo R were flown, one task being abortive due to technical failure. No movements of major importance were seen.

430 Squadron Log

From 10 August through the 12th heavy fighting was raging to the north and south of the pocket forming around the German army. The battle to the west at Mortain continued. The enemy, badly scarred by the devastating attacks of the rocket Typhoons and fighter bombers inflicted on his tanks and motor vehicles, seemed to have finally decided that he would not move in daylight hours unless absolutely necessary.

Of eleven tactical reconnaissance operations, 430 Squadron carried out on 10 August, seven reported "no movements seen." Of the six operations carried out on 11 August, three reported "no movement;" and of twelve on the 12th there were six so reported.

Furthermore, for some reason our direct taskmaster, Dempsey's Second British Army staff, seemed either to have bogged down or there was a new man on staff who did not know how to use the reconnaissance squadrons at his disposal. For the first and only time the squadron log recorded a situation like this:

> Very few tasks were received from Army this morning; consequently, no sorties were flown until this afternoon.

There was a dearth of tasking notwithstanding that the sky was cloudless, visibility was excellent and there was a hell of a lot of fighting going on out there.

Of the tactical reconnaissance operations on 10 August in which movement was reported, one was into the Mortain area where the Germans were throwing all their weight in the counterattack thrust ordered by Hitler. This was to be the only Mortain Recce 430 Squadron was tasked to do during the period of the German assault that had started on 7 August. The sector belonged to the Americans who were successfully holding off the onslaught of the German Panzer divisions pulled in from the Caen/Falaise area and elsewhere. It was likely, however, that by the morning of 10 August Montgomery wanted to have one of his own 'eyes' take a look at the situation rather than rely totally on reports from his Americans.

Thus at 08:35 hours that morning, with F/O Ken Gillmor as cover, I was airborne out of B.8 headed for Mortain. It was an excellent flying day. Visibility was unlimited except for 5/10ths scattered cloud at 1,500 feet. In the Mortain sector immediately behind the German lines there was clear evidence of the heavy battle that was still being fought. I saw much scattered activity but no concentrations of vehicles or troops. So my report on debriefing after returning to B.8 at 10:15 hours had to be general: "Considerable movement and MET observed in the entire area."

Of the 12 August operations two TAC/R missions reported German movement. Significantly, both were eastbound inside the pocket toward what, as of the night of 12 August, was to become the notorious Falaise Gap. The first was an 08:45 to 09:45 hours TAC/R by F/O J.A. 'Butch' Lowndes with S/L Ken Hay-Roe in the Falaise, Argentan, Sées, Briouze, Domfront area. There was no cloud that

Cal Bricker

Bob Gill

Ed Winiarz

Vince Dohaney

Red Moore

Belli-Bivar

Top two, L to R: Dennis Whittaker, Jim Prendergast
Middle, L to R: Jack Watts, Clem St. Paul, Pappy Dunn, Ken Gilmor
Bottom, L to R: Bobby Clark, Dick Manser, Ed Geddes

L to R: S/L Harold Day, W/C Bunt Waddell, W/C John Godfrey, G/C Ernie Moncrieff, S/L T. Williams, S/L Smokey Stover

morning but the usual haze was present, cutting visibility down to five miles. What Butch Lowndes saw as he flew west out of Argentan along the main highway to Briouze was six German tanks lumbering eastward at Fromentel, only ten miles west of Argentan. Montgomery later wrote:

> After four days' fighting around Mortain, the enemy had suffered enough and began to pull back his Panzer divisions to meet the threat to his flanks: particularly on the south, where hitherto protection had been afforded by inadequate battle groups. The enemy plan was evidently to extricate as many troops as possible, both Panzer and infantry, from the salient and reform a north-south line much further to the east.[1]

Butch Lowndes' information about the enemy tanks would have been of enormous value if it had been passed on to the Americans who, with the French Armored Division of Leclerc as part of Patton's Army, were at that moment thrusting up toward Argentan from the south.

The next significant report of 12 August was that of F/L Jim Prendergast flying with F/O Ken Charman in a TAC/R over precisely the same route taken by Lowndes and Hay-Roe, but twelve hours later.

Prendergast's observations were the first clue that the enemy was indeed packing up and starting to head for the Seine:

> no cloud, hazy, visibility 3 miles. 30 MET moving northeast out of Sées. Much movement from Sées to Q-4640.

Sées, a town lying ten miles to the northeast of Argentan, was a place upon which roads converged from several directions. Q-4640 was the pinpoint where the highway running north from Sées intersects at a seven-mile distance with a main east-west road. Montgomery, who had available to him the composite intelligence reports of four Mustang tactical reconnaissance squadrons, had enough information from us to conclude:

By 12 August reconnaissance reports clearly showed a general trend of enemy movement to the east from the Mortain area through the 'neck' between Falaise and Argentan and on towards the Seine ferries. But the enemy was still fighting back hard and apparently trying to stand his ground within the salient; it was reasonable therefore to assume that this movement comprised the rearward elements of the German forces, and that if we could close the jaws of our 'short' enveloping movements across the Falaise-Argentan neck, we should have in our grasp the bulk of the fighting formations of von Kluge's forces.[2]

Prendergast's find was the first trickle which soon was to turn into a flood.

In the next few days, strapped in our Mustangs flying at low level over the pocket, we would watch the Germans gather, form columns of vehicles in broad daylight and drive "on towards the Seine ferries" through the Falaise-Argentan Gap that General Patton ought to have closed on 12/13 August when two of his armored divisions arrived at Argentan.

On 12 August when I circled in the smooth late evening air in a cloudless, hazy sky midway between and about a mile overhead Falaise and Argentan, I saw the war from a vantage point allowed only a few. But if I could have soared higher with the penetrating eyes of an eagle I would have seen all the forces in the Battle of Normandy arrayed before me.

Three miles to the north of Falaise astride the road to Caen, I would see the flashes of the guns of the 2nd and 3rd Canadian Infantry Divisions and of the 4th Canadian and 1st Polish Armored Divisions, all fighting in a regrouping action behind which they would mount a new operation, Tractable, an attack that could not get under way any earlier than 14 August.

To the south some 7 or 8 miles from where I was circling was the town of Argentan. The distance between the Canadians standing astride the road to Caen, a few miles north of Falaise at Quesnay, and Argentan, was a formidable 20 miles. In Argentan I would have still been able to see

German troops. But on its southern approaches and to the west and east, I would have been able to see tanks and armored vehicles of General Patton's XV Corps moving north under General Haislip. More particularly they were Leclerc's 2nd French Armored Division on the west and to the southeast the American 5th Armored Division under General Oliver. Ahead of them, straight north up the road to Falaise until my eyes reached the rear of the horde of German armor and guns fighting off the Canadians to the north of Falaise, I would be able to see only a few enemy forces, — a mere handful of tanks, guns, troops, to stand in the way of the advance of Patton's armor under Leclerc and Oliver. Virtually nothing.

Then looking far to the west toward Mortain, I would have seen the beginnings of the German Seventh Army starting to withdraw under the permission of the Fuhrer, granted that day. The Mortain counterattack had failed, but not before Hitler had thrown into the bulging pocket enormously valuable reinforcements of tanks, guns and troops in a last-ditch effort. In that pocket to the west of me and north beyond Falaise was what was left of the whole of the German Seventh Army and the remnants of its Panzer Army. The pocket was enormous. Hundreds of thousands of men, thousands of vehicles, hundreds of tanks, an entire army, all were in a pocket with only one mouth, the Falaise Gap. I was circling over it at the moment. It was twenty miles wide. Through it the first of the escaping, retreating German vehicles were beginning to move.

The opportunity to complete the encirlement was at hand, the very objective that Bradley and Montgomery had agreed upon a few days earlier. But there was no way the Canadians, Poles and the British Army could break through north of Falaise to 'rush' south past Falaise to Argentan; they were pinned down where they were.

No, if the ring was to be closed with the two German Armies inside the pocket, it would have to be done by Patton and it would have to be done forthwith. In a signal at 21:30 hours, 12 August, Haislip, the commander of XV Corps, notified Patton that he was about to capture his last assigned objective, Argentan. If Patton would authorize XV Corps to proceed north of Argentan, Haislip was ready to move the

American Armored Division through Leclerc's French Division at Argentan for the drive north to meet the Canadians.

Patton's response was prompt. In a message at 04:40 hours on 13 August, Patton instructed him to push slowly in the direction of Falaise along the Argentan-Falaise road, which would also be the left boundary of his advance. On arriving at Falaise, Haislip was to "continue to push on slowly until . . . contact (with our allies) was made."

When a 5th Armored Division patrol had attempted to advance north on the morning of the 13th, they were stopped by German guns from the high ground north of Argentan, which inflicted damage on both the French and American attacking groups. In the afternoon a patrol from Leclerc's division entered Argentan, reaching the center of town, but on the arrival of German tanks, it quickly retired. Neither of the probes north was in strength, although all the necessary American armored force was in place to easily move through the German defenders.

Meanwhile, the six tanks, which Lowndes had seen at about 09:00 the morning before moving easterly on the main highway about ten miles west of Argentan, had arrived in the Argentan sector. They were elements of 1 SS and 2 Panzer Divisions. The 116 Panzer as well with infantry and artillery had also arrived late on the 13th. Even so, it was obvious to the German commanders that three emaciated Panzer divisions would not be able to hold for any length of time. The slim defensive line could have been eliminated at the bidding of the XV Corps units at Argentan.

On the morning of 13 August, General Dietrich, the Commander of Fifth Panzer Army, sent to the headquarters of Army Group B a signal that clearly stated the precarious posture of the German forces at that moment:

If the front held by the Panzer army and the Seventh Army is not withdrawn immediately and if every effort is not made to move the forces toward the east and out of the threatened encirclement, the army group will have to write off both armies. Within a very short time resupplying the troops with ammunition and fuel will no longer be possible. Therefore, immediate measures are necessary to move to the east before such movement is definitely too late. It will soon be possible for the enemy to fire into the pocket with artillery from all sides.[3]

Astonishingly enough, the German line at Argentan did hold, not because of the defenses in place, but because Patton was told to stop further movement to the north. Patton then informed Haislip he was not to go north of Argentan and he was to withdraw any of his elements that might be "in the vicinity of Falaise or to the north of Argentan."

That directive given by Patton created the notorious Falaise Gap. It was probably the most costly, controversial order given in the European theatre during World War Two.

As a result of that order and the subsequent creation of the Falaise Gap, in the next six days thousands of vehicles, armor, horse-drawn artillery and thousands of troops would move through the Gap, making their way to the ferries of the Seine and sanctuary on the banks beyond, ready and able to fight another day.

What that order meant in terms of escaping German forces could only begin to be measured after the closing of the Falaise Gap during 19/20 August, a full week after the decision had been taken to create it.

13

17 August 1944   OPERATIONS: 9 TAC/R's were
flown, a total of 18 sorties. F/O E. J.
Geddes and F/O K. G. Gillmor on a
TAC/R, were attacked by 20 plus
F.W. 190's near Mantes-Gassicourt.
No damage was done but both
aircraft became separated and the
task was abandoned. The last light
sorties observed large amount of
tanks, M.T., staff cars, etc. moving
east out of the Falaise-Argentan
pocket. At the same time, news was
received tonight of 100 American
tanks in Versailles.

430 Squadron Log

From 13 August onward the pace of the enemy's withdrawal
had accelerated rapidly as the Gap continued to remain
open. TAC/R's of the pocket began on the 13th with
"impression of considerable activity in Briouze;" and "in
the Argentan-Falaise area 44 MET." On 14 August "40 plus
MET moving northeast out of Laigle and movement in
Laigle itself;" and in the Domfront area a "column of tanks
and MET, 50 MET in field." On 15 August "20 plus MET in
convoy at Domfront;" "In the Evrecy, Laigle area 30 MET;"
"Open MET had passengers who waved white flags on
approach of aircraft."

During a TAC/R of mine that day at about 16:30 hours,
I watched with amazement from an altitude of about 1,000
feet as horse-drawn guns and armored cars moved eastbound
in the area about 30 miles to the west and north of Argentan.
I reported "25 ambulances on the road" 10 miles west of

Argentan also headed eastbound. The enemy was out in the open and was being hit very hard by fighter bombers of the XIX United States Air Force and by our Typhoons and Spitfires. The large number of ambulances we were seeing quickly gave rise to the suspicion that the Germans were painting the protective red crosses on their military vehicles in order to save themselves.

On 16 August F/O Butch Lowndes with F/O Al Light-body on a first-light TAC/R in the Falaise-Argentan Gap area reported "200 plus MET, armored cars, artillery, ambulances" moving east. Later in the day in the same area, F/L Dick Manser with F/L Ken Charman saw "50 plus MET moving northwards toward Falaise at Putanges;" while Prendergast and Lightbody found "30-50 MET" in the Falaise area.

During the late evening of 13 August I had been tasked to lead a TAC/R well to the east in the Dreux, Evreux area in the flat country leading toward the Seine. St. Paul, Winiarz, and Iverson were with me. It was a clear evening with high cirrus clouds and good visibility of up to 20 miles and beyond. We were flying at 3,000 feet, about 25 miles outside the bombline well into enemy territory. In the Dreux area, I picked up the dust of a large number of rapidly moving vehicles ahead of me but slightly to the right. They were still too far away to identify. Before I was in a position to pinpoint their location I checked my map. They were at least 30 miles beyond the bombline. Therefore they had to be German!

In the front of my mind was the rough lesson I had learned about bomblines two weeks before. This time, however, I was satisfied that I could with impunity ring up Group Control Center to bring in the Spitfires and Typhoons. First I had to be sure the target was big enough to warrant it.

As we got closer I could see they were tanks going hell bent, dust billowing behind them as they charged in column down a flat French side road eastward toward the Seine. I estimated that there were about twelve of them, certainly a number that justified a call for the fighter bombers and rocket aircraft. Pinpointing their location I was just about to call GCC when my eyes told me there was something a little different about those tanks. No. They didn't look like Tigers or any other German tank I had seen.

My God, they're Shermans! But they're 30 miles beyond the bombline! I later learned that they were Patton's tanks charging for Dreux, leaving Normandy, the pocket and the Falaise Gap far behind. Incredible! I did not call GCC.

14 August was a beautiful, sunny, warm summer day in the Falaise Gap. Fields of golden grain stood ready for harvest on the rolling farmlands north of Falaise where once again long columns of Canadian and Polish armor sat ready to roll into the battle behind the preliminary attack of Canadian bombers and then the artillery.

At 11:37 hours the artillery fired its marker shells for the bombers and Operation Tractable was under way. Its purpose was to take Falaise "in order that no enemy may escape by the roads which pass through, or near it."

For Tractable, General Simonds used similar techniques to those he used in Totalize. He transported his troops in armored vehicles in massed columns, but this time it was done in daylight. He would attack without any surprise whatsoever.

The first-light bombing support raid in the morning was successful but a second in the afternoon at 14:00 hours comprising some 417 Lancasters, 352 Halifaxes, and 42 Mosquitoes that delivered 3723 tons of bombs again involved another horrifying short bombing. By this time the frequent, costly, incomprehensible short bombings had convinced many army commanders and certainly their troops that they would be far better off to leave the air force at home. The casualties inflicted by Bomber Command were almost as bad as those caused by the enemy. In this bloody bombing the 12th Field Regiment RCA suffered 21 killed, more died of wounds, and 46 wounded. The Royal Regiment of Canada had 6 killed and 52 missing.

Nevertheless, Tractable pressed forward and by the afternoon of the 16th, the South Saskatchewan Regiment with the Cameron Highlanders of Canada and a squadron of the Sherbrooke Fusiliers Regiment cleared the town. On the left, the 4th Armored Division and the Polish Armored

Escaping German vehicles: Falaise Gap area

Escaping German vehicles: Falaise Gap area

Division had been directed toward Trun near Chambois, east of the Gap, where eventually the Americans would link up with them to close it.

With the taking of Falaise on the 16th, the yawning Gap had been reduced to 15 miles, still a wide enough opening to attract every enemy vehicle, tank, and soldier in the pocket.

Patton, meanwhile, had been sitting at Argentan from 12 August onward, under orders not to advance north to Falaise. Furious, Patton decided that he could no longer hold Haislip's four divisions there. Finally, on the morning of 14 August, he called Bradley, urgently requesting that two of Haislip's four divisions at the Argentan shoulder be turned loose for a fast dash to the Seine. Bradley gave permission:

> If Montgomery wants help in closing the gap, I thought, then let him ask us for it. Since there was little likelihood of his asking, we would push on to the east.
>
> In his advance to the Seine, Patton was to split Third Army three ways with one corps on the south headed toward Orléans, another in the center directed on Chartres, while Haislip, on the north, struck toward Dreux, 40 miles this side of Paris.[1]

It was Haislip's tanks that I had found racing toward Dreux about 21:00 in the evening of the 14th.

Meanwhile, inside the pocket the enemy was in disarray. On 15 August the fighters and fighter bombers of the American XIX and IX Tactical Air Commands in their P47's and P51's joined the Spitfires and the Rocket Typhoons of the British and Canadians of the 2nd Tactical Air Force. They began constant, ravaging attacks on lines of German motor vehicles moving in columns within the pocket, — the Kessel as the Germans called it — heading toward the Falaise Gap. The Germans were free from air attack only when by luck they found themselves within the Allied bombline. The 'Jabos', as the enemy called the fighter bombers, ranged back and forth unimpeded over the pocket, blasting every target they could find. The pocket was now becoming a cauldron of German wreckage and dead. Notwithstanding the risk of death from the air, the German Army had no choice but to move in the open by day. By 17 August, it seemed as though the whole German Army was heading toward and through the Gap. The men of what was originally estimated to be at least 12 German divisions in the pocket, including Panzers, had only one thing in mind — to get out.

Von Kluge himself was fired by Hitler on 17 August. At dawn on 15 August he had mysteriously set out to the front with his son, a wireless truck and a small escort. Von Kluge disappeared. He was completely out of contact until 22:00 hours that evening. This strange action caused Hitler, now paranoid, to believe that von Kluge had established contact with the enemy with a view to surrendering himself and his forces. Ironically, von Kluge had replaced Field Marshal von Rundstedt as Commander-in-Chief West because von Rundstedt had made a remark that indicated to Hitler that he believed the only solution to the Allied invasion of Normandy was to make peace with the enemy.

On page 4 of the *Times* of London of Tuesday, 15 August 1944, there was a curious article entitled "American Third Army."

> It was stated last night that General Bradley has been appointed Commander-in-Chief of the American Fighting Forces in France, which included, besides the original First Army, a new Third Army. The name of the commander of the Third Army was not revealed.

That terse statement caused another tempest in a teapot in that the British thought it meant that Montgomery had been demoted and that he was no longer in charge. Again, everyone, including Montgomery, was upset with the overpowering Americans. There had to be quick action to save the sensitive British face. In the next edition of the *Times* on Wednesday, 16 August, page 4 had this:

GENERAL MONTGOMERY'S COMMAND

It is officially stated at Supreme Allied Headquarters that the announcement of General
Bradley's command of the 12th Army Group in no
way affects the position of General Montgomery as
over-all Commander of all Allied Ground Forces
in France under General Eisenhower.

Immediately below that brief report was the first
mention of General Patton. Now all the world would know
that he was leading the spectacular successes of the
American Third Army:

GEN. PATTON'S PROMOTION

From Our Own Correspondent
NEW YORK, Aug. 15
Simultaneously with the announcement that
General Patton is commanding an army in France,
the Senate Military Affairs Committee in Washington this morning finally confirmed his per-
manent promotion to the rank of Major General.
The committee had held up action on this promotion since last October because of a "soldier-
slapping" incident during the Sicilian campaign,
but on General Eisenhower's announcement of
General Patton's new command, the committee
decided that he had been "disciplined sufficiently."

In the *New York Times* on Wednesday, 16 August the
news of Patton was front page:

PATTON IS THE THIRD ARMY'S CHIEF

Senators confirm his promotion

Supreme Headquarters, Allied Expeditionary
Force, Aug. 15 — Lieut. Gen. George S. Patton, Jr.,

is the tactical genius who has driven the rampant United States Third Army across Brittany, through LeMans and then northward through Alençon and Argentan, completing the southern jaw of the trap on the Nazi Seventh Army. The controversial, gravel-voiced General Patton has been leading an army literally born in battle Aug. 1st. It has been on the offensive since the day it was created and never has let up a minute.

The long, glowing, news report about Patton also contained a piece that eloquently told of the dramatic change in the fortunes of George Patton with the stunning announcement of his leadership of the Third Army:

Today Senator Albert B. Chandler, Democrat of Kentucky, who led the fighting in committee against the elevation of General Patton, presented the committee's decision to the Senate.

Senator William Langer, Republican of North Dakota, interposed objections, contending that a full complement of the Senate should be present to act on such a matter. Senator Chandler asked to be heard before the confirmation was blocked.

Mr. Chandler said he had changed his position. It had been changed for him, he said, by General Patton's performance in the Normandy-Brittany campaign. Again, he told the Senate, General Patton was leading American soldiers to victory in arms, and again he had showed himself to be "the greatest tank commander in the world."

Senator Langer withdrew his objections. The confirmation was effective immediately.

The American public had their hero once again.

On 17 August all the squadrons in the British and Canadian manned 2nd Tactical Air Force operating out of Normandy received a controversial order that was attributed to Montgomery's headquarters. The bombline was to be moved well east of the Gap between Falaise and Argentan. From that moment forward, none of the Typhoons and Spitfires of the British 2nd Tactical Air Force or the Thunderbolts and Lightnings of the IX United States Air Force could attack any enemy vehicles, troops, or other targets of opportunity within the pocket or the Gap. So far as we could see there were still tens of thousands of troops in the pocket, which was now becoming severely compressed. Tanks, horsedrawn artillery, ambulances, and vehicles of every kind were moving in broad daylight toward the Gap under our very eyes. As 83 Group Intelligence Summary of Operations No. 67 stated (our 39 Recce Wing was part of 83 Group), "we were debarred from attacking the Western-most enemy."

For all the pilots this was an astonishing order. It gave the Germans carte blanche, and, without fear of attack, time to gather their tanks and vehicles into orderly columns, then to drive and march out of the pocket and the Gap toward the Seine. However, once they reached the open area a few miles to the east of the Gap they lost the bombline protection and were subject to air attack.

At the time it was said that the Polish Armored Division, fighting to the left of the Canadians coming down the Falaise road, had been attacked by our own Spitfires or Typhoons in the close quarter of the converging battle, and that Montgomery had given in to the pleas of his army commanders to call off the attacks for fear of further incidents.

We fighter recce pilots believed that if there was any problem with pinpointing or identifying enemy targets, whether they were 100 yards or 50 away from our own troops on the ground, we, the ace map readers, the bloodhounds, should have been given the job of leading in the Spits, Thunderbolts, Lightnings, and Typhoons. We should have been the battleground Pathfinders. As we saw it that solution would have been a far better practical alternative than taking the unbelievable route of denying our massive tactical air forces the opportunity to attack and destroy German forces now in full, organized retreat out of the pocket through the Gap.

Two other factors influenced the decision to issue the

order that tied the air forces' hands. The first was the army
commander's typical inability to understand fully the
capability of the air forces available to do his tasking. This
inability leads to distrust, particularly when the air force
has, as has been seen, made some grievous, costly errors in its
close, heavy bombing support of the army assaults. It is true
that at the time of the Falaise Gap the Canadians, British
and Poles had had more than their share of short bombings
in daylight by Bomber Command and the USAF. They were
understandably furious with the air force. However, in our
opinion as the people in and over the battlefield, the answer
was not to emasculate us but to task the air commanders to
come up with a solution that would ensure there was no
repeat of the close quarter attack on the Poles.

The second factor came from the many reports by the
fighter recce pilots and others of an over-abundance of
sighted ambulances; for example, my own report on the 15
August when I counted 25 vehicles with red crosses on them
eastbound on the main highway ten miles west of Argentan.
General Freddy deGuingand, Montgomery's chief-of-staff,
later gave this explanation for moving the bombline away,
well to the east of the Gap and forbidding the Allied fighter
bomber and rocket aircraft from attacking:

> We were kept pretty busy with the various pro-
> blems connected with the battle of the 'pocket'.
> The co-ordination of air support was the most
> difficult of them all. When once the area had
> become reduced there was a great danger of the
> Tactical Air Forces supporting each Army Group
> becoming mixed up. It was very difficult to select
> bomb-lines that would suit everyone. Eventually
> the task of co-ordination was given to Coningham.
> During this time pilots reported a large pro-
> portion of the enemy's vehicles were carrying Red
> Cross flags and emblems. It was obvious that this
> was merely a ruse to avoid having their transport
> attacked. I believe these flags were even seen on
> tanks. What were the pilots to do? The decision
> was to avoid attacking them, for it was thought
> that the Germans in their present mood might well

take reprisals against our prisoners and wounded.
A difficult decision, but probably the right one.[2]

That line of reasoning might have been valid at Montgomery's headquarters, but to the young pilots, cruising
back and forth over the bulging pocket, our guns and rockets
turned off, the result simply was that we could not believe
anyone could give such an order. However, given it was and
it was obeyed. The cost in vehicles and enemy troops that
might otherwise surely be destroyed or forced to surrender
was enormous. As a gross error in tactical battlefield judgment the 17 August order moving the bombline east away
from the overflowing pocket and Falaise Gap must qualify
as one of the gravest in the utilization of assembled air power
in World War II.

The earlier decision that kept Patton's forces from
proceeding north from Argentan on 12/13 August, thereby
creating the Falaise Gap, when combined with the injunction against pocket and Gap attacks by the fighter bombers
and rocket aircraft of the Allied Tactical Air Forces,
produced the first thwarting of what Professor Percy
Schramm, commenting on these events from the German
viewpoint, described as the first "opportunity the enemy
had during this retreat-operation to cut off and destroy a
whole army." The second thwarting would occur on 19
August.

On that day I would be witness to an event that was
to demonstrate the costliness and stupidity of the order
debarring air-to-ground attacks in the pocket and the
Falaise Gap.

14

19 August 1944   OPERATIONS: F/O R.H. Rohmer and
F/O E.F. Geddes TAC/R 13:00/13:45
10/10's at 5,000'. Visibility 10-15
miles. Column of armor 250 plus
moving east 232233. 100 plus moving
east at 220240. 10 tanks 181228. 20
tanks at 190172. 10 vehicles at 196215.
430 Squadron Log

On 17/18 August the flood of Germans through the Falaise
Gap was in full flow. At last light on 17 August F/L Gill had
reported in the Argentan area "300 tanks, staff cars, ambulances on all roads, general direction east through entire
area." The morning of the 18th brought a report from F/L
J.R. Manser: "All roads leading into Vimoutiers from south
and southwest completely jammed with MET. Crossroads at
468510 same condition." Vimoutiers was 15 miles northeast
of Argentan and the reported crossroads was at Exmes and
lay 10 miles due east of Argentan. Other reports from our
aircraft over the Falaise Gap reported "all roads active with
enemy tanks, guns, MET moving east;" "200 MET moving
east and southeast;" "200 MET and tanks crossing river and
moving east four miles south of Vimoutiers;" "1,000 plus
vehicles jammed in area" north of Argentan.
    From the Falaise Gap east to the Seine the main roads
were filled with tanks, vehicles, and guns, desperately
fleeing from the Kessel. F/L E.S. Dunn reported hundreds of

MET moving east toward the Seine River crossing of Bonnières, northwest of Mantes-Gassicourt.

The enemy was in full flight. Furthermore he was escaping through the Gap that had been open for seven long and, for the Allied forces, costly days, and was now free from Allied air attacks in the pocket and Gap.

With F/O E.F. Ashdown, I arrived over the Gap shortly after 13:00 hours in the afternoon of 19 August, flying low at about a thousand feet. I was astonished by what I saw. Crossing the main road to Falaise three miles northwest of Argentan was a column of every imaginable type of vehicle, a mixed bag of trucks, horsedrawn artillery, tanks, ambulances, anything that could move. They were two abreast on a dirt road leading northeast toward Pommainville. The head of the column was stopped at a fork in the road about 400 yards east of the paved Falaise-Argentan road. The body of the double line column of vehicles stretched snake-like westward across the Falaise-Argentan road toward the small village of Commeaux. Around it the enemy had been gathering in the fields and under trees over the previous twenty-four hours. They were now moving, jockeying into position, forging their way onto the roads leading into the tail of the seemingly endless column.

At its head at the fork in the road there were two staff cars. At my low altitude, I could plainly see their occupants standing beside them, apparently attempting to decide which road to take. There before me in the long double line stretching westward was the largest, most vulnerable "target of opportunity" I had or ever would see. If they were not attacked and destroyed the enemy troops and their equipment below me would move out and escape to fight again another day.

But my number two and I could not attack. We fighter recce pilots still flew under the injunction that prevented us from going after ground targets. Even worse, the Army's order prohibiting any attacks against the enemy in the pocket or the Falaise Gap was in full force. Therefore, it was futile to call up Group Control Center to report the column because the Air Force had been rendered impotent. There was no choice but to watch as the occupants of the staff cars got back into their vehicles and the column began to move out unimpeded along the south fork in the road. The intelligent Germans below me had long since deduced that through some incomprehensible decision made by their enemy, they were at least for that moment, safe from any air attack. They could probably no more believe the incredible decision that I could sitting above them.

Instead of being destroyed upon the spot that entire column snaked its way out of the Falaise Gap. Two days later, in a jeep, I went down four miles of the roads it had followed. There was not a single destroyed or damaged vehicle, no evidence that the enormous, fleeing force had passed that way except for the bloated carcasses of a few dead horses along the roadside and one destroyed Tiger tank.

While the order prohibiting air attacks in the Falaise Gap might have been incomprehensible to me, it certainly was not to the Army elements that had been hit by our own aircraft. That very day, 19 August, the 51st (Highland) Division of 1 British Corps lodged a complaint to 21st Army Group about attacks that had occurred the day before. They complained of 40 separate incidents resulting in 25 vehicle casualties but, more important, 51 personnel casualties.

However, it was the Polish Armored Division that had been truly suffering. Not only had these brave fighting men suffered heavy losses during the bomber raids on 8 and 14 August, they were now being hammered by our tactical aircraft. In the late hours of the 18th its headquarters reported:

"Units and brigade headquarters have been continually bombed by own forces. Half the petrol being sent to 2nd Armoured Regiment was destroyed through bombing just after 1700 hrs."[1]

During the three-day period 16-18 August, 72 Polish soldiers were killed and 191 wounded through attacks from our own aircraft, while throughout 2 Canadian Corps, 77 were killed and 209 wounded. As a result, the Canadian Army headquarters lodged a strong demand for measures to be taken so that such incidents would not happen again.

Whatever the justification for the prohibitory order, the sight of that long, two-abreast German column moving out the Falaise Gap was a spectacle I will never forget. It was an event that should never have been allowed to happen.

Montgomery's telephone instruction to Bradley to close the Gap by having Haislip's XV Corps push on from Argentan toward Trun and Chambois was not given until the afternoon of 16 August. As the distinguished Canadian military historian, Colonel C.P. Stacey, commented:

> The action that might suitably have been taken on 13 August when Patton was prevented from crossing the army boundary south of Argentan, was taken now . . . The intention seems to have been simply to disregard the army group boundary, for there is no record of a change in it at this moment.[2]

To this time, Montgomery's order to Bradley on 16 August has been the only known directive given by Montgomery concerning the Falaise Gap during the period 12 through 16 August.

The fact that Montgomery gave Bradley the order to cross the boundary between the American and the British-Canadian Armies and move toward Chambois to close, is in itself of significance for it demonstrates that, without doubt, it was Montgomery and only Montgomery who could have given permission for Patton to advance north of Argentan on 12 August or any time thereafter. Bradley had no authority to permit Patton to proceed north to Falaise on 12 August. He could only order him to stop — unless Montgomery himself gave the order to advance. As to the timing of the Montgomery verbal order, Stacey says:

> It seems likely, in fact, that Montgomery telephoned Bradley about the same time at which he telephoned Crerar [3:30 p.m., 16 August]. This is rendered the more probable by the statement of General Patton (*War As I Knew It*, 109-10) that it was at 6:30 p.m. on the 16th that Bradley telephoned him and ordered him to attack towards Trun.[3]

At the same time he gave orders to Bradley to advance

north of Argentan, Montgomery issued concurrent orders to the First Canadian Army to thrust south east from Falaise. The intention expressed by the commander of 2nd Canadian Corps on 18 August was in keeping with the Montgomery directive: " 'To link up with U.S. forces and hold line of River Dives.' "[4]

Finally, after bloody battles throughout the Trun-Chambois area, the First Canadian and First United States Armies made contact at Chambois in the evening of 19 August, the Polish Armored Division claiming the first meeting. But it was not the end of the Gap battle.

Early in the morning of the 20th, remnants of the German Seventh Army's formations made an all-out attempt to break out at St. Lambert-sur-Dives and make contact with elements of 2 SS Panzer Corps, then fighting in a westward direction from Camembert under orders from the new Commander-in-Chief West, and also Commander of what was left of Army Group B, Field Marshal Walter Model. On 18 August, immediately after he had taken over from von Kluge on the 17th, (von Kluge committed suicide 18 August) Model ordered that the Seventh Army and what was left of Panzer Group Eberbach were to be rescued from the pocket as quickly as possible. The attack on the 20th resulted from Model's orders.

The German Army Group situation report for the day states in part:

> In bitter close fighting, about 40-50 per cent of the encircled forces managed to break out and join hands with the 2nd SS Panzer Corps. At St. Lambert-sur-Dives, the battle for a breach lasted for five hours.[5]

There was further fierce fighting in the Chambois area during 21 August, but by the end of that day the battle had ceased. The Falaise Gap no longer existed but a veritable fountain of controversy has cascaded from it over the intervening decades.

How many men escaped from the pocket through the

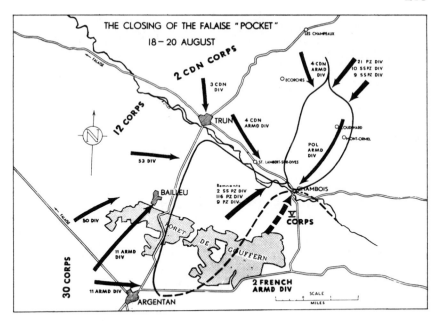

THE CLOSING OF THE FALAISE "POCKET"
18 – 20 AUGUST

Falaise Gap? This has been a question of speculation among military historians. However, from the information now available it is apparent that the numbers were sufficiently high that the Germans were to claim the mass escape as a victory of their own.

On the matter of the number of Germans opposing the Allies in Normandy, Stacey concludes that "it appears likely that the Germans deployed about 740,000 men of their army in Normandy south of the Seine."

German Army Group B reported that its casualties from 6 June until the time of the beginning of the Gap, 12/13 August, were 158,930. Reserving a figure of 200,000 troops for the area of Normandy to the east of Caen, it can be concluded that the scale of the force opposite the American and British-Canadian Armies during the first two weeks in August and, therefore, in the pocket would have to be in the range of 400,000 men. It would require that kind of strength at a minimum to withstand the tremendous Allied forces on Normandy soil. Eisenhower recorded that:

> By July 2, 1944, we had landed in Normandy about
> 1,000,000 men, including 13 American, 11 British

and 1 Canadian divisions. In the same period we put ashore 566,648 tons of supplies and 171, 532 vehicles.[6]

Stacey says, "By 1 September the Allies had landed according to contemporary records, 826,700 military personnel in the British area and 1,211,200 in the U.S. area of Normandy."[7]

According to the America military historian, Dr. Forrest C. Pogue:

> on the evening of 19 August, elements of General Hodges' V Corps met Polish tankers to complete the encirclement of *Seventh Army* and parts of *Fifth Panzer Army*, an estimated 125,000 men.[8]

Given these conservative estimates, it was likely that from 12 August when Hitler approved the order to withdraw from the pocket and Mortain, some 275-300,000 men had to be accounted for. The Allies took some 50,000 prisoners out of the pocket "and only 10,000 German dead were counted on the battlefield when the pocket was closed at last on 19 August." That would put the number of men who escaped from the pocket in the range of 210,000, plus those who escaped during the linking counterattack in the Trun and St. Lambert-sur-Dives area on 20/21 August when some 30,000 to 35,000 enemy soldiers got away.

Therefore, notwithstanding the mass destruction wrought on the enemy from the air and by artillery it is likely that between 200-250,000 men escaped through the Falaise Gap. With them went enormous numbers of tanks, vehicles and huge volumes of war material.

It is also likely that the column I saw in the early afternoon of 19 August did not escape. Blumenson wrote that in the late afternoon of the same day, "Polish tanks surprised a long column of German vehicles and armor moving bumper to bumper on the Chambois-Vimoutiers highway." This column could well have been mine.

In the Gap area lying between Pierrefitte, Argentan, Chambois, Vimoutiers and Trun, the carnage and destruction were staggering. According to Stacey:

British investigators of No. 2 Operational Research Section found 187 tanks and self-propelled guns, 157 lightly armored vehicles, 1778 lorries, 669 cars and 252 guns, a grand total ot 3043 guns and vehicles. This was in addition to 1270 vehicles (including 90 tanks, 31 self-propelled guns and 60 other guns) representing an admittedly incomplete count of those left in "the pocket" — defined as the general area Falaise—Condésur-Noireau—Vassy—Tinchebray—Barenton—Domfront—La Ferte-Macé—Argentan.[9]

Notwithstanding the scale of the Allied victory in Normandy as evidenced by the heavy destruction or capture of the Seventh Army's equipment and that of its Panzer Army with thousands of their personnel; and notwithstanding the boast of Montgomery that his victory "was to be acclaimed as the greatest achievement in military history," that victory could have been far more decisive if the entire German Seventh Army and the Panzers had been completely encircled by Patton's Third Army thrusting forward from Argentan toward the Canadians and Poles north of Falaise on 12/13 August.

To have allowed the escape of a substantial part of the German Seventh Army and its supporting Panzer Army without an all-out attempt to complete the encirclement from the south must rank as one of the most costly blunders in World War II. It must be judged as a military disaster painted over by the glowing facade of the glory of the victory acclaimed as the greatest achievement in military history. In truth the massive German escape through the Falaise Gap made it anything but such an achievement.

The future cost of that escape was paid in Allied lives and casualties in the subsequent fall and mid-winter battles on the threshold of Germany. Furthermore, the successful withdrawal from the pocket of substantial forces was claimed by the Germans as one of the great passages of arms of the war. It was an achievement that must have encouraged and enabled Hitler to keep on fighting, thereby extending the war for several months; whereas a complete and total annihilation of the Seventh Army and the Fifth

Panzer Army as hoped for by Eisenhower might well have seen the termination of hostilities in northwest Europe months in advance of its ultimate conclusion in 1945. Indeed, if the battle of Normandy had been a total Allied success, the seeds of a negotiated armistice between the Germans and the Western Allies might have grown into reality in August 1944.

The psychological impact of an Allied total victory in Normandy would have been crushing for Hitler, his general staff, and the German people. General Bodo Zimmerman, von Rundstedt's Operations Officer, would later say: " 'But for the existence of unconditional surrender, we might well have folded up right there and then.' "[10]

Had hostilities ceased on the Western Europe front at or about mid-August 1944, the face of modern Germany might well look quite different. By 13 August when the pocket could first have been closed, the Russian army had yet to set foot on German soil. The ramifications for the Soviets in the partition of Germany had peace occurred at that moment can only be conjecture. I have often speculated whether the Western Allies would have joined with Germany to do battle with the Soviets had they refused to halt.

While an armistice or peace was on the minds of the German generals who could see the futility of continuing with the fighting, that certainly was not Hitler's position. Having survived an assassination attempt, he was more dedicated than ever to fight to the end. But a complete, clean, total victory over his forces in Normandy might have changed even his demented mind.

However, the question was never put to the test because the victory was anything but clean. With the mass of men, equipment, and tanks that had victoriously escaped from the Falaise Gap and the Kessel, the Fuhrer could now mount his lines of defense in Holland and in the approaches to Germany.

15

Conclusion

Who was it who was responsible for the controversial order
that stopped Patton at Argentan on the night of 12 August?
Why was the action that "might have won us a complete
battle of annihilation" not taken? Indeed, why was it
ordered that the encirclement not be completed?

In the end, Patton and his shocked Third Army had to
look on helplessly as their quarry fled through the Gap.
For him it was an unbelievable, incomprehensible catas-
trophe. In his diary entry of 16 August, he wrote concerning
the events of 12/13 August:

> "After I had telephonic orders to halt from Leven
> Allen . . . I again called him at 1215 and asked if he
> had any orders to permit me to advance [north
> beyond Argentan]. I told him . . . it was perfectly
> feasible to continue the operation. Allen repeated
> the order [from Bradley] to halt on the line and
> consolidate.

I believe that the order . . . emanated from the 21st
Army Group and was either due to [British]
jealousy of the Americans or to utter ignorance of
the situation or to a combination of the two. It is
very regrettable that XV Corps was ordered to halt,
because it could have gone on to Falaise and made
contact with the Canadians north of that point and
definitely and positively closed the escape gap."[1]

It is of significance to note at this point that there was a
substantial factual discrepancy in Eisenhower's recollections when he wrote *Crusade In Europe,* some years after the
event, against his account of the situation written the day
it happened. The reference here is to his account of Bradley's
obtaining Montgomery's concurrence on the swing north to
Argentan. Eisenhower said in his book that he was with
Bradley when he telephoned Montgomery, but in his own
memorandum for his diary made the day of his visit, he
found that Bradley had already acted on the idea of turning
north and had already secured Montgomery's agreement.

Another example of the faultiness of memory exists in
Bradley's own recollections seven years after the event. He
recalls telephone conversations on which hinged the question of the responsibility for the order preventing Patton
from going north of Argentan.

George helped settle my doubts when on August 14
he called to ask that two of Haislip's four divisions
on the Argentan shoulder be freed for a dash to the
Seine.[2]

Bradley's recollection is wrong. Patton did not call
Bradley on the telephone. He went to see him. The following is an extract from Patton's diary written 14 August 1944,
the very day of the event:

"In exactly two weeks the Third Army has ad-
vanced farther and faster than any Army in the
history of war . . .

"To visit Haislip whom we found quite
pepped up. I told him of my plan to move the

XX Corps on Dreux and the XII Corps on
Chartres.

"I then flew back . . . to see Bradley and sell
him the plan. He consented, and even permitted
me to change it so as to move XX Corps on
Chartres, the XV Corps on Dreux, and the XII
Corps on Orleans. He will also let me keep the
80th and give Middleton an infantry division from
the First Army to replace the 6th Armored in
Brittany.

"It is really a great plan, wholly my own, and I
made Bradley think he thought of it. 'Oh, what a
tangled web we weave when first we practice to
deceive.'

"I am very happy and elated.

"I got all the Corps moving by 2030 so that if
Monty tries to be careful, it will be too late."[3]

Patton saw Bradley. He flew back to see him.

This clear example of the quite human flaw in
Bradley's recollection of the events on 14 August 1944
brings into serious question the verbatim accuracy of his
seven year memory of telephone conversations and of orders
verbally delivered in the crucial period 12 August through
the 14th, when the high tempo and fluidity of the battle
situation forced a reliance on verbal instructions by telephone, wireless or in person as opposed to being written.
Furthermore, recollected conversations of years back cannot
but be shot full of inaccuracies. Nevertheless, Bradley, in
A Soldier's Story, attempted to recall verbatim conversations
and the line of reasoning that led him to the decisions
he'd made seven years earlier. What Bradley wrote in 1951 —
while Montgomery was still alive — was:

Meanwhile Monty labored on the north with
slackening success. After five days of attack he had
pushed his Canadian pincer only half the way to
Falaise. Thus when Haislip reached Argentan on
the evening of August 12, he found Monty stalled
on the north with an 18-mile gap separating the
British and American forces.

Patton telephoned me that evening from LUCKY FORWARD [Patton's headquarters] near Laval.

"We've got elements in Argentan," he reported. "Let me go on to Falaise and we'll drive the British back into the sea for another Dunkirk."

"Nothing doing," I told him, for I was fearful of colliding with Montgomery's forces. "You are not to go beyond Argentan. Just stop where you are and build up on that shoulder."[4]

Bradley went on to amplify why he held Patton at Argentan:

At the same time I was reluctant to chance a head-on meeting between two converging Armies as we might have done had Patton continued on to Falaise. For any head-on juncture becomes a dangerous and uncontrollable maneuver unless each of the advancing forces is halted by a pre-arranged plan on a terrain objective.[5]

Bradley knew full well that the Panzers and infantry were holding the Canadians and Poles in check well north of Falaise. There could be no possible danger of their colliding head on so long as the German forces stood between them. In point of tactics, Patton's armor and infantry attacking the Germans from the rear would have had an enormously beneficial effect for the Canadians and Poles.

Moreover, Bradley knew that the boundary line between the British-Canadian and the American forces had been set by Montgomery, who was the sole arbiter of those lines. The dividing line running east-west had been placed by Monty at a point south of Argentan. Even so, in granting earlier approval for Haislip to go 12 miles north of the British-U.S. boundary to Argentan, Montgomery "happily forgave us our trespasses and welcomed the penetration." At least that was Bradley's later recollection.

The line between the British-Canadian and American

armies was fixed and rigid. There was no possible way that Bradley could have authorized Patton to proceed north from Argentan without first getting Montgomery's concurrence. The British general was the sole and only field arbiter on boundaries. Therefore, one apparent reason that caused Bradley to not allow Patton to advance was that Bradley had no authority to allow him to cross the line and go north. That was quite apart from any concern for colliding with Montgomery's barely moving, far-distant forces some 18 to 20 miles to the north.

Another odd statement was made by Bradley. He was a stickler for discipline in observing the chain of command, and had never taken any major decision without having cleared it with his superior, Montgomery. Bradley claimed:

> In halting Patton at Argentan . . . I did not consult with Montgomery. The decision to stop Patton was mine alone. It never went beyond my CP.[6]

Was Bradley's recollection faulty on this point as well?

Bradley went on to explain the consequences of what he recalled as his instructions to Patton to advance no further:

> Meanwhile, as we waited impatiently for Monty at Argentan, the enemy reinforced that gap. Already the vanguard of Panzers and SS troops were sluicing back through it toward the Seine. But instead of redoubling his push to close that leak, Monty shifted his main effort against the pocket farther west. Rather than close the trap by capping the leak at Falaise, Monty proceeded to squeeze the enemy out toward the Seine. If Monty's tactics mystified me, they dismayed Eisenhower even more. And at LUCKY FORWARD, where a shocked Third Army looked on helplessly as its quarry fled, Patton raged at Montgomery's blunder. George was doubly irritated for having been forbidden to close it himself. But Monty had never prohibited and I never proposed that U.S.

222

forces close the gap from Argentan to Falaise. I was quite content with our original objective and reluctant to take on another.[7]

Bradley's recollection that Monty had never prohibited was wrong. What Bradley had forgotten or overlooked in the seven years that had passed since the event, was that by refusing to move the boundary line at Argentan, Montgomery did in fact prohibit Patton's First Army from closing the gap from Argentan to Falaise. It was totally inherent in the rigid boundary line. The only person who could alter that line was Montgomery. Even the Supreme Commander, Eisenhower, could not move it unless he was prepared to take over command of the forces in the field and relegate Montgomery to accepting the command of only the 21st Army Group. At that point in time Eisenhower was not in a position to take that step either politically or militarily.

Eisenhower supported Bradley's position to hold Patton at Argentan, a decision the Supreme Commander had apparently made almost exlcusively on the matter of the boundary lines. On 12 August:

I was in Bradley's headquarters when messages began to arrive from the commanders of the advancing American columns, complaining that the limits placed upon them by their orders were allowing Germans to escape. I completely supported Bradley in his decision that it was necessary to obey the orders, prescribing the boundary between the army groups, exactly as written; otherwise a calamitous battle between friends could have resulted.[8]

It is passing strange and out of Bradley's pattern of dealing with his superior, Montgomery, if his recollection was correct that he did not discuss the Argentan boundary line on the night of 12 August 44, either with Montgomery himself or with deGuingand, Monty's chief-of-staff and confidante, the man who protected his "Chief" from the world and represented him in the highest councils. Bradley was in touch with both of them by telephone or message on a daily basis.

In the hindsight of several years Bradley thought that he had been content with the original objective of Argentan and reluctant to take on another. Also, in retrospect, he doubted Patton's ability to spin a line across the narrow neck and hold it.

In fact, the German forces that could have impeded Patton's northward thrust on the night of 12 August and into 13 August were extremely light. Furthermore, "as a matter of fact, we had reconnaissance parties near the town when we were ordered to pull back," Patton wrote in 1947. The town was Falaise. The reconnaissance parties were elements of Leclerc's French Armored Division.

Instead the Americans sat at Argentan until mid-afternoon of the 16th when Montgomery telephoned Bradley, belatedly ordering him to push on from Argentan toward Trun and Chambois. Even so, Montgomery did not move the boundary line between the armies north from Argentan. The thrust northeast he ordered was to be another "trespass." The War Diary of Air Vice Marshal S.C. Strafford of the Advance Allied Expeditionary Force states this in the record of 19 August 1944:

American staffs, both air and ground had repeatedly complained of the difficulty caused by the position of the inter/Army Group boundary and had expressed the view that it had delayed the crossing of the ARGENTAN/FALAISE gap by the northern thrust of the American columns from ARGENTAN. To enable the American air to support their own columns, arrangements had been specially agreed between 2 TAF and Ninth Air Force yesterday that Ninth Air Force fighter/bombers should come into the 2 TAF area in close support of the American columns and only answering calls for ground attack from their V.C.P.'s. The Americans were satisfied with this as far as it went, but their view was that they must have complete freedom to support their land operations. *The AVM expressed the urgent need for the issue by 21 Army Group in their role of G.H.Q. Land Forces, of an order clearly laying down what the present inter/Army Group and inter/Army boundaries were. There was certainly confusion of thought on this in the last few days, as on the British side, it was shown on maps East and West through Argentan, while in HQ 12 US Army Group letter of instruction No. 5 dated 17th August 44, it was shown as South of ARGENTAN.* This order at the same time gave the First Army task of driving further North of the Boundary to seize the area CHAMBOIS, TRUN. AVM discussed this with Chief of Staff 21 Army Group (de Guingand) in front of map, but before the discussion was completed, Chief of Staff 21 Army Group was called away to the telephone and did not return to the meeting.[9]

When Montgomery finally made the call to Bradley ordering him to send Patton's troops from Argentan northeast to Chambois on the 16th, Bradley concurred.[10]

On the record, and without any doubt, General Montgomery was responsible for drawing the line east and west through Argentan beyond which Bradley or Patton under him could not proceed. Furthermore, Montgomery was in touch with the battle position of the American forces at all times. They were, after all, under his command.

The order Bradley gave to Patton was the only order he could have given unless Montgomery approved of a request of Bradley to let Patton go north, a request Bradley claims not to have made. In the alternative, Montgomery himself could have ordered Patton to go north, doing so of course through Bradley. He did not do so.

On 10 August Montgomery knew that the Canadians and Poles were unable to move south from Falaise and were therefore unable to close the Gap with the Americans at Argentan as required by the "rush" plan to which he was committed and which he himself claimed to have ordered. Again, it was within Montgomery's sole and exclusive authority to order Patton to go north. It was not within

Bradley's competence. There was no way Bradley unilaterally would or could order Patton north. However, if on the night of 12/13 August Montgomery had given the order to change the inter/Army boundary line or had agreed to let it be changed at Bradley's request, the situation would have been quite different. There would have been no Falaise Gap.

Even deGuingand was later to admit:

> It is just possible that the gap might have been closed a little earlier if no restrictions had been imposed upon the 12th Army Group Commander as to the limit of his northward movement.[11]

In his position as alter ego to Montgomery, deGuingand was completely aware of his Chief's sensitivity in the matter of boundary lines between British-Canadian and American armies.

DeGuingand had seen Montgomery's intense anger and bitterness over Eisenhower's clandestine attack on him in the presence of Churchill only a few days before on both 26 and 27 July. Monty was totally convinced that this plan of pivoting at Caen was completely misunderstood, not only by Eisenhower but by the SHAEF staff of whom the most critical was Tedder, his own countryman. In accordance with the brilliant plan that he, Montgomery, himself had devised, the Americans were now swinging around under the Germans, trapping the enemy in a pocket. With great publicity, credit, glory and public applause Bradley and Patton had broken out, were traveling rapidly, fanning across France while he, Montgomery, and his British-Canadian armies and the Polish Armored Division were sitting north of Falaise pounding away at the Germans, barely able to move and still pivoting.

For the sake of face, for the sake of his job, and in order to deprive the Americans of the undeserved ultimate credit and glory they would receive if it was they who completed the encirclement by driving north to Falaise; and in order to avoid the avalanche of criticism he would be subjected to for again not moving and having to let the Americans do it for him — for all these reasons something had to be done. What could he do? Or not do?

226

The answer is that Montgomery would deny the Americans the opportunity to go north of Argentan, to drive forward to Falaise to complete the encirclement. He would hope by some miracle that his own forces might finally break through the German wall still standing between his troops and Falaise. But even if they did not, his attitude toward the Americans was so antagonistic and vengeful that he would not move that Argentan boundary line.

Again, in any historical account of those few days, there is no record of any action on Montgomery's part in relation to the Argentan inter/Army boundary line until his order on the afternoon of 16 August. All historic conclusions have been that Montgomery did nothing, even though he knew that Patton's army was at Argentan and that Bradley had ordered Patton not to go across the line.

Such is not the case.

On the evening of 12 August at his headquarters, by that time located in the Forêt de Cerisy a few miles southwest of Bayeux, Montgomery gave a verbal order to Freddie deGuingand. It was passed on by him directly to Bradley.

As it happened, Brigadier E.T. Williams, one of Monty's own staff, was with deGuingand in the latter's van at Montgomery's headquarters when the order was given. The American military historian, Dr. Forrest C. Pogue, interviewed Williams on 30-31 May 1947, just three years after the event. Williams enjoyed a high reputation for having a remarkably clear and accurate memory. Pogue took notes of what Williams told him. It will be recalled that 2nd French Armored was Leclerc's Armored Division under Patton. Under instructions from Patton, Leclerc had pushed on slowly toward Falaise from Argentan on the evening of 12 August. These are Pogue's notes, never before published:

Falaise Gap — Remembers was in Freddie's (deGuingand) truck near Bayeux when 2d French Armored made its swing up and crossed the road towards Falaise. Monty said tell Bradley they ought to get back. Bradley was indignant. We were indignant on Bradley's behalf. DeGuingand said, "Monty is too tidy." Monty missed closing the sack. Freddie thought Bradley should have been allowed to join Poles at Trun. Bradley couldn't understand. Thought we were missing our opportunities over inter/army rights. However, it should be pointed out that Monty regarded Bradley as under his command; therefore his decision was not made on the basis of inter/army considerations. Master of tidiness. He was fundamentally more interested in full envelopment than this inner envelopment. We fell between two stools. He missed the chance of closing at the Seine by doing the envelopment at Falaise.

Montgomery gave the order not to advance north of Argentan to deGuingand, who passed it to Bradley who gave it to Patton. Montgomery gave the order. An indignant Bradley complied. He had no choice.

There is no mystery as to the responsbility for creating the infamous Falaise Gap and for the escape of tens of thousands of troops, and tanks, vehicles, guns and material from the pocket to fight again another day. The man who gave the order was Montgomery. Even if he had not given the order, which is now clear he did, he failed or refused to move the boundary line.

Either way, the creator of the Falaise Gap — Patton's Gap, the Gap Patton ought to have been permitted to close — and its consequences was not General Omar N. Bradley. It was General Sir Bernard Law Montgomery.

Endnotes

Chapter One

[1]Ladislas Farago, *Patton: Ordeal and Triumph* (1963; rpt. New York: Dell Publishing Co. Inc., 1976), p. 349.

[2]Farago, *Patton: Ordeal and Triumph*, p. 262.

[3]Wilmot, *The Struggle for Europe* (London: Collins, 1957), p. 262.

[4]Farago, *Patton: Ordeal and Triumph*, pp. 527-8.

Chapter 2

[1]Farago, *Patton: Ordeal and Triumph*, p. 356.

[2]Anthony Cave Brown, *Bodyguard of Lies* (New York: Harper & Row, 1975), p. 460.

[3]Bernard Law Montgomery, *Montgomery of Alamein: Normandy to the Baltic-Invasion* (1947; rpt. London: Corgi Books, 1974), II, p. 213.

[4]Montgomery, *Alamein*, p. 213.

[5]Ibid., p. 231.

[6]F. de Guingand, *Operation Victory* (London: Hodder & Stoughton Limited, 1947), p. 318.

[7]Farago, *Patton: Ordeal and Triumph*, p. 405.

[8]Ibid., pp. 407-408.

[9]Ibid., p. 408.

Chapter 3

[1]Montgomery, *Alamein*, p. 238.

[2]David Irving, *The Trail of the Fox* (1977; rpt. New York: Avon Books, 1978), p. 412.

Chapter 4

[1]Montgomery, *Alamein*, pp. 282-3.

[2]de Guingand, *Operation Victory*, p. 314.

[3]Brown, *Bodyguard of Lies*, p. 652.

[4]Ibid., p. 659.

Chapter 5

[1]Brown, *Bodyguard of Lies*, p. 364.

[2]Montgomery, *Alamein*, p. 300.

[3]Bernard Law Montgomery, *The Memoirs of Field-Marshall Montgomery* (London: Collins, 1958), p. 254.

[4]Montgomery, *Alamein*, p. 300.

Chapter 6

[1]Montgomery, *Alamein*, p. 305.

[2]Ibid., p. 305.

[3]Ibid., pp. 313-4.

[4]Ibid., p. 313.

[5]Brown, *Bodyguard of Lies*, p. 709.

Chapter 7

[1]Brown, *Bodyguard of Lies*, p. 736.

[2]Farago, *Patton: Ordeal and Triumph*, p. 420.

[3]Ibid., p. 420.

[4]Dwight D. Eisenhower, *Crusade in Europe* (New York: Doubleday & Co. Inc., 1948), p. 267.

Chapter 8

[1]Montgomery, *Alamein*, p. 328.

[2]Ibid., pp. 330-1.

[3]Ibid., pp. 335-6.

[4]Montgomery, *Memoirs*, p. 257.

[5]Ibid., p. 255.

[6]Ibid., p. 256.

Chapter 9

[1]Brown, *Bodyguard of Lies*, p. 771.

[2]Ibid., p. 771.

[3]Montgomery, *Alamein*, p. 341.

[4]Forrest C. Pogue, "The Breakout and Pursuit to the Seine," *The Supreme Command, U.S. Army in WWII, European Theatre of Operations,* Part 4, Vol. 3 (Washington: Office at the Chief of Military History, Department of the Army, 1961), p. 198.

[5]Pogue, *The Supreme Command,* p. 200.

[6]Omar N. Bradley, *A Soldier's Story* (New York: Holt, Rinehart & Winston, 1951), p. 355.

[7]Martin Blumenson, *The Patton Papers: 1940-1945* (Boston: Houghton Mifflin Company, 1972), p. 490.

[8]George S. Patton, *War as I Knew It* (New York: Houghton Mifflin Company, 1947), p. 96.

[9]Montgomery, *Memoirs,* pp. 260-1.

[10]Winston Churchill, *The Second World War, Triumph and Tragedy,* Vol. 6 (Boston: Houghton Mifflin Company, 1953), pp. 29-30.

[11]Montgomery, *Memoirs,* pp. 261-2.

Chapter 10

[1]Patton, *War As I Knew It,* pp. 97-98.

[2]Ibid., p. 98.

[3]Charles R. Codman, *Drive* (Boston: Little, Brown, 1957), pp. 158-9.

[4]Montgomery, *Alamein,* p. 352.

[5]Ibid., p. 353.

[6]Mathew Cooper, *The German Army 1933-1945: Its Political and Military Failure* (London: Macdonald and Janes, 1978), p. 508.

[7]Bradley, *A Soldier's Story*, p. 350.

[8]Ibid., p. 350.

[9]Ibid., p. 352.

[10]Montgomery, *Alamein*, p. 341.

[11]de Guingand, *Operation Victory*, p. 397.

Chapter 11

[1]Montgomery, *Alamein*, pp. 357-8.

[2]Brown, *Bodyguard of Lies*, p. 784.

[3]Ibid., p. 785.

[4]Blumenson, *The Patton Papers*, p. 503.

[5]Eisenhower, *Crusade in Europe*, p. 275.

[6]Bradley, *A Soldier's Story*, p. 372.

[7]Eisenhower, p. 275.

[8]Bradley, *A Soldier's Story*, p. 375.

[9]Montgomery, *Alamein*, p. 364.

[10]Ibid., p. 364.

[11]James Wellard, *General George S. Patton, Jr. — Man Under Mars* (New York: Dodd, Mead & Co., 1946), p. 161.

234

[12]Blumenson, *The Patton Papers*, p. 501.

[13]Codman, *Drive*, pp. 158-9.

Chapter 12

[1]Montgomery, Alamein, p. 367.

[2]Ibid., p. 367.

[3]Martin Blumenson, *The Duel for France* (Boston: Houghton Mifflin Company, 1963), p. 197.

Chapter 13

[1]Bradley, *A Soldier's Story*, p. 379.

[2]de Guingand, *Operation Victory*, p. 325.

Chapter 14

[1]C. P. Stacey, *The Official History of the Canadian Army in the Second World War: The Victory Campaign*, Vol. III (Ottawa: Queen's Printer, 1955-60), p. 257.

[2]C. P. Stacey, *The Victory Campaign*, p. 251.

[3]Ibid., p. 251.

[4]Ibid., p. 256.

[5]Ibid., p. 262.

[6]Eisenhower, *Crusade in Europe*, p. 270.

[7]Stacey, *The Victory Campaign*, p. 272.

[8]Pogue, *The Supreme Command*, p. 215.

[9]Stacey, *The Victory Campaign*, p. 265.

[10]Brown, *Bodyguard of Lies*, p. 772.

Chapter 15

[1]Blumenson, *The Patton Papers*, pp. 508-9.

[2]Bradley, *A Soldier's Story*, p. 378.

[3]Blumenson, *The Patton Papers*, p. 510.

[4]Bradley, *A Soldier's Story*, p. 376.

[5]Ibid., p. 377.

[6]Ibid., p. 377.

[7]Ibid., pp. 376-7.

[8]Eisenhower, *Crusade in Europe*, pp. 278-9.

[9]Unpublished War Diary.

[10]Bradley, p. 379.

[11]de Guingand, *Operation Victory*, p. 325.

Bibliography

Allen, Colonel Robert, S. *Lucky Forward: The History of Patton's Third U.S. Army*. New York: Vanguard Press, 1947.

Belfield, Eversley and H. Essame. *The Battle for Normandy*. London: Batsford, c. 1965.

Blumenson, Martin. *The United States Army in World War II, The European Theatre of Operations* (Vol. 3 of 14), *Breakout and Pursuit* (Part 5 of 8). Washington, D.C.: Office of the Chief of Military History, Department of the Army, 1961.

Blumenson, Martin. *The Dual for France, 1944*. Boston: Houghton Mifflin Company, 1963.

Blumenson, Martin. *The Patton Papers*. Boston: Houghton Mifflin Company, 1972.

Bradley, Omar N. *A Soldier's Story*. New York: Holt, Rinehart & Winston, 1951.

Brown, Anthony Cave. *Bodyguard of Lies*. New York: Harper & Row, 1975.

Chalfont, Alun. *Montgomery of Alamein*. London: Weidenfeld and Nicolson, c. 1976.

Churchill, Winston S. *The Second World War, Triumph and Tragedy* (Volume 6 of 6). Boston: Houghton Mifflin Company, 1953.

Codman, Charles R. *Drive*. Boston: Little, Brown, 1957.

Command Decisions. U.S. Department of the Army, Office of the Chief of Military History. Kent Roberts Greenfield, general editor (with an introduction by Hanson W. Baldwin), c. 1959.

Cooper, Mathew. *The German Army 1933-1945: Its Political and Military Failure*. London: Macdonald and Janes, 1978.

Craven, Wesley Frank, and Cate, James Lea, ed. *The Army Air Forces in World War II, Europe: Argument to V-E*

Day, Volume III (of VII), (January 1944 to May 1945). Chicago: The University of Chicago Press, 1951.

Eisenhower, Dwight David. *Crusade in Europe.* New York: Doubleday & Co., Inc., 1948.

Essame, Hubert. *Patton: A Study in Command.* New York: Scribner, 1974.

Farago, Ladislas. *Patton: Ordeal and Triumph.* New York: Dell Publishing Co. Inc., 1976.

de Guingand, Major-General Sir Francis K.B.E., C.B., D.S.O. *Operation Victory.* London: Hodder & Stoughton Limited, 1947.

de Guingand, Major-General Sir Francis, K.B.E., C.B., D.S.O., *Generals at War.* London: Hodder & Stoughton Limited, 1964.

Harkins, General Paul D. *When the Third Cracked Europe: The Story of Patton's Incredible Army.* Harrisburg, Pa.: Stackpole Books, c. 1969.

Irving, David. *The Trail of the Fox.* New York: Avon Books, 1978.

Lyall, Gavin. *The War in the Air: The Royal Air Force in World War II,* edited by Gavin Lyall. New York: William Morrow, 1969.

Johnson, Group Captain J.E., DSO, DFC. "The Killing Ground" in *The War in the Air,* edited by Gavin Lyall. New York: William Morrow, 1969.

Lewin, Ronald. *Montgomery as Military Commander.* New York: Stein and Day, c. 1971.

Maule, Henry. *Caen: The Brutal Battle and Breakout from Normandy.* Newton Abbot, England, Vancouver: David and Charles, 1976.

Montgomery, Bernard Law, 1st Viscount. *The Memoirs of Field-Marshal The Viscount Montgomery of Alamein, K.G.* London: Collins, 1958.

Montgomery, Bernard Law, 1st Viscount. *Normandy to the Baltic.* London: Hutchinsom & Co. Ltd., 1947; London: Corgi Books, 1974.

Nicholson, Colonel G.W.L., C.D., *The Gunners of Canada: The History of the Royal Regiment of Canadian Artillery.* Toronto: McClelland and Stewart, c. 1967-1972.

North, John. *North-West Europe, 1944-5: The Achievement of 21st Army Group.* London: H.M. Stationery Office, 1977.

Barnard, Lieutenant-Colonel W.T., E.D., C.D. *The Queen's Own Rifles of Canada, 1860-1960: One Hundred Years of Canada.* Don Mills, Ontario: Ontario Publishing Company, c. 1960.

Patton, George S., Jr. *War As I Knew It.* Annotated by Colonel Paul D. Harkins. Boston: Houghton Mifflin Company, 1947.

Pogue, Forrest C. *George C. Marshall: Education of a General 1880-1939.* With the editorial assistance of Gordon Harrison. Forward by General Omar N. Bradley. New York: Viking Press, 1963.

The RCAF Overseas: The Sixth Year, (Volume 3 of 3). Royal Canadian Air Force Historical Section. Toronto: Oxford University Press, 1944-49.

Semmes, Harry Hodges. *Portrait of Patton.* New York: Appleton-Century-Crofts, 1955.

Speidel, Hans. *We Defended Normandy.* Translated by Ian Colvin. London: Jenkins, 1951.

Stacey, Colonel C.P., O.B.E. *Canada's Battle in Normandy: The Canadian Army's Share in the Operations, 6 June - 1 September 1944.* Ottawa: King's Printer, 1946.

Stacey, Colonel C.P., *The Official History of the Canadian Army in the Second World War:* (Volume III of III). *The Victory Campaign: The Operations in North-West Europe 1944-1945.* Ottawa: Queen's Printer, 1955-60.

Thompson, Reginald William. *Montgomery, The Field Marshal: A Critical Study of the Generalship of Field-Marshal the Viscount Montgomery of Alamein, K.G., and of the Campaign in North-West Europe, 1944/45.* London: Allen & Unwin, 1969.

The United States Army in World War II, The European Theater of Operations (Vol. 3 of 14), *The Supreme Command* (Part 4 of 8). Washington, D.C.: Office of the Chief of Military History, Department of the Army, 1961.

Wellard, James Howard. *General George S. Patton, Jr., Man Under Mars.* New York: Dodd, Mead & Co., 1946.

Wilmot, Chester. *The Struggle for Europe.* London: Collins, 1957.

Wood, Alan. *The Falaise Road.* Toronto: Macmillan Co. of Canada, Ltd., c. 1944.